John Stoughton

Religion in England under Queen Anne and the Georges, 1702-1800

Vol. 2

John Stoughton

Religion in England under Queen Anne and the Georges, 1702-1800
Vol. 2

ISBN/EAN: 9783337324285

Printed in Europe, USA, Canada, Australia, Japan

Cover: Foto ©Lupo / pixelio.de

More available books at **www.hansebooks.com**

UNDER

QUEEN ANNE AND THE GEORGES.

1702–1800.

BY

JOHN STOUGHTON, D.D.,

AUTHOR OF "ECCLESIASTICAL HISTORY OF ENGLAND," ETC.

VOLUME II.

London:

HODDER AND STOUGHTON,
27, PATERNOSTER ROW.
MDCCCLXXVIII.

CONTENTS OF VOL. II.

CHAPTER XVI.

Accession of George III., 4.—Character of the New King, 7.- Bishop Warburton, 9.—New Bishops, 11.—Death of Archbishop Secker, 13.—Countess of Huntingdon, 14.—Archdeacon Blackburn, 17.—Subscription, 19.—Revision of Prayer Book, 21.—Dissenting Deputies, 22.—Concession to Dissenters, 25.—Roman Catholics, 29.—The Gordon Riots, 31.—Catholic Relief Bill, 37.

CHAPTER XVII.

Test and Corporation Acts, 39.—Parliamentary Debates, 40.—French Revolution 41.—Dr. Price, 43.—Edmund Burke, 44.—Excitement, 46.—Dr. Priestley, 48.—Unitarians, 51.—Quakers, 52.—Changes in the Episcopate, 55.

CHAPTER XVIII.

Episcopal Church in America, 65.—Consecration of Bishops, 68.—Colonial Bishoprics, 70.—British Factories, 75.

CHAPTER XIX.

Cathedral Services, 76.—The Clergy, 80.—Dr. Parr, 83.- Cox and Crabbe, 85.—White and Kennicott, 86.—Paley, 88.

Orthodox Theologians, 91.—Evangelicals, 93.—Venn and Romaine, 94.—John Newton, 96.—Thomas Scott, 99.—Bedford Row Chapel, 103.—Richard Cecil, 104.—Joseph Milner, 106.—Theophilus Lindsey, 111.—The Universities, 113.—Charles Simeon, 116.—Boyle Lectures, 118.—Bampton Lectures, 119.

CHAPTER XX.

Dr. Johnson, 121.—The Poet Cowper, 124.—John Thornton, 129.—Robert Raikes, 130.—William Wilberforce, 131.—Neighbourhood of London, 136.

CHAPTER XXI.

Whitefield's Death, 141.—Wilks and Rowland Hill, 142.—Surrey Chapel, 145.—Countess of Huntingdon, 146.—The Countess's Connexion, 150.—Tonbridge Wells, 152.—The Countess's Chaplains, 154.—Fletcher of Madeley, 156.—Ordination in Spa Fields Chapel, 161.—Death of the Countess, 162.

CHAPTER XXII.

Methodism, 163.—Methodist Troubles, 164.—Wesley's Authority, 167.—William Grimshaw, 169.—Methodist Controversy, 170.—Fletcher's "Checks," 171.—Toplady, 174.—Coke and Clarke, 176.—First Methodist Chapel, 178.—Methodist Magazine, 179.—"Deed of Declaration," 179.—American Methodism, 181.—Wesley's Dissent, 185.—Methodist Preachers, 187.—Wesley's Death, 197.—The Conference in 1791, 199.—Questions Respecting Sacraments, 201.—Alexander Kilham and the New Connexion, 203.—Methodism and the Establishment, 205.

CHAPTER XXIII.

Presbyterians, 207.—Learned Men, 210.—Academies, 214.—Presbyterian Ministers, 217.—Dr. Langford and Job Orton, 217.—Dr. Taylor, 220.—Dr. Price, 222.—Dr. Priestley, 224.—Mrs. Barbauld, 227.—The Octagon Chapel, 228.—Methodism and Presbyterianism, 229.—Scotch Presbyterianism, 230.

CHAPTER XXIV.

Congregational Academies, 233.—Thomas Harmer, 240.—Dr. Boothroyd, 243.—Dr. Edward Williams, 244.—Old Independency, 246.—Dr. Wilton and John Clayton, 249.—Samuel Lavington, 251.—John Howard, 252.—Thomas Toller, 255.—Persecution, 257.—Yorkshire Nonconformity, 259.—Congregationalism in Lancashire, 262.—Gloucester, 267.—Wiltshire, 269.—Warwickshire, 271.

CHAPTER XXV.

General Baptists, 273.—Whiston, 275.—New Connexion, 276.—Articles of Faith, 277.—Particular Baptists, 278.—Robert Robinson, 281.—Baptist Churches, 284.—Beddome and Stennet, 286.—Pearce and Sutcliff, 287.—Dr. Ryland, 288.—William Carey, 290.—Baptist Missions, 293.—Andrew Fuller, 295.—Robert Hall, 299.

CHAPTER XXVI.

Quakers, 303.—Quaker Testimonies, 305.—John Gurney, 306.—Quaker Legislation, 309.—Quakers and Methodists, 314.—Social Life of Quakerism, 317.—Norwich Friends, 231.—Yearly Meetings, 323.—Swedenborgianism, 324.

CHAPTER XXVII.

Views of Christian Union, 328.—Combined Efforts, 329.—Evangelical Magazine, 331.—Missionary Society, 336.—The Ship *Duff*, 340.—Tahiti, 343.—Missionary Fathers, 344.—Constitution of the Society, 347.—Village Itinerancy, 349.—Religious Tract Society, 352.—British and Foreign Bible Society, 355.—Church Missionary Society, 357.

CHAPTER XXVIII.

State of Religion, 362.—Preaching, 363.—Public Meetings, 364.—Sunday Schools, 365.—Theological Literature, 368.—German Philosophy, 372.—Church and Dissent, 374.—Statistics of Dissent, 377.—Spiritual Life, 378.—Henry Martyn, 378.—Legh Richmond, 383.—Cornelius Winter, 384.—A Mast Maker at Sheerness, 387.—A Scotch Artisan, 389.—A Laborious Student, 391.—Losses and Gains, 395.—Progress, 397.

RELIGION UNDER GEORGE III.

VOL. II.   B

CHAPTER XVI.

1760-80.

GEORGE the Second died on the 25th of October, 1760, and was buried at Westminster on the 11th of November. He expressed a wish that his remains and the remains of his Queen should be interred together; consequently his own coffin, with that of his consort, were placed in a single sarcophagus, and the sides of the two coffins being withdrawn, their ashes commingled. Through the eyes of Horace Walpole we witness the funeral obsequies in the historical Abbey Church of England :—

" The procession through a line of footguards, every seventh man bearing a torch, the Horse Guards lining the outside, their officers, with drawn sabres and crape sashes, on horseback, the drums muffled, the fifes, bells tolling, and minute-guns—all this was very solemn." At the Abbey door the Dean and Chapter, " in rich robes, the choir and almsmen bearing torches," received the royal corpse; " the tombs, long aisles, and fretted vault all appearing distinctly," as the interment took place at night.

Secker, as Archbishop of Canterbury, of course was present, and he relates :—

" Nov. 11 was the late King's funeral. I was at several

Committees of Council in relation to it, but nothing passed there worth writing here. I did not put on weepers with my other mourning, and few of the bishops and other clergy did, and those were chiefly the younger and gayer. They were indeed appointed, but in conjunction with directions about coats, swords, etc., and the clergy in general had not usually worn them; nor did I understand that such of the clergy as omitted them now were blamed. I went to the great door of Westminster Hall in my coach, which was allowed to stay there all the time. They who walked first in the procession filled the stalls before they who walked last came, so that I and the Lord Keeper and Lord Privy Seal, etc., stood for some time in the middle of the choir; but afterwards we went to a bench in the N.E. corner, and stayed there. I got home to Lambeth about 11."

This passage occurs in a MS. volume[1] in the handwriting of Archbishop Secker, who also supplies a minute account of certain incidents connected with the accession of George the Third, which may here be appropriately introduced. As member of the House of Lords and an officer of State, he took part in the proclamation of the new King :—

"I thought to go on," he says, "to Temple Bar, and then return to the House, but could not for the crowd till I had got to Fleet Ditch." "I believe no Lord's coach but mine went much further than Charing Cross."

---

[1] The documents are entitled "Court Papers," and are preserved amongst the MSS. in Lambeth Library, No. 1130. They are full of interesting particulars.

On Monday, the 27th of October, he conversed with his Majesty respecting needful alterations in the Prayer for the Royal Family.

"The King sent for me into a room, where he was alone, and told me that as the Royal Family was numerous, and he was unwilling to put in any of his brothers and leave out his uncle, and many names might hereafter make confusion, he thought it would be best to insert only the Princess Dowager of Wales in particular. I assented to it; and then I took the opportunity of assuring him of my duty and best services. He said very graciously, that he had no doubt on that head, and that I was one of his oldest acquaintance, having baptized him on the day he was born, after once doubting whether he was alive, as Mrs. Kennon, the midwife, had often told him."

Secker, it may be added, not only baptized, but also confirmed the young prince; and after the accession he performed the ceremony at the marriage of the King with the Princess Charlotte of Mecklenberg. On Sunday, Nov. 2nd, the Archbishop writes:—

"The King hoped the proclamation against vice and profaneness would be regarded, and have a good effect. I answered, that such proclamations had been apt to be considered as matters of course, but that his example, I was persuaded, would give life and vigour to this. He replied that he thought it was his principal duty to encourage and support religion and virtue. I applauded this sentiment in few words highly, and mentioned it afterwards in conversation as his."

On a later occasion, after presenting an Address from the clergy of the Diocese of Canterbury, the Archbishop states:—

The same day "I read to the King on his throne the Address of the Bishop of London and Chapter of St. Paul's and Clergy of London and Westminster, first acquainting him in a few words that the Bishop, being unable, had desired me to do it. This the Bishop did in imitation of what was done March 13, 1701, when also the Bishop of London was indisposed. This Address was brought me from the Bishop, as also the speech which I read to the Princess of Wales in his name, and that of his clergy, after I had spoken my own compliment for Canterbury."

Secker carefully preserved numerous letters and notes relating to the Coronation of George the Third, and amongst them occurs the following statement relating to a circumstance which has been differently represented [1] :—

"At the Communion the King asked me if he should not take off his crown. I said the Office did not mention it. He asked if it would not be more suitable to such an act of religion. I said, 'Yes; but the Queen's crown could not be taken off easily.'"

The Archbishop remarks a few sentences before:—

"When I had put on the crown, the ladies pinned it to the Queen's head-dress or hair. The King then asked,

---

[1] See Stanley's "Hist. Memorials of Westminster Abbey," p. 101.

'What must be done?' I said, 'As ladies' heads are used to be covered, it would not be regarded.' He put off his crown immediately; and all the peers that saw it took off their coronets. Archbishop Wake's MS. directs both the King and Queen to take off their crowns. His printed form doth not."

Whatever might be the political faults of George the Third, and no doubt they were great, of his personal virtues, and the sincerity of his religious faith, there can be no doubt. Traditions of his devoutness still linger amongst the stories of old times at Windsor; and they include anecdotes of his sympathy with religious people of different denominations. He spoke with respect of the worthy pastor of an Independent Church in the town; was very considerate in allowing Nonconformist servants in the household ample opportunities for devotional services;[1] and it is related that once passing by a Methodist meeting house surrounded by a tumultuous rabble, he said, "The Methodists are a quiet, good kind of people, and will disturb nobody; and if I learn that any persons in my employment disturb them, they shall be immediately dismissed." His desire that every child in his dominions should be enabled to read the Scriptures is well known.

---

[1] My memories of Windsor extend over nearly half a century; and in what I have said I speak from personal recollections of what was well known in my early days.

After the accession of George the Third, the Dissenting Ministers of the three denominations in London, according to established custom, had an audience with his Majesty, and presented a loyal Address.

"Illustrious and ancient descent," they said, "princely education, prime of life, early piety and virtue, love of probity and truth, regard to liberty and the rights of conscience, and your known affection to this your native country, peculiarly endear your Majesty to all your subjects, and promise them everything their hearts can wish from the best of kings." They then refer to the war which was going on, and express their hope of "such a peace in Europe as shall effectually support the Protestant religion and liberties," an object the Dissenters ever kept in view throughout their political activity, and which on occasions of this kind they habitually recognised. "We recollect with joy and unfeigned gratitude," they went on to say, "that glorious era which settled the succession to the throne of Great Britain in your Majesty's royal house, and perpetuated to these nations, under God, the free and undisturbed enjoyment of all their civil and religious liberties; and we humbly beg leave to assure you, most gracious Sovereign, that, entirely confiding in your Majesty's Government, we shall not fail, from dictates of conscience and gratitude, to be examples ourselves of loyalty and duty, and to inculcate on all who attend our ministry, that submission and obedience to your Majesty's authority and government." " I thank you for this loyal affectionate Address," replied his Majesty ; "you may be assured of my protection, and of my care and attention to support the Protestant interest, and to maintain the Toleration inviolate."

In January, 1760, just before the new accession, Warburton was consecrated Bishop of Gloucester. "Nothing of a private nature," said Mr. Pitt, afterwards Earl of Chatham, "had given him so much pleasure as his bringing Dr. Warburton upon the Bench."[1] At a time when pre-eminent devotedness to the clerical calling, and a zealous discharge of its most spiritual duties, was, to say the least, not regarded as a chief qualification for the Episcopate, this appointment is not surprising. Such a distinguished scholar and thinker had claims above most men to a Bishopric, when Bishoprics were deemed proper rewards for service in the republic of letters ; but beyond that, Warburton had little to recommend him. A critic like Salmasius, "who seems to have erected his throne on a heap of stones, that he might have them at hand to throw at the heads of all who passed by ;" a man voracious of praise, and expecting compliments to be returned with interest ; a rector who

---

[1] Hurd's " Life of Warburton," prefixed to the " Divine Legation," vol. i. p. 44.

never visited his parish ; and a dignitary charged with
neglecting spiritual duties, could not be expected to
win the hearts or edify the lives of either the clergy
or the laity of his diocese. Nor did he make any
mark in the House of Lords. Some dreaded his
promotion, as though a second Atterbury would now
appear; "but," says his biographer, "he had neither
talents nor inclination for parliamentary intrigue or
parliamentary eloquence."[1] In a celebrated Triennial Charge, in the year 1761, he throws an odd light
on Episcopal practices, for he observes that it was a
habit in old times for a new bishop to give some
intimation how he was lifted into so eminent but
hazardous a station; but now the clergy had become less solicitous to know "whence their bishop
had dropped down among them." After warning
his auditors against "*fanaticism*, whether spiritual
or literary ; *bigotry*, whether religious or civil ; and
infidelity, whether philosophical or immoral," he
urged them to diligence in study, especially in theological learning; and after an allusion to the Universities, not at all complimentary,—it should be
recollected he had never been at Oxford or Cambridge,—he poured forth his satire on the popular religious literature of the day, comparing "the smaller
Divinity to the flies and lice of Egypt from the dust
of the land." It "meets you in your desk, and lies

---

[1] "Hurd's Life of Warburton," p. 45.

hid in all you taste and handle. The artful disguise, too, is no less taking than the plenty. And as Flaminius, host of Chalcis, entertained his guest with a magnificent variety of viands, and all from the hog-sty, so the whole of this delicious cookery comes from as dirty a place — I mean a bookseller's garret." What would be thought of such an Episcopal charge in the present day?

Warburton had a profound contempt for the Methodists, pronouncing Whitefield a madman, and Wesley little better—a judgment in which too many were ready to concur. No acts of Episcopal diligence and zeal are recorded in Warburton's life; and when he died, the periodicals of the day, with the exception of the *Westminster* and *Gentleman's Magazines*, were silent respecting the man who had been all his life tormented by literary ambition.

In the first year of George III. several bishops died: Hoadly, of Winchester; Sherlock, of London; Gilbert, of York; this occasioned several changes in the Episcopal Bench. Dr. Drummond, as Archbishop of York; Dr. Thomas, as Bishop of Salisbury; Yonge, as Bishop of Norwich; and Green, as Bishop of Lincoln, kissed the royal hand on the same day. All this happened before the coronation; and Newton, as Bishop of Bristol, passed through the ceremony soon afterwards.

The frank autobiography of the last prelate takes us behind the scenes, not at all to his advantage.

After an offer of the Deanery of Westminster, with the Bishopric of Rochester,—when, as he says himself, "the Bishop of Bristol did not think it worth his while to make the exchange, having something better in view,"—Mr. Grenville endeavoured to obtain for him, in 1764, the see of London, on the decease of Dr. Osbaldeston. The Duke of Bedford joined in the recommendation; but his Majesty, who "was very gracious in his answers, and was pleased to say many kind things of the Bishop of Bristol," was "unluckily, somehow or other, partly engaged, and had given some kind of promise for Bishop Terrick, in Lord Bute's administration, which he thought himself now obliged to fulfil." This was not the only time, Newton tells us, with the air of a disappointed man, that Dr. Terrick stood in his way. When the Primate of Ireland was thought to be dying, in 1764, Mr. Grenville "sounded a particular friend of the Bishop of Bristol, to know whether the Primacy would be agreeable to him." After the Archbishop was gone, Mr. Grenville sent for Dr. Newton and assured him he could readily obtain for him the royal appointment to the vacant see. But the Bishop, "having fully considered the matter before in all points of view, declined the offer with all possible gratitude, assigning his reasons for so doing, and expressing how much happier he should be with a translation to a bishopric in England, not naming any one in particular." It is curious to learn how the

Minister classified the sees. They were of two kinds—"bishoprics of business, for men of abilities and learning; and bishoprics of ease, for men of family and fashion." Of the former he reckoned Canterbury, York, London, and Ely, on account of its connection with Cambridge; of the latter, Durham, Winchester, Salisbury, and Worcester. But the ambitious Bishop lost his chance of further preferment when Mr. Grenville resigned office in 1765.[1]

In 1768, Secker, Archbishop of Canterbury, ended his days. It is said that he "was never acceptable nor agreeable at Court, nor ever had due weight and influence there." The sway of appointments, once to a large extent in the hands of the Primate, had by degrees been engrossed by the Ministers of State, and "bishops were regarded as little better than ciphers, even in their own churches." Twenty old royal chaplains were discarded, and as many new ones appointed, without the privity of his Grace; but members of the Royal family did not scruple to write to him in recommendation of clergymen whom they wished to serve.[2] On the Primate's decease,

---

[1] " Life of Dr. Thomas Newton," p. 112-157.

[2] In the *Court Papers*, Lambeth MSS, is a note from the Princess Amelia, asking on behalf of a clergyman, for a living of £100 a year; and another follows, thanking him for his compliance. I may add that the Archbishop preserved letters he received from his Majesty's Ministers, announcing victories by the Prussians over the Russians and Austrians, and by the English over the French Fleet. He also inserted the following

Dr. Newton calculated that Dr. Terrick, Bishop of London, would be promoted to Canterbury, and he hoped he should himself be raised to the Metropolitan see; but his hopes were dashed to the ground—"Diis aliter visum," he despondingly exclaimed, "The higher powers made a different arrangement."[1]

Dr. Cornwallis, Bishop of Lichfield and Dean of St. Paul's, succeeded Secker; and in noticing his career as Primate, the Countess of Huntingdon crosses our path. In the latter half of the eighteenth century she attained the zenith of her influence, and during the first ten years of that period, as well as before, through the services of Whitefield, who acted as her chaplain, produced a striking effect upon the minds of many noble personages. In her town house, crowds of titled people filled the drawing-room, to hear the much-talked-of preacher. There sat Lord Chesterfield, who, after listening to an eloquent sermon, returned thanks with characteristic courtli-

---

charges he had to pay after the King's accession." A note of fees due for swearing His Grace, Thomas, Lord Archbishop of Canterbury, one of the Lords of His Majesty's most honourable Privy Council, on the 17th day of March, 1761.

To the Clerks of the Council	£10
To the Under Clerks	4
To the Under Keeper of the Council Records	6
To the Council Chamber Keepers	5
To the Under Keeper	1
	£26

[1] "Life of Newton," p. 163.

ness; and there, too, Lord Bolingbroke might be seen and heard, inviting the orator to visit him, and endeavouring "to pass from infidelity to Calvinism if he could."[1] A centre of religious power in the circles of fashionable life, the Countess watched the conduct of prelates, being much concerned at what she heard respecting entertainments at the archiepiscopal palace; for Mrs. Cornwallis created great scandal by her balls and her routs, and by the splendour of her equipage. Lady Huntingdon aimed at putting an end to all this, which had become the talk of the town; and for that purpose she waited on his Grace. He was highly offended at this interference, and his wife went so far as to ridicule her ladyship in conversation with some fashionable friends. The Countess, hearing she had been called a hypocrite by Mrs. Cornwallis, sought an interview with the King.

"Madam," said he, "the feelings you have discovered, and the conduct you have adopted on this occasion, are highly creditable to you. The Archbishop's behaviour has been slightly hinted to me already; but now that I have a certainty of his proceedings, and most ungracious conduct towards your ladyship, after your trouble in remonstrating with him, I shall interpose my authority, and see what that will do towards reforming such indecent practices." "I have been told so many odd stories of your ladyship, that I am free to confess I felt a great degree of curiosity to see if you were at all like other women; and I am happy in

---

[1] Southey's "Life of Wesley," vol. ii. p. 167.

having an opportunity of assuring your ladyship of the very good opinion I have of you, and how very highly I estimate your character, your zeal, and abilities, which cannot be consecrated to a more noble purpose."

He then spoke of the talents of some of her ladyship's preachers, who he understood were very eloquent men. "The bishops," said he, "are very jealous of such men;" and he went on to mention a conversation he had lately had with a dignitary he would not name. This person had complained of the conduct of Lady Huntingdon's students and ministers, who had made a disturbance in his diocese. "Make bishops of them—make bishops of them," said the King. "That might be done," replied the Bishop; "but, please your Majesty, we cannot make a bishop of Lady Huntingdon." "It would be a lucky circumstance if you could," added the Queen;" to which the King added, "I wish there was a Lady Huntingdon in every diocese in the kingdom."

The result of the interview soon appeared in the following letter, which is probably an unparalleled piece of correspondence between a King and an Archbishop, at any rate in modern times :—

"My good Lord Prelate,—I could not delay giving you the notification of the grief and concern with which my breast was affected, at receiving authentic information that routs have made their way into your palace. At the same time, I must signify to you my sentiments on this subject, which hold these levities and vain dissipations as utterly inexpedient, if not unlawful, to pass in a residence for many centuries devoted to divine studies, religious retirement, and the extensive exercise of charity and benevolence; I add, in a place where so many of your predecessors have led their lives in such sanctity as has thrown lustre on the pure religion they professed and adorned.

"From the dissatisfaction with which you must perceive I behold these improprieties, not to speak in harsher terms, and on still more pious principles, I trust you will suppress them immediately; so that I may not have occasion to show any further marks of my displeasure, or to interpose in a different manner. May God take your Grace into His almighty protection! I remain, my Lord Primate, your gracious friend,

G. R."[1]

Whilst appointments to high places were made in the manner already described, several clergymen were much dissatisfied with the terms of subscription. Francis Blackburn, Archdeacon of Cleveland, a learned, clever, and honest man, of firm decision, and of courage bordering on audacity, fond of writing, ready with his pen, addicted beyond measure to controversy, attacking Warburton, and Butler, and intensely disliking Secker, appears to have been an Arian of the same type as Samuel Clarke. It is plain that he differed from the formularies of the Church in many respects; and it seemed to be a main object ever before him to seek a change in the law of clerical subscription.

He anonymously published in 1766 a book entitled "The Confessional," in which he relinquished a posi-

---

[1] "Life and Times of the Countess of Huntingdon," vol. ii. p. 283

tion he had once held, namely, that the Church formularies were entitled to a wide interpretation; he now attacked the principle of subscription altogether, contending that Churches had no right to make creeds, and that every creed contains material decisions from which an intelligent Christian, who has duly examined the Scriptures, may not unreasonably dissent.[1] He also affirmed that to impose interpretations of the Bible is to interfere with the right of private judgment, so vigorously asserted at the period of the Reformation; and that to adopt Burnet's latitudinarian defence of the Articles was to plunge into "embarrassed and fluctuating casuistry." If subscribers believed the Articles to be true, they certainly believed them to be true in one precise uniform sense; "if so," he asked, "what is there in our constitution to warrant an expositor to allow men to subscribe in different senses?" It was Blackburn's idea, that Burnet had little faith in his own theory of subscription, and that he was pressed by Archbishop Tillotson into a service which he reluctantly performed.[2]

The force of the Archdeacon's arguments is irresistible when applied to what is called "religious toleration" in general; but the right, or otherwise, of imposing subscription upon the ministers of a Church

---

[1] "Confessional," Blackburn's Works, vol. v. p. 175.
[2] Ibid., pp. 241–225

is another question, and however that may be settled, certainly the fact remains, that the law of subscription did not prevent the existence within the pale of the Establishment of a wide diversity of opinion on the very points assumed to have been settled by the Thirty-nine Articles.

In 1771 proposals were made for an application to Parliament on the subject. It was urged that the clergy ought to be "delivered from this yoke of bondage" and that "orthodoxy," in the mouth of a Protestant, should only mean agreement with Scripture. In accordance with such proposals, a meeting of London clergymen was convened at the Feathers Tavern, where a petition drawn up by the zealous Archdeacon was adopted. It asserted the rights of conscience, the free exercise of reason and judgment in the study of Scripture, and then it prayed for the undoubted Protestant privilege of interpreting Scripture without being bound by any human explications; and it was asked that at the Universities and elsewhere similar relief might be granted. With the prayer were joined expressions of loyalty, and the abhorrence of popish principles felt by the petitioners. The document received 250 signatures, including those of thirty or forty physicians and lawyers.

The petition, presented to the House of Commons in February, 1772, by Sir William Meredith, was opposed as a blow for "the absolute destruction of the Church," and supported on the ground that some of the Articles were "incomprehensible and self-contradictory." The principal men on the Opposition side sustained the prayer; and when it was urged that sectaries would make their way into the Church, if subscription were relaxed, Sir George Saville exclaimed, addressing the Speaker, "Sectaries, Sir, had it not been for sectaries, this cause had been tried at Rome. I thank God it is tried here."[1] He replied to Burke, who opposed the petition, and said that, for himself, he would not set bars in the way of those who were willing to enter and labour in the Church of God; and, it should be added, that the Solicitor-General—the question being considered an open one—appeared during the course of the debate in antagonism with his colleagues; for, said he, "The Universities, which prepare for all the learned professions, and rear fit members of Parliament, ought not to be confined to those of a particular creed; and we must reform them, if they will not reform themselves."[2]

The proposal to receive the petition was negatived by 217 to 71; but in our own time the object of the petitioners has been partially accomplished by an alteration in the terms of subscription, and by the abolition of certain tests at the Universities of Oxford and Cambridge.

---

[1] "Parliamentary Hist.," vol. xvii. p. 245.
[2] Ibid. same debate.

The Service for King Charles's day, as might be expected, strengthened the reasoning against subscription ; and by a remarkable coincidence, the sermon preached on the 30th of January that year, by Dr. Nowell, the Commons' Chaplain, helped the argument on the side of the petitioners. It is a curious fact, that the Speaker and four members only were present on the occasion, and, as a matter of form, the House returned thanks for the discourse. When printed, it was found to be a high-flown oration of the Sacheverell type ; and consequently a distinguished member moved that it should be burnt by the hangman, a very awkward proposal, whilst a vote of thanks for it stood recorded in the journals. The thanks were expunged, and the debates which they occasioned gave "fresh force and edge" to the matter of subscription. A motion followed for repealing the Act for observing the 30th of January, on the ground that the Service was no less than blasphemous, a parallel being drawn in it between King Charles and the blessed Saviour. Sir Roger Newdigate, member for the Oxford University, defended the Service, and took with him 125 votes against 97.

When attempts to obtain relief from subscription failed, there followed a movement for revising the Prayer-Book. An appeal was made on this behalf to the Bishops, by a Kentish Incumbent, who urged, that if, by such a revision, Dissenters were not brought back to the Church, the Church itself would have the satisfaction of knowing it had done its duty in removing blemishes and sweeping stumbling-blocks out of the paths of conformity. Dr. Percy and Dr. Porteus both favoured the idea, and Archbishop Cornwallis looked on it without prejudice; but in February, 1773, his Grace returned a formal answer, that, in the opinion of the Bench, nothing could prudently be done in the matter.[1]

Coincident with these circumstances was an attempt to prevent dormant claims on the part of the Church to landed estates or other property;[2] consequently several prelates became alarmed lest concerted attacks from different directions should be made on the rights and safeguards of the Establishment. The alarm increased when the Dissenters put in a claim to be relieved from the pressure of a clause in the Toleration Act, requiring that their ministers should subscribe to the doctrinal Articles. They felt encouraged to take this step by arguments adduced during the debates just noticed—arguments irrefragable in reference to the liberties of those who were not included within the State Church.

The Dissenting Deputies continued their activity through the reign of George III. in extending the liberties of their brethren. They now completed an

---

[1] " Life of Bishop Porteus," p. 40.
[2] Mr. Henry Seymour, in 1772, introduced but could not carry what was called the Church Nullum Tempus Bill. Mahon's (Lord Stanhope's) " Hist. of England," vol. v. p. 302.

important measure which they had steadily pursued for some years. By a London Corporation bye-law, Nonconformist citizens had long been annoyed through the imposition of fines for not serving as Sheriffs, the fines so imposed being, it is said, employed in the erection of the Mansion House. As the Corporation Act rendered every person incapable of holding a civic office, who had not within a year received the Lord's Supper in the Church of England, and as the Toleration Act had repealed the penal consequences of Dissent, some argued that on these grounds the Metropolitan system might be resisted with effect, and be eventually extinguished. Accordingly, when, in 1754, three Dissenters were elected who declined to serve, and actions were brought against them, resistance was made through the encouragement of the Deputies, at first not successfully. In 1757, the Sheriff's Court decided in favour of the Corporation; but in 1762 a judgment was obtained in the Court of Hustings, favourable to the defendants. The Corporation endeavoured to set this aside by writ of error before the House of Lords, in the month of January, 1767, when Lord Mansfield delivered a memorable speech, and the case ended with a second reversal of what had been done in the Sheriff's Court.[1]

The Deputies, in March, 1772, took another step in

---

[1] "Hist. and Proceedings of the Deputies," pp. 27-38.

the path of religious liberty. By the Toleration Act, Protestant Dissenting Ministers and Schoolmasters were exempted from penal laws against Nonconformity only on condition of their taking the oaths of allegiance and supremacy, and also subscribing to a declaration against Popery, and to the doctrinal Articles of the Church of England. To relieve them from the last of these requirements, it was proposed to substitute the following words, "We believe that the Holy Scriptures of the Old and New Testament contain a revelation of the mind and will of God, and that we receive them as the rule of our faith and practice." The enforcement of the objectionable clause of the Toleration Act had fallen into desuetude; still it might at any moment be revived; and while it remained written in the statute book, it left upon Nonconformists a stigma and reproach. Sir Henry Hoghton, continuing his adoption of the cause promoted by the Deputies, brought a Bill before the Commons, proposing the alteration just mentioned. He was seconded by Sir George Saville; and the Bill having passed the Lower House, reached the Lords. The Bill was there thrown out by a large majority. Several of the bishops, alarmed at this activity on the part of Nonconformists, set their faces against the measure, some of them backing their arguments against concession by certain passages from the works of Socinian divines. Lord Camden, Lord Shelburne, Lord Mansfield, and Lord Chatham, however, supported the Bill; and perhaps it was on this occasion that the last-named nobleman uttered his famous witticism descriptive of the English Establishment, as "Popish in its Liturgy, Calvinistic in its Articles, and Arminian in its clergy."[1]

In 1773, the Bill was re-introduced to Parliament in an amended form, On this occasion Burke came forward as the advocate of concession ; and when told that connivance was all which Dissenters could expect, inquired indignantly, "What, sir, is liberty by connivance, but a temporary relaxation of slavery?"[2] The idea of connivance exasperated the most eloquent of the Peers. "I hear," says Lord Chatham with characteristic warmth, writing at the time to a friend, "I hear in the debate on the Dissenters, the Ministry avowed enslaving them, and to keep up the cruel penal laws, like blood-hounds coupled up, to be let loose on the heels of these poor conscientious men, when Government pleases, *i.e.*, if they dare to dislike some ruinous measure or to disobey orders at an election."[3] The Bill was thrown out once more. But in 1779,. Sir Henry Hoghton and his friends succeeded in their endeavours. An Act was passed enabling

---

[1] Mr. Gladstone calls it "a shallow witticism, little worthy of so illustrious a man."—" Church Principles," p. 462.
[2] May's " Constitutional History," vol. iii. p. 93.
[3] " Chatham's Correspondence," vol. iv. p. 259. Letter to Lord Shelborne.

Nonconformist ministers and schoolmasters to pursue their calling without any subscription to the Thirty-nine Articles. At first no other subscription was substituted; but afterwards, in consequence of a motion by Lord North, it was required that a declaration should be made by persons seeking to be qualified under the Act, that they were Christians and Protestant Dissenters, and took the Scriptures as their rule of faith and practice.[1]

In 1774 and 1776 there occurred three remarkable accessions to the Episcopal Bench. In the first of these years, Brownlow North became Bishop of Worcester; and in 1780 he reached the splendid see of Winchester. Descended from the Norths, who figured in the previous century, and brother to Lord North, the favourite Minister of George III., his chances of preferment from birth and rank were obvious; his dignified appearance and courtly manners, no doubt, being regarded as special qualifications for his position as prelate of the Garter, an office attached to the Winchester episcopate. Judging from his portrait in magnificent knightly mantle, with his collar and his St. George, his pleasant face surmounted by a ponderous wig, he must have looked eminently fitted to figure at Court, and to grace state ceremonials; but when we learn that he was absent from his diocese for years during long continental

---

[1] May's " Constitutional History," vol. iii. p. 94.

travels,[1] we cannot pronounce him an exemplary bishop.

The same year Richard Hurd obtained the see of Lichfield and Coventry, to be exchanged in 1781 for that of Worcester. Though of humble birth, he seems to have been a man of polished manners; and at Hartlebury Castle, when he received his mother, a farmer's wife of no education, he would " with stately courtesy " lead her up to the head of the table—an incident to the credit of his character as a son and a gentleman. The "terse, neat little thin man" does not seem, with all his graciousness, to have made many friends, if we are to believe the accounts given of him by some; yet, on the other hand, it is said, "piety and goodness were so marked on his countenance, which is truly a fine one, that he has been named, and very justly, 'the Beauty of Holiness.'" Indeed, in face, manner, demeanour, and conversation, he seemed precisely what a bishop should be, and what would make a looker-on,—were he not a bishop, and a see vacant,—cry out, " Take Dr. Hurd, that is the man."[2] The opinion thus expressed does not indicate any appreciation of the Episcopal office beyond that of its relation to superior society; and with such reference George III. pronounced him "the most naturally polite man he had ever known."[3] The

---

[1] Nichol's " Literary History," vol. vi. p. 658.
[2] Madame D'Arblay made the remark.
[3] Kilvert's " Life of Hurd," p. 199.

aristocratic Brownlow North could not have maintained Episcopal dignity more sumptuously than the plebeian Richard Hurd; for when the latter went a quarter of a mile from the Castle to Hartlebury Church, it was in his coach, with servants in full dress liveries; and when he went to the Bristol Hot Wells, a favourite resort amidst fatigues of office, he was accompanied by a retinue of twelve attendants.[1] Hurd added to qualities like those of North, some which North did not possess; for Hurd was a literary man, the friend and biographer of Warburton, and author of works which fill eight volumes, including "An Introduction to the Study of the Prophecies concerning the Christian Church in general, and in particular, concerning the Church of Papal Rome." Warburton praised him as one of the best scholars in the kingdom; and Hurd repaid the obligation in the eulogiums he conferred on Warburton. A very different man from either was Dr. Beilby Porteus, appointed to Chester in 1776, to London in 1787. Though not belonging exactly to the Evangelical school, he looked upon it with favour, and promoted its objects, such as a better observance of the Lord's day, the establishment of Sunday Schools, the encouragement of lay activity, and, at a later period, the support of the British and Foreign Bible Society.

In further tracing the connection between religion

---

[1] Kilvert, p. 200.

and the State, we meet, in the year 1778, with a relaxation of penal laws bearing on Roman Catholics. Since the days of Elizabeth, they had been subjected to heavy persecution, and what arose out of political disaffection continued long after such disaffection had ceased. Catholic worship in public was proscribed, and the disciples of an ancient faith were driven into holes and corners, if they would celebrate their religious rites; of which circumstance mementos may be found in concealed chambers of old decaying mansions in different parts of England. The Revolution did not place Roman Catholics on the same footing with orthodox Dissenters; and in 1700, an Act of Parliament offered a reward of £100 for the discovery of any priest who dared to celebrate the offices of his Church. Yet Roman Catholics seem to have taken courage; and we find Doddridge saying in one of his letters, "The growth of Popery seems to give a general and just alarm. A priest from a neighbouring gentleman's family makes frequent visits hither, and many of the Church people seem popishly inclined."[1]

The Rebellion of 1745 excited fresh indignation against English and Scotch Papists, because of the sympathy which some of them had manifested toward the grandson of James II. In this instance, as is often the case, the innocent suffered with the

---

[1] "Doddridge's Correspondence," vol. iii. p. 182.

guilty; and inoffensive people were sometimes harassed quite as much as their rebellious neighbours. Such persons pleaded their loyalty in an address to George III., trusting that their irreproachable conduct for many years sufficiently proved the honesty of their character as citizens; and, in 1778, Sir George Savile, supported by Mr. Dunning, proposed the repeal of penalties, enacted in 1700—that priests should be imprisoned, that the estates of Roman Catholics educated abroad should be forfeited in favour of Protestant heirs, and that they should be incapable of holding real property. The statute of 1700, indeed, had not been rigidly enforced, yet instances of its execution had occurred; and there was nothing but public opinion to prevent the revival, at any moment, of this tremendous power of oppression. These disabilities were now removed, the Bill to that effect easily passing through both Houses; one Whig Bishop, Hinchcliffe of Peterborough, alone opposing it in the Lords[1]. The effect was soon apparent. In 1780, as compared with 1767, the number of Roman Catholics increased from 67,916 to 69,376.[2] They could now live in peace. Nobody could interfere with any priest who said mass in a family chapel, or in a public church. One situated at Oscott, near Birmingham, approached "through green meadows

---

[1] "Parl. History," vol. xix. pp. 1137-1145.
[2] Census, 1851. Report on Religious Worship, sect. ci.

and silent lanes," witnessed the performance of Catholic rites, whilst many of the poor in the neighbourhood knelt at the altar. At a later period, especially at the time of the French Revolution, Catholic exiles sought refuge within our shores; they provided for themselves churches, and established monastic institutions, and, in 1794, a stately mansion amidst the charming woods of Ribblesdale was transformed into the famous Stoneyhurst College.

There is a class of people who import into Protestant zeal a popish-like intolerance. Many such were living in 1780, and with the cry of "No Popery," heightened by the recent Act of Relief, they proceeded to form Protestant Associations, under the leadership of George Gordon, a young nobleman, described by his admirers as a staunch Whig, an enemy to the American War, and a friend to the liberties of the people; by others, as "a silly booby," "a laughing-stock," "a make-game," and a "fellow with a twist in his head." He called a public meeting at Coachmakers' Hall, in Noble Street, Foster Lane, where a petition was prepared for the repeal of the Act of 1778; and it was resolved that all the Members of the Association should meet in St. George's Fields, on the Surrey side of the river, at 10 o'clock in the forenoon of Friday, the 2nd of July. On that summer day, 50,000 or 60,000, some say 100,000, people assembled in an open space, once famous for violets growing in "the water ditches," where, later on, mobs gathered for political purposes oddly described by Archbishop Laud in the "History of His Troubles." The members of the Association and their friends, wearing blue cockades, came to listen to Lord George, and then to convey a huge petition professedly containing 120,000 names, to the House of Commons. Many readers will remember the excitement in April, 1848, when the Chartists assembled on Kennington Common for a different purpose, but in a somewhat similar manner. Unfortunately the wise precautions taken in the latter instance were not adopted in the former; and with only parish beadles and helpless watchmen to keep the peace, the Protestant mob had it their own way. They marched in three detachments, under banners inscribed with the words "*No Popery;*" and at Charing Cross were joined by numerous allies on horseback and in carriages. The narrow streets were blocked up with swelling multitudes, and Palace Yard was soon packed by a riotous mob. Lord Mansfield, who had recently told a jury to acquit a Catholic priest charged with celebrating mass, had his carriage windows broken; and, having scrambled into the House of Lords, "he sat quivering on the woolsack like an aspen." The Archbishop of York had his lawn sleeves torn off and flung in his face. The Bishop of Lincoln, on his way to Parliament, sought refuge in a house, from which he escaped, according to rumour, in a woman's dress, along the leads. The populace saluted Lord

Bathurst as "the Pope," and an "old woman;" "the notion of Pope Joan," as Horace Walpole said, "being thus split into two." A gentleman in black, riding in the Duke of Northumberland's carriage, was pronounced a Jesuit confessor, and his Grace's pocket picked of watch and purse. Other acts of violence followed, and the temporal peers were treated worse than the spiritual ones. At the same time the mob rushed into the lobby of the Commons' House with shrieks of "No Popery! No Popery! Repeal! Repeal!" The Serjeant at Arms and other officers were defied, much to the amazement and terror of the members in cocked hats and big wigs sitting within St. Stephen's Chapel, then boxed up with galleries, like a Dissenting meeting house. From the top of the stairs, Lord George harangued his friends, telling them to persevere, and calling out the names of obnoxious members—Lord North and Mr. Burke amongst the rest. At length, the House divided on the question of receiving the monster petition; 8 voted for it, and 194 against it.

The "Protestants" now became furious, and proceeded to burn down the chapels of Popish Embassies. Next evening they attacked the dwellings of Roman Catholics in Moorfields; on and on the excitement rolled, the blue cockades appearing all over the city and the suburbs. Savile House, in Leicester Fields, was assailed; and then the miserable fanatic who had taken the lead in the business began to disavow all share in the riots. Gibbon wrote, "Forty thousand Puritans, such as they might be in the time of Cromwell, have started out of their graves;" but here the historian is seen at fault, for nothing like this had ever been seen during the Civil Wars. Escaped from the control of their leaders, the fanatic multitudes continued their excesses, still burning with professed religious zeal—still shouting "No Popery! No Popery!" Then came the conflagration of Newgate, the flames mounting up to heaven; the sky black with smoke; embers flying over the neighbouring houses; prisoners in chains rushing about the streets; "any one might get in, and, what was never the case before, any one might get out." Lord Mansfield's House, in Bloomsbury Square, was fired, his furniture, books, and curiosities were burnt whilst his cellars were drained; the flames in different parts of the City not being extinguished until the 9th of July. "The sight," says Dr. Johnson, "was dreadful, thirty-six fires all blazing at one time."[1] Lord George was tried for treason and acquitted, but he died in Newgate. "He began his career as a midshipman, he ended his career as a Jew."[2] An odd antithesis; but, beyond all doubt, he was a mad fanatic during part of a life, which ignominiously terminated in Newgate. It is amusing to find in the newspapers of the day, certain advertise-

---

[1] Lord Mahon (Stanhope) vol. vii. pp. 28, 31.
[2] Ibid. vol. vi. p. 240.

ments—whether they proceeded from regard to trade or religion we cannot say—in which the advertisers assure the public, that Mr. Bicknell, his Majesty's hosier, is as true and faithful a Protestant as any in his Majesty's dominions, and also, that they have the best authority for saying, that "his Majesty's wine merchants and many others, are also Protestants."[1]

Roman Catholics, then as now, were not all of one mind on a question, which more than any other aroused the opposition of Protestant Englishmen—namely, the Pope's Infallibility, in connection with a claim to the power of deposing sovereigns from their thrones. The Rev. Alban Butler, the learned author of "Lives of the Saints," in one of his letters on "Bowyer's History of the Popes," distinctly remarked that, "though some private divines think that the pope, by the assistance of some special providence, cannot err in the decisions of faith solemnly published by him with the mature advice of his council, or the clergy, or the divines of his Church, yet it is denied by others; the learned Bossuet and many others, especially of the school of Sorbonne, have written warmly against that

---

[1] *London Courant*, June 8, 1780, quoted by "Lord Mahon," vol. vii. p. 36. I would add to the above account, that an aged friend of mine was present at the burning of Newgate, and used to describe the fearfulness of the spectacle, and the religious frenzy of the period.

opinion. No Catholic looks upon it as an article or term of communion." "Mr. Bowyer never found the infallibility of the pope in our creed, and knows very well that no such article is proposed by the Church or required of any one."[1] This passage has a seasonable importance just now, read in the light of the conclusion reached by the recent Vatican Council; but the main purpose for its introduction is to show that some English Catholics of the last century were averse to the ultramontane theory, the maintenance of which by others had greatly prejudiced their cause, and had hindered the progress of political freedom. In 1782 a committee was formed of liberal laymen in communion with Rome, to attend to the affairs of the Roman Catholic body in England; and Mr. Charles Butler, known as the author of works on Romanism, acted as secretary. They proposed that a new oath of allegiance should be framed, protesting against the temporal authority of the pope, his right to excommunicate kings and absolve subjects, and the assumed idea, that Catholics were not bound to keep faith with Protestants. A committee was formed with the title of *Protesting Catholic Dissenters*, and resisted certain decisions of their bishops, as "encroaching on their natural Civil and Religious rights." Even attempts were made to

---

[1] Life of Butler prefixed to his "Lives of the Saints," vol. i. p. xiv.

obtain the power of appointing bishops by the clergy and people.[1] Persons supporting these views were numerous and influential, including several noblemen; but the four Vicars Apostolic, who, sheltered by the Act of 1778, could publicly exercise priestly and episcopal functions, disliked the appellation of "Protesting Catholic Dissenters"; and in discussions on the subject, a leading part was taken by the learned Dr. Milner, agent for the bishops of the Western and Northern districts. He became acquainted with Pitt, Fox, Dundas, and Wyndham, and also with Bishop Horsley, upon whom he made a very favourable impression. A Bill brought in by Mr. Mitford in 1791, for the relief of "Protesting Catholic Dis-

---

[1] Dr. Schaff in his "History of the Creeds," p. 90, states that the Archbishop of St. Louis, Peter Richard Kenrick, was an opponent of the infallibility dogma in the Vatican Council, but afterwards submitted. "In a lengthy and remarkable speech which he had prepared for the Vatican Conncil, but was prevented from delivering by the sudden close of the discussion, June 3rd, 1870, he shows that the doctrine of papal infallibility was not believed either in Ireland, his former home, or in America; on the contrary that it was formally and solemnly disowned by British bishops prior to the Catholic Emancipation Bill." See Friedrich's "Documenta," vol. i. pp. 189–226. Oxenham, in his translation of Döllinger's "Reunion of Churches," p. 126, says that in Keenan's "Controversial Catechism," the doctrine of papal infallibility is repudiated as an article of the Catholic faith, and treated as a Protestant calumny: but that since 1871, the leaf containing this assertion is cancelled and another substituted. Schaff, p. 102.

senters," provided for the enforcement of a new and modified oath of abjuration; but through Milner's influence Fox helped to defeat the proposal.[1]

---

[1] "Parl. Hist.," vol. xxix. pp. 113–115, 664. May's "Constit. Hist. of England," vol. iii. p. 107.

CHAPTER XVII.

1780–1800.

A CONSIDERABLE time having elapsed since the last application to Parliament for a repeal of the Test and Corporation Acts, the committee of Dissenting Deputies in 1786 determined to re-open the question; and in 1787 waited on Mr. Pitt to solicit his offices on their behalf. On the 28th of March in that year a motion was made for the repeal, by Mr. Beaufoy, seconded by Sir Henry Hoghton, and supported by Charles James Fox, Lord Beauchamp, and William Smith. The usual arguments were urged on both sides. After a debate in the House of Commons of seven hours, the motion was negatived by 178 to 100. Not discouraged by this defeat, the deputies renewed their exertions in 1789, when Mr. Beaufoy again made a motion, seconded by Sir Henry Hoghton: "That the House resolve itself into a committee to consider so much of the Acts of the 13th of Charles II. for regulating Corporations, and of the 25th of Charles II. for preventing dangers from popish recusants, as renders it necessary for persons holding places of trust under the Crown to receive the sacrament." So ran the new motion; but the attempt failed like the former, only that the majority dropped to 124 against 104, a result which encouraged the Dissenters. In 1790 they returned to the subject, and solicited Mr. Fox to lead their cause. Mr. Fox gave notice on the 15th of February, 1790, that in the month of March he would bring in a Bill for the repeal of the Acts. He did so in a speech of great power.

The conduct of the Dissenters, he said, had been uniformly peaceable, the State had nothing to apprehend either from their disloyalty or ambition. He wished he could say as much of all other sects. The High Church party, which had happily been dormant for a great number of years, was now reviving. It had not been dead as he had hoped, but had only, for a time it seems, lain asleep. Their constant cry had ever been "the Church is in danger." He was sorry to observe some dignitaries of the Church, men of distinguished talents, whom he held in great respect, join in the absurd alarm, and express their affected and chimerical apprehension of danger upon the present occasion. Were there not many avowed Dissenters both in that and the other House of Parliament? Yet no danger was ever entertained from that circumstance to the constitution. "But," say the party, "if you make a Dissenter an exciseman there will be danger."[1] Mr. Pitt contended that the Establish-

---

[1] "Parl. Hist.," vol. xxviii .p. 394. Fox's speech is reported at length. The whole debate covers above sixty columns.

ment would be imperilled by the removal of tests, because Dissenters, admitted to office, would use all legal means for subverting what they disliked, and Burke, vehement in his opposition, dwelt with warmth upon the hostility towards the Church recently manifested by Dr. Price and Dr. Priestly. Upon a division the supporters of the measure were defeated by a majority of nearly three to one.[1] It may appear wonderful to many that this piece of intolerance in the legislation of England should be retained for nearly forty years after that period—especially as it remained practically abortive, except in the way of casting a reflection upon Dissenters ; for an annual Act ever since 1727 was passed to indemnify those who accepted office without qualifying themselves according to the law.[2] But the circumstances and the spirit of the times, so different from our own, must be taken into account, not to vindicate or excuse, but to explain, at least in part, the conduct of many politicians at that crisis.

It is impossible to understand the nature and issue of the debate just noticed without glancing at the French Revolution, and at the effect it produced on English society. The meeting of the States General had been held in May, 1789, and had proclaimed liberty and equality. The third Estate had declared

---

[1] Ayes, 62 ; Noes, 149.
[2] May's " Constit. Hist.," vol. iii. p. 82.

itself the National Assembly, and had absorbed all
power within its own hands. The people had risen
against the troops, and the Bastille had been razed
to the ground in the summer of the same year. The
nobility had emigrated. The rights of man, the abolition of feudal and aristocratic privileges, and the
liberty of the press had been authoritatively asserted.
The palace of Versailles had been attacked, and the
king brought to Paris. It takes away one's breath
to enumerate the startling events which occurred in
a few short months. Of course Englishmen felt the
deepest interest in these astounding changes. They
were divided into two parties. Some thought only
or chiefly of the previous history of France, a history
of misgovernment in the State, and of corruption in
the Church; of oppression on the side of rulers, and
endurance of wrong on the side of the ruled; of
the most frightful abuse of political power, and the
most frightful perversion of religious truth. In the
troubles which befell the royal family and the upper
classes, they saw the just Nemesis of Providence—the
necessary consequence of previous tyranny and un-
righteousness. The overthrow of so much evil gave
them satisfaction. An age of wickedness had come
to an end; a better day seemed about to dawn.
They were full of hope. Others thought only, or
chiefly, of the disturbance of order; of the convul-
sion of society; of the sufferings endured by men and
women brought up in the lap of luxury; of the dis-

appearance of chivalry and refinement amidst the surging waves of democratic vulgarity; of the shock given to thrones; of the tottering position of the Church; of growing licentiousness under the name of liberty, and advancing infidelity under the name of reason. To such beholders the heavens were overspread with thunder-clouds, while, where they stood, they felt the throes of a coming earthquake.

Dr. Richard Price may be taken as a type of the first class. He was a learned Presbyterian minister, a metaphysician and moralist, a financier and politician. His four dissertations on Providence, Prayer, the State of virtuous men after death, and Christianity, are sufficient to support his fame in the first two respects; and, as to the last two, there can be no doubt of his brilliant genius and great influence. He had sympathized with America in the War of Independence, and enjoyed the confidence of Dr. Franklin. On the 4th of November, 1789, in the midst of the changes just enumerated, he preached a sermon at the Meeting House of the Old Jewry. He chose for his subject "the Love of our Country," upon which he dilated at some length, dwelling upon truth, virtue, and liberty as those "blessings in which the interest of our country lies, and to the attainment of which our love of it ought to direct our endeavours."[1] At the close of the discourse, the

---

[1] Fourth Edition of the Discourse, with additions.

preacher burst forth into an impassioned eulogium upon what had been effected by the French Revolution up to that time [1]—some while, it should be noticed, before the Reign of Terror, and the execution of Louis XVI. The Declaration of Rights, proclaimed in Paris, expressing principles which are now adopted by almost all Englishmen, fired Dr. Price with the utmost enthusiasm, and opened bright prospects of national prosperity on the other side the Channel.

From Richard Price we must turn to Edmund Burke, the philosophical statesman, who—after having advocated reform as one of the leaders of the Whig party, now paused in his career, and turned round to look at things in a new light—may be taken as a type of the other class. Price's sermon attracted his attention, and, in reply, he wrote and published in 1790 his elaborate "Reflections on the Revolution in France." He denounced the discourse as the declamation of a man connected with literary caballers, intriguing philosophers, and political theologians; and, in contrast with Price's glowing hopes, Burke painted scenes of desolation and misery. The queen startled when asleep by the voice of the sentinel crying out to save herself by flight; ruffians, reeking with blood, rushing into her chamber; the king, the queen, and their infant children forced to abandon their palace swimming with blood, polluted by

---

[1] Pp. 49, 50.

massacre, and strewed with scattered limbs and mutilated carcases. With all this he contrasted the conservatism of England. "We are not the converts of Rousseau; we are not the disciples of Voltaire; Helvetius has made no progress among us; atheists are not our preachers; madmen are not our lawgivers." "We know, and it is our pride to know, that man is, by his constitution, a religious animal; that atheism is not only against our reason, but our instincts, and cannot prevail long." "We are resolved to keep an established Church, an established monarchy, and an established aristocracy, each in the degree it exists, and no greater."[1] Though Price's sermon contains a great deal to which all liberal politicians in the present day would subscribe, there are passages in it which crossed the prejudices and aroused the fears of the Tory citizens at that season of excitement; but, on the other hand, Burke attributed to Price designs for which no warrant is given in the discourse; and said a great deal which it would be difficult to reconcile with the principles of the Revolution of 1688.[2] Dr. Price of course opposed the

---

[1] "Reflections," pp. 91, 162, 179, 181, 192, 216, 225.

[2] It is remarkable that in Scotland, as well as England, Christian ministers regarded events in France with great satisfaction. Robinson, the historian, in a sermon heard by Lord Brougham, in 1788, at Edinburgh, spoke of events then passing on the Continent, which would produce an event which our neighbours would ere long have to celebrate like to that which

Test and Corporation Acts, and, in common with many of his Dissenting friends, zealously sought their repeal. Burke, looking at the question through the medium of the French Revolution, fancied he saw in their repeal the destruction of a breakwater against mischievous changes in Church and State. Nothing can be more futile than his reasoning, regarded in the light of subsequent history; the Test and Corporation Acts are gone, and are now confessed by all parties to have been sources of weakness, not props of strength, to the political and ecclesiastical constitution of the country. But the terror produced in so many quarters by the Revolution sufficiently accounts for the resistance made at the time to the Bill introduced by Fox. In 1791 came the flight of Louis XVI.; in 1792 the sway of the Jacobins and the abolition of Royalty; in 1793 succeeded the execution of the monarch and the Reign of Terror; in 1794 the execution of the queen. Tragical events occurring from month to month in Paris created a profound sensation throughout England. The two parties on this side the water came into more determined collision than ever. Those who thought with Price, made the best they could of the frightful excesses committed, and anticipated the purification of the social atmosphere by passing storms. Those who thought with

---

had then called them together.—See Brougham's Life, vol. i. p. 27; and Stanley's "Church of Scotland," p. 128.

Burke, insisted upon the correctness of his predictions, and the justness of their fears. As is ever the case in times of excitement, each party saw little but what was wrong and mischievous on the side assailed, little but what was right and good on the side espoused. Even religious people excused the violence of the Parisian democrats. What they read in the *Morning Chronicle*, the liberal organ of the day, they construed in favour of the cause of reform and freedom ; but other religious people regarded the state of French affairs with the utmost horror. Politics pervaded every circle, to the exclusion of other subjects. Few there were who did not rank with Fox and Price, or with Pitt and Burke. The trials of Hardy, Tooke, Thelwall, and others, agitated London to an extent, says an old friend, now passed away, " which I have never seen equalled, though my life is fallen in times and events of the most prodigious and portentous character." [1] Some, however, with a wise discrimination, separated between the good and evil abroad, and between the religious and the irreligious elements commingled at home. Whilst they maintained the political rights of society, they detected and exposed the universal and destructive tendencies of infidelity. No one did this so effectually as the Rev. Robert Hall, in his sermon on the subject. [2]

---

[1] "Autobiography of the Rev. W. Walford," p. 113.
[2] " Hall's Works," vol. i., p. 13.

Though Dissenters had obtained a measure of relief in 1772 and 1773, there was a strong feeling manifested against them in 1790 and 1791. When Burke, in March, 1790, read to the House of Commons extracts from the writings of Priestly and others, he conveyed the impression that Nonconformity was inimical to the Church of England, and that the Establishment had fallen into greater danger than the Church of France a year or two before. This great politician also, in his "Reflections on the French Revolution," inveighed against the introduction of politics into Nonconformist pulpits, saying that "no sound ought to be heard in the Church but the healing voice of Christian charity;"[1] forgetting that politics, on the other side, were as vehemently advanced in cathedrals and parish edifices; indeed, that sometimes "they resounded with language, at which Laud would have shuddered, and Sacheverel would have blushed."

Under the inspiration of Burke's book and Burke's speeches, increased by sermons preached at church, there rose once more throughout the country a cry of "the Church in danger," and the "Familiar Letters to the Inhabitants of Birmingham," by Dr. Priestly, who opposed the Establishment, while he praised the Constitution of England, augmented the tumult. This gentleman was the most original English philosopher of his age. His works on Electricity, Light and Air, what-

---

[1] "Reflections on the French Revolution," p. 92.

ever their literary merits or demerits, are of a nature to secure for him a very high place in the history of scientific investigation, and his experiments in chemistry, which led to most important discoveries, were all the more creditable on account of the immense difficulties which he had to overcome. He turned all his observations to valuable account, and the "discovery of truth seems to have been, in every case, his real and undisguised object."[1] A Royal proclamation dated July 11th, 1791, denounced "a certain scandalous and seditious paper" printed and published at Birmingham, and offered £100 for the discovery of the writer. The seditious paper thus condemned invited the people to celebrate the destruction of the Bastille in Paris, and also attacked the English Parliament as venal, the English Ministers as hypocritical, the English clergy as oppressors, the reigning family as extravagant, and the crown as too heavy for the head that carried it. Though the infamous placard made its appearance in Birmingham, it is said to have been concocted in London. At all events, a party assembled at a tavern in the town to celebrate the triumph of the French Revolution, and another party, assembled at another tavern, the same day, to toast Church and King. Outside, mobs hissed and hooted, but the dinners passed off without disturbance in-

---

[1] Thomson, in his "Annals of Philosophy," vol. i., and his "History of the Royal Society," gives a high character to Dr. Priestly.

doors. After the first company had separated, the rabble broke into the room, declaring that they "wanted to knock the powder out of Priestly's wig," encouraged in their exploit, it is reported, by what had been said in a speech delivered at the other celebration. Soon after, Priestly's meeting house was in flames. Another meeting house shared the same fate. Then the mob marched to Fair Hill, where Priestly lived, and destroyed his dwelling, his furniture, his books, and his philosophical instruments. When the riot began, the Doctor was quietly at home, having been absent from the dinner, and he now refused to accept on the part of his friends, defence against the ruffians, because he had scruples as to resisting persecution by force. He and his family were conducted to a place of refuge, and then the work of demolition was accomplished.[1] From the 14th to the 17th of July Birmingham fell into the hands of the rioters. Scenes in London eleven years before were re-enacted; houses of prominent Dissenters were consumed; wretches got drunk in a wine cellar, and perished in the very flames they had kindled; warehouses were plundered and atrocities committed, Nonconformists being selected as the victims of the abounding furies. The magistrates at first were content with issuing an appeal to "Friends and Brother Churchmen," to desist, since the damage, amounting to £100,000,

---

[1] *Annual Register.*

would fall on the parishes. At last, Light Dragoons rode into the town, the mobs dispersed, several culprits were tried, and three of the number executed.

The Unitarians, to whom Priestly belonged, suffered more than other Dissenters from penal enactments. The 9th & 10th of William III., for suppressing blasphemy and profaneness, proscribed the public maintenance of Socinian opinions; and though the law was not put in operation it remained on the Statute Book, to the discredit of a respectable body of citizens. Mr. Fox, in May, 1792, proposed to repeal so much of the law as affected Unitarians. Referring to the prejudices against this denomination, he said Dr. South had traced their pedigree from wretch to wretch, back to the devil himself; but that these descendants of the devil were now his clients, and he claimed, on their behalf, the same toleration as was accorded to orthodox Nonconformists; at the same time, he pointed to the Birmingham riots as the natural result of bigotry and persecution. Burke again appealed to the facts of the French Revolution as a warning to this country; and described Fox's clients as allies of the Jacobins, and disciples of Tom Paine. Fox's motion was defeated by 142 against 63.[1] Party rancour increased, and politics being mixed up with religion,—sedition, and treason, no less than

---

[1] "Parliament. Hist.," vol. xxix. p. 1372.

heresy and schism, were laid to the charge of certain Dissenters.[1]

It will be remembered that in 1736, Quakers had applied to Parliament for the abolition of vexatious methods of enforcing tithes; and a measure for that purpose passed the Commons, but was defeated by the Lords. Under the old law still in existence, Friends were exposed to much hardship, and in 1796 seven of them were in York Castle, without any prospect of deliverance. Mr. Sergeant Adair, on the 21st of April that year, proposed a Bill to facilitate the recovery of tithes, without the infliction of imprisonment. Again the Bill passed the Commons, but the Archbishop of Canterbury headed an opposition in the Lords, on the ground that there remained no sufficient time for the consideration of so important a question; a course of proceeding in exact accordance with a precedent set in the same House on the previous occasion of the Quaker appeal.[2] The next session the Bill reappeared, when Sir William Scott, afterwards Lord Stowell, declared the opinions held by the Quakers were of such a nature as to affect the civil rights of property, and therefore he considered them as unworthy of legislative indulgence.

---

[1] The prosecution in November, 1792, of William Winterbotham, a Baptist minister, affords a striking example of the injustice of the government at that time. See " State Trials."

[2] See " Parl. Hist.," vol. xxxii. p. 1022, and the first vol. of this Hist. p. 243.

If one man had conscientious scruples against the payment of tithes, to which his property was legally liable, another might object to the payment of rent as sinful, while a third might hold it irreligious to pay his debts. If the principle of indulgence were ever admitted, the sect of anti-tithe Christians would soon become the most numerous and flourishing in the kingdom—a course of reasoning quite beside the mark, as the Quaker did not seek to be relieved from tithe payments, but only from the cruel method of enforcing them. They had conscientious scruples about voluntary payment; but they were prepared quietly to suffer distraint upon their property for that purpose. What they complained of was, the oppressive litigation and the unrighteous imprisonment to which they were exposed; and therefore it could be replied that the tithe owner would be enabled by the proposed Bill to recover his demands by summary distress, instead of punishing a conscientious and peaceable neighbour, by an ignominious and painful incarceration. The Speaker decided by a casting vote for going into committee on the Bill, but the Bill was afterwards lost by a majority of sixteen.[1]

Before closing this review of the relations of the State to religion, it is proper to notice a check which Parliament, towards the end of the century, put upon simoniacal practices in the Establishment. In 1783

---

[1] "Parl. Hist.," vol. xxxii.; May's "Const. Hist.," vol. iii. p. 113.

an appeal was made to the House of Lords from a decision of Lord Loughborough respecting what were called Bonds of resignation. Laymen having rights of presentation, received from a clerk, when presented to a living, a bond to resign when called upon to do so. The practice not only put the clergy in a state of dependence inconsistent with their office as ministers of the gospel, but also frequently involved a simoniacal contract, by which a patron obtained money for presentation to a benefice actually vacant. Lord Loughborough had decided that such bonds were legal, but in 1782 the House of Lords reversed that decision.

Again, in 1800 another practice of a kindred description disappears. It had become common upon purchasing an advowson to take a lease of the tithes, glebe, and parsonage house for 99 years, on a peppercorn rent, and to enter into possession of the premises, and the profits, as if there had been an actual resignation. The Bishop's authority to refuse acceptance of a resignation, if he thought it proceeded from improper motives, could be thus set aside ; and scandalous manœuvres thus crept into the Establishment. The Bishop of London saw the mischief, and determined to do what he could to terminate it. He therefore refused to institute a clergyman, who had taken a lease of the kind described, and after long and expensive litigation accomplished his object. "The abatement of these evils was the first breaking in upon that great crust of abuses, which had been long hardening around the Church of England." "The commencement of the next century witnessed an attack upon the monster evil of non-residence and pluralities."[1]

Within the last twenty years of the eighteenth century some important changes occurred on the episcopal benches. Dr. Robert Watson rose to the see of Llandaff, in 1782. A Westmoreland boy, admitted at Cambridge as a sizar dressed in a coarse mottled coat and blue yarn stockings, he won a scholarship, became a Tutor and a Fellow, qualified himself in the course of a few months for the professorship of chemistry, and seven years afterwards we find him Regius Professor of Divinity. He prided himself on being the "self-taught professor," and in other ways exhibited originality and independence. He wrote letters under the signature of "a Christian Whig," with the view of abolishing subscription. He vindicated the French Revolution in a sermon, which made much noise, but gave great offence at court; and, what chiefly recommended him as a theologian, he wrote an "Apology for Christianity," in answer to Gibbon. His promotion to Llandaff arose from a desire on the part of Lord Shelburne, the Prime Minister, to gratify the Duke of Rutland, Watson's friend, and next to secure the support and service of

---

[1] Perry's "Hist. of the Church of England," vol. iii. p. 485.

a very able man as partisan in the House of Lords. Instead of proving a pillar to the administration, the independent prelate advocated the equalization of episcopal revenues, greatly to the disgust of his friends, and the embarrassment of the administration. Yet he helped the Whig party by some clever speeches, and threw himself into politics, to the neglect of sacred responsibilities. He had before held a professorship, an archdeaconry, and two rectories, as sinecures or nearly so; and now he completely set aside diocesan duties, yet grumbled at the sacrifices he made for the cause of civil and religious liberty. Hence, Robert Hall said of him, "having married public virtue in his early days, he seemed for ever afterwards to be quarrelling with his wife."[1] His most popular book —a book with an unfortunate title, like the preceding one,—is "The Apology for the Bible," which appeared in 1798, and won for him a theological reputation such as he had not before possessed. It was followed by a still more popular publication, "An Address to the People of Great Britain," energetically supporting the war against France, showing that the opinion Watson had formed of the Revolution underwent a change as he watched its ambitious and sanguinary developments.

In 1783 the brilliant scenes at Lambeth were overshadowed by the death of Archbishop Cornwallis, and

---

[1] "Works," vol. vi. p. 125.

the primacy was offered to two prelates; first to Dr. Lowth, then Bishop of London, who declined the honour, because of personal infirmity and domestic affliction; and next to Dr. Hurd, who preferred remaining at Hartlebury, where he was diligently engaged in the collection of a magnificent library. The two are said to have united in recommending Dr. Moore, then Bishop of Bangor, for the vacant post; a clergyman whose rise in the Church had been most remarkable. Born in the city of Gloucester, the son of a butcher, he entered Pembroke College, Oxford, where he so well succeeded in his studies, that he was chosen by the Duke of Marlborough as tutor to his son. The story goes, that the Duchess would not allow him to sit at the family table; but after having thus mortified the young man, she in the time of her widowhood, actually offered him her own hand. He declined the honour, which so pleased her son, that he did all in his power to promote Moore's preferment. It is said of him, that "he avoided all activity but that of Christian piety and spiritual duty, and scarcely took any part in political disputes." Neither did he take "any steps to inflame the minds of the Dissenters on the one hand, nor to alarm the friends of orthodoxy on the other."[1] Dr. Prettyman, who assumed the name of Tomline, became Bishop of Lincoln in 1787, and at the same time obtained the

---

[1] Nichols' "Lit. Anecdotes," vol. viii. p. 95.

Deanery of St. Paul's. Tutor to Mr. Pitt, he had served him as secretary when the great statesman was chancellor of the exchequer, and also when first lord of the treasury. Partly as a reward for these services, Tomline received his preferments; but he had other recommendations. Not only as a scholar, but as a theologian he made some mark in English literature—his "Elements," and his "Refutation of Calvinism," showing very plainly how opposed he was to "evangelical" sentiments. He lived far into the present century, and it is recorded of him, in contrast with his brother of Llandaff, that during the thirty-three years of his episcopate, he regularly performed a triennial visitation,—a thing never done by any of his predecessors.

A much abler man than Tomline, and if not so original as Watson, yet a far more accomplished theologian, and a much greater pulpit orator—indeed Watson does not appear to have excelled in that respect—was Dr. Samuel Horsley. His literary fame rests chiefly on his letters in reply to Dr. Priestly; a production remarkable for its learning, acuteness, and general ability, but sadly wanting in the courtesies of controversy. The imperiousness of the orthodox disputant weakened the cause, which, in other respects, the letters were calculated to strengthen and promote. He assailed the doctrines of Unitarianism with unmerciful vehemence, and forgot the distinction between principles and persons. In controversy Horsley much more resembled Goliath of Gath, "the staff of whose spear was like a weaver's beam," than that Divine Master, who would not "break the bruised reed, nor quench the smoking flax." It is true, that Priestly did not resemble the reed or the flax; but Horsley comes before us as the kind of man, who cared little about the temper of his opponents, whether gentle or otherwise, being borne away by the fierce storms in his own heart. Lord Chancellor Thurlow, as Lord Chancellor, gave him a stall at Gloucester, saying that those who defended the Church ought to be supported by the Church, and in 1788 he became Bishop of St. David's. He figured in Parliament as a supporter of Pitt's administration, and whilst his overbearing spirit did not adorn his character, his political opinions were thought by many quite inconsistent with the liberal genius and spirit of the English constitution. He was translated to Rochester in 1793, and to St. Asaph in 1802. In the pulpit Horsley appeared to great advantage. His sermons are masterpieces of eloquence; and if some of them contain specimens of Biblical interpretation, ingenious, but doubtful; others present instances of truth and originality in rare combination;[1] and in one case at least—his sermons on the Syrophenician woman[2]—Horsley evinces a mastery over the human

---

[1] For instance, Sermons xv.–xviii. and xx.–xxix.
[2] Sermons xxxvii. xxxviii.

affections, no less than over the human understanding. Many an eloquent sermon has been preached in Westminster Abbey, but perhaps rarely, if ever, was there one so effective as that delivered by Horsley in 1793. It was on the anniversary of the execution of Charles I., and a few days after Louis XVI. had been guillotined. Those who are old enough to remember people who lived during the French Revolution know well through what a state of excitement our forefathers then passed ; how terrified they were, and no wonder, at the tidings coming over from Paris of blasphemy and murder ; and how their fears magnified disaffection existing in their own country into a prelude and sign of like enormities. Just then, the sermon alluded to was preached ; the House of Lords attended the service ; the temporal peers on the south side, the Bishops on the north. Horsley, in his lawn sleeves, and with a manner never to be forgotten, burst out into a peroration in which he combined the regicides of England and the regicides of France. "Oh my country," he exclaimed, "read the horror of thy own deed in this heightened imitation, and lament and weep that this black French treason should have found its example in that crime of thy unnatural sons." And as the words fell on the ears of assembled lords, they rose, with one accord, from their seats, and remained standing to the end of the discourse. The Deanery fell vacant that year through the death of Dr. Thomas ; and it is commonly thought that this preferment was immediately bestowed on Horsley, as a reward for his eloquence. " His despotic utterances," observes the present occupant of the office, very unlike to him in this respect, " remain in the tones of his chapter orders:" "We the Dean do peremptorily command and enjoin," etc.; and it is further related that he wore his red ribbon in every time and place, like Louis XIV., who went to bed in his wig. An overbearing style is apparent enough in his writings, especially in his controversial letters; but it ought to be added, as an instance of the mingling of very different qualities in the same person, that his stay in office was marked by special consideration for the welfare of his ecclesiastical subordinates, and that when he died at Brighton, in 1806, " the choir of Westminster Abbey attended his funeral at Stoke Newington, to testify their gratitude."[1]

Within two years after Horsley succeeded to St. David's, another episcopal appointment took place which requires notice. Dr. George Horne attained to high distinction in the University of Oxford, and in 1768 rose to be Principal of Magdalen College. Cultivating pious veneration for Scripture, he erroneously feared the results of criticism pursued by Dr. Kennicott, who collected various readings for his Hebrew Bible; he also adopted, to some extent, the system of philosophy and the method of interpretation, which

---

[1] Stanley's " Memorials of Westminster Abbey."

bears the title of "Hutchinsonianism." John Hutchinson was a clergyman of the Church of England, who died in 1737. Addicted to the study of natural science as well as divinity, he sought to blend the two systems into one; and, making the Bible a test of philosophy, he aimed at bringing astronomy, and everything else into accordance with what he took to be the meaning of Revelation. He wrote a curious work entitled "Moses' Principia" in reference to the law of gravitation, taught in "Newton's Principia." Horne published a pamphlet, now almost entirely forgotten,[1] in which he did not question the mathematical calculations of Sir Isaac, but treating gravitation as a power left unexplained by our great philosopher, he proceeds to attempt a solution of the mystery on the Hutchinsonian principle of a Divine plenum in nature. Further, according to the Hutchinsonian method, he found mystical meanings in the Old Testament, where other people could not. His "Commentary on the Psalms" speedily attained an immense popularity, and never will devout minds fail to derive edification from its perusal; the Introduction

---

[1] The pamphlet is entitled "A Fair, Candid, and Impartial State of the Case between Sir Isaac Newton and Mr. Hutchinson, in which is shown how far a system of physics is capable of mathematical demonstration; how far Sir Isaac's, as such a system, has that demonstration; and consequently, what regard Mr. Hutchinson's claim may deserve to have paid to it." I have before me the second edition, 1799.

to it by its tender beauty continues to inspire admiration in the minds of many unprepared to accept his comments. His "Letter to Dr. Smith," on the death of Hume, and his "Letters on Infidelity," written afterwards, display sharpness of wit, which, however entertaining to those who agree with the excellent author, scarcely tends to conciliate or convince the sceptic. As a preacher, Horne excelled in a style of composition and delivery, then uncommon with orthodox divines. He sought to make his pulpit addresses popular, not with the view of catching applause, but that he might win over multitudes to the service of his Master. He had not the stiff orthodoxy of Tomline, or the original genius of Watson, or the overwhelming force of Horsley; but he had in his gentle piety, amiable manners and devotional zeal, episcopal qualifications which went beyond theirs. When he had been made Bishop of Norwich in 1790, after having been Dean of Canterbury for nine years, a Norwich clergyman wrote to a friend,—"Report tells us, that the Dean of Canterbury is to be our Bishop." "Yes," replied a clerical friend in the metropolis, "so I hear, and I am glad of it, for he will make a truly Christian Bishop." "Indeed," rejoined the other; "well I do not know him myself, being a Cambridge man; but it is currently reported at Norwich, that he is a Methodist." Such talk reflects the habit of the times; every new Bishop excited curiosity, and every one more earnest than others incurred the epithet of "Methodistical."[1] Horne seems to have been too feeble at the time of his appointment to accomplish much. "Alas!" he exclaimed, as he entered the old palace doorway, "I have come to these steps at a time of life when I can neither go up them nor down them with safety."[2] He retained his see only about two years, a circumstance often forgotten when mention is made of *Bishop* Horne's Commentary. It was published fourteen years before his consecration.

---

[1] "Life of Horne," prefixed to his Works, vol. i. p. 177.
[2] Ibid. p. 160.

CHAPTER XVIII.

1780-1800.

THE war of American Independence broke out in 1775, and as the fight at Lexington and the battle on Bunker's Hill were reported on this side the Atlantic, intense excitement arose amongst Englishmen, concerned for the integrity of the empire. Not only in its political issues, but in its ecclesiastical complications, it interested a great number of persons. The American Episcopal Church was a branch of the English Establishment. The Book of Common Prayer was read from the time of the introduction of religion into Virginia, on the shores of Chesapeake Bay, as on the banks of the Thames; for the terms of the Charter in 1606—granted to a colony formed there by Episcopalians—prescribed that in the new settlement, "the true word and service of God should be preached, planted, and used, according to the rites and doctrines of the Church of England." This settlement, like other colonies under the English Crown, came within the capacious boundaries of the Metropolitan see of London; and ecclesiastical authority on the side of the mother country, and submission on the side of the daughter state continued until the outbreak of war between them. The Virginian clergy were intensely loyal; a circumstance which brought them into collision with Revolutionary authorities. The American Republic, born out of the struggle, was inspired with a passion for religious liberty, and knew no difference between Episcopalians, Presbyterians, Baptists, and other bodies; but Episcopalians, whether clerical or lay, exposed themselves to serious consequences, by assuming a position which opposed the new government. If Monarchism could not tolerate Republicanism, neither could Republicanism tolerate the antagonism of monarchical champions. The resisting clergy, therefore, had to suffer what they called persecution for political acts, though power on the part of the new rulers seems to have been considerately used; for when soldiers marched into a church where there officiated a pious Episcopalian,—who had said "it was in the power of Washington to close the church, but not to make the clergy relinquish their duty," and who fearlessly continued service in the presence of armed men,—no violence followed: firmness saved the assembly from further wrong. Washington was an Episcopalian, and so was Jefferson;[1] and when

---

[1] Bishop Wilberforce (in his "American Church," p. 175), calls him "the Deist Jefferson," but I have before me an autograph letter by Jefferson, dated Aug. 10, 1823, in which, replying to some application for pecuniary help, he says, "The principle that every religious sect is to maintain its own teachers and

the war was over, and American Independence established, they continued in the same religious profession as before; but the Revolution snapped the bond between Episcopalianism on the one side of the water and Episcopalianism on the other. The Church of Virginia no longer remained part of the great London diocese, and it became necessary when peace returned that some arrangements should be made to produce and maintain a consistent organic independence in that and other colonies where Episcopalianism took root. It should be added that as the Episcopal Church in America was severed from the mother Church in England, so also it was severed from state ties in its own land. This was accomplished not without a struggle. "It gave rise," says Jefferson, "to the severest contests in which I have ever been engaged." But there was moderation in the beginning, at least on the side of the popular party; for, whilst Non-Episcopalians were exempted from contributing

---

institutions is too reasonable and too well established in our country to need justification. I have been from my infancy a member of the Episcopalian Church, and to that I owe and make my contributions. Were I to go beyond that limit in favour of any other sectarian institution I should be equally bound to do so for every other; and their number is beyond the faculties of any individual. I believe therefore that in this, as in every other case, everything will be better conducted if left to those immediately interested. On these grounds I trust that your candour will excuse my returning the enclosed paper without my subscription; and that you will accept the assurance of my great personal respect and esteem. Th. Jefferson."

to Episcopalian Church funds—to the clergy were secured arrears of salary with their glebes, their plate, their buildings, and their books. The Episcopalian clergy were thrown, like other clergy, upon the voluntary principle. In this respect a Virginian rector came to be on the same footing as a New York Presbyterian, or a Boston Congregationalist; but permission to retain ecclesiastical property on the same terms as before, came to be revoked; and so at length thorough equality was established.

After the close of the American war, and the establishment of Independence, the Episcopalians of that country made a great effort to organize their Church upon the principles to which they were attached. A meeting of Episcopalians was held in 1783, at New York, and they elected Dr. Seabury to the episcopal office. He sailed to England to obtain consecration, but difficulties at once made their appearance. Without an Act of Parliament, it was said, the Bishops could not consecrate an American subject; for no subject of a foreign state could take the oath of allegiance, and that was essential for consecration in this country. One door was open. Though consecration was impossible in England, where Episcopacy is part of the state, it was not impossible in Scotland, where it is unestablished. Independently of legal obstacles on this side the Tweed, there were other considerations to recommend an application to Bishops on the other side. The recent war had exasperated the States against England. "From the Churches of England and Ireland," said the son of Bishop Berkley, who had lived in America, "she will not now receive the Episcopate, if she might; I am persuaded that many of her sons would joyfully receive Bishops from Scotland." "A Bishop," he had remarked just before, "consecrated by the English or Irish Church, would find considerably stronger prejudices against him in the revolted colonies, than would one who had been called to the highest order by a Bishop or Bishops of the Scotch Church—our Bishops, and those of Ireland, having been nominated by a sovereign, against whom the colonists have rebelled, and whom you have never recognised."[1] Dr. Seabury therefore turned his thoughts to Scotland. The Scotch Bishops were applied to, and they regarded the application with favour, but new difficulties arose; it was said the scheme was contrary to the judgment of the two English Archbishops. This turned out to be an overstatement; they would not sanction nor would they oppose the contemplated step. The ceremony, therefore, was performed at Aberdeen, in November, 1784, by the Bishops of Aberdeen, Ross, and Moray. After consecration, Dr. Seabury signed, on behalf of his American brethren, articles of friendship between the sister Churches.

But this did not satisfy all American Episcopalians.

---

[1] Wilberforce's "American Church," pp. 198, 9. Seabury's MSS.

They wished to obtain clerical orders from Canterbury. The Episcopal Convention forwarded an address to the Primate, and after a time the Archbishop expressed a readiness, in which his brethren shared, to grant episcopal succession to the American Church, provided the ecclesiastical constitution adopted was worthy of approval. Some alterations had been made by the Convention in the Liturgy, some things had been omitted, and some things had been left to the option of the clergy. Concessions were made on both sides, and it was finally arranged that the Apostles' Creed should be left untouched; that the Nicene Creed should remain in use; and that reading the Athanasian symbol should be left to the discretion of the clergy. Some other changes were allowed, and the King approving of the arrangement, a consecration of American Bishops took place in the chapel of the Archbishop of Canterbury, on the 4th of February, 1787.

The same year the diocese of Nova Scotia was constituted by letters patent from London, dated August the 8th. It is the oldest of British Colonial dioceses, and the first Bishop was Dr. Inglis, who had been a missionary in New York, in connection with the Propagation Society. In Nova Scotia the condition of the Episcopalian Church at the time must have been truly deplorable. "Food I have but barely," says De la Roche, a devoted missionary of that communion, "as to raiment I have it not; I am in great distress, for I receive no additional benefits from the people here; they confer already too great a favour, in their own sense of the matter, on a Church of England minister to countenance him by keeping in the Church."[1] Strong prejudices, no doubt, at the time existed against the system, and this can easily be accounted for by traditions of English Episcopacy, handed down from the Puritan fathers of the American Colonies; but patience, and devotedness to the spiritual interests of the people, in due course overcame opposition to a large extent, and a very considerable increase in the number of Episcopalians in Nova Scotia arose from the influence of American loyalists, attached to the Church of England, who fled from the United States, after the War of Independence. In a letter dated the 28th of October, 1782, the writer, a clergyman, speaks of three hundred persons who had just arrived at Annapolis, and were soon to be followed by three times that number. Halifax, also, became so thronged with refugees, mostly Episcopalians, that house rent rose to an enormous degree, and the provisions of life reached an exorbitant price.[2] A Bishop of the diocese, son of Dr. Inglis first appointed to the diocese, writing many years afterwards, gathered up traditions of the early Episcopalian settlers.

---

[1] Hawkins' "Missions of the Church of England," p. 359.
[2] Ibid. p. 372.

" I have lately been at Shelburne, where nearly ten thousand of them, chiefly from New York, and comprising many of my father's parishioners, attracted by the beauty and security of a most noble harbour, were tempted to plant themselves, regardless of the important want of any country in the neighbourhood fit for cultivation. Their means were soon exhausted in building a spacious town, at great expense, and vainly contending against indomitable rocks, and in a few years the place was reduced to a few hundred families. Many of them returned to their native country, and a large portion of them were reduced to poverty. . . . Some few of the first emigrants are still living. I visited these aged members of the Church. They told me that, on their first arrival, lines of women could be seen sitting on the rocks of the shore, and weeping at their altered condition. It is a happy circumstance that the church, built soon after the arrival of the settlers, and consecrated by my father in 1789, has been carefully preserved, and is in excellent condition." [1]

An increase of population favourably disposed towards Episcopacy at once increased the responsibilities of those who were pledged to sustain the mission, and encouraged the spirit of faith and hope ; a circumstance to which, in an anniversary sermon, before the Propagation Society, for 1784, Dr. Butler, Bishop of Oxford, referred by saying :—" An infant Church is rising under the favour and protection of the Government in Nova Scotia ; and it is of a

---

[1] Hawkins' " Missions of the Church of England," p. 373.

singular description, consisting of honourable exiles under the pastoral care of fellow sufferers."[1]

Six years after the formation of the Bishopric of Nova Scotia, that of Quebec was created by letters patent. Archbishop Secker had said, in 1776, that King George III. had repeatedly expressed himself in favour of American Episcopates, and had promised, if objections were imagined to be against other places, a Protestant Bishop should be sent to Quebec, where there was a Popish one, and where there were few Dissenters to take offence.[2] That Dissenters did take offence is too true; but the offence, if excusable on grounds adverted to already, was also unjustifiable, and partook of that very exclusiveness to which the existence of Dissent was a standing protest. Now in Quebec, as in other parts of Canada, Episcopalians were supplied with all the institutions and privileges which their conscientious convictions led them to desire.

Looking at the extent of our colonial empire at the close of the last century, it is remarkable that no more dioceses were instituted at that time. Nova Scotia and Quebec were the only English Episcopal folds existing abroad down to so late a period as 1814, when the see of Calcutta was created. Ten years more elapsed before Jamaica became a Bishopric.

---

[1] Hawkins, p. 374.
[2] Ibid. p. 393.

Since then a large number of Colonial Diocesans have been appointed, amounting, in 1877, altogether to sixty-six.

It may be added that the establishment of American Independence put an end to the operations of the Propagation Society in that part of the world, which now became the United States. The termination of missionary relationship between the two countries was marked by a graceful acknowledgment on the part of the Clerical and Lay Delegates assembled in the New Republic in 1785. "All the Bishops of England, with other distinguished characters, as well ecclesiastical as civil, have concurred in forming and carrying on the benevolent views of the Society for Propagating the Gospel in Foreign Parts; a society to whom, under God, the prosperity of our Church is in an eminent degree to be ascribed. It is our earnest wish to be permitted to make, through your Lordships, this just acknowledgment to that venerable society."[1] The Bishopric of Connecticut then existed alone; in 1787 arose the Bishopric of Pennsylvania, and in 1875 the American Bishoprics reached the number of fifty-nine.

Relieved from responsibilities in so wide a field, the society concentrated their efforts upon Newfoundland and Nova Scotia, and soon afterwards upon Canada and New Brunswick. Coincident with this

---

[1] Hawkins, p. 345.

change in the society's labours was a slight effort in Sierra Leone after its acquisition by the British Crown in 1787. An itinerant missionary had been sent there in 1752. A native, ordained in England, arrived on the Gold Coast in 1765, and a catechist reached Sierra Leone in 1787. No Bishopric was established there until 1850.

From the commencement, the society had been charged with the care of British "factories beyond the seas," in addition to the colonies. After religious assistance had been rendered to English residents in Amsterdam and Moscow,[1] a trust fund was originated in 1761 for the benefit of a college at Debretzen in Hungary; and in 1768 another fund was collected by the authority of a Royal Letter, in aid of the Vaudois Churches in Piedmont.

---

[1] There were factories at Moscow and Archangel, "first fruits of the otherwise abortive effort made by the fleet of Edward VI. to discover the rich territories of Cathay." The services of the Church in these places were conducted by a chaplain, at first in a private dwelling, afterwards in a Church on ground given by the Russian Emperor. Anderson, vol. iii. p. 78.

CHAPTER XIX.

1780–1800.

SEVERAL special services, in certain chief temples of the national religion, are recorded as having occurred in the forty years now under review. A famous Handel Festival was held in Westminster Abbey, in the early summer of 1784, when the immortal oratorio of that master of music, who had been interred in Poet's Corner just a quarter of a century before, seems to have produced a deep impression; for a Dissenting preacher, addressing his congregation in a country town, thus refers to the circumstance:—

"When I attended the oratorio of the 'Messiah' some years ago in Westminster Abbey, where were the King and royal family, between two and three thousand auditors, and twelve hundred performers, the chorus was performed—'Worthy, Worthy, the Lamb.' I thought it would have been too much for me; I felt it thrill through my whole frame, the hair of my head almost stood up, and the ground trembled under my feet."[1]

---

[1] Toller's "Short Discourses," p. 116.

To the metropolitan cathedral of St. Paul's royal visits were paid. George II. never appeared there in state, but when George III. recovered from his mental malady, in 1789, he, with Queen Charlotte, the Prince of Wales, and other members of his family, attended Divine worship in the City, to return thanks for the Divine mercy, and on the occasion six thousand children lifted up their voices to God in the service of song. Again, in 1797, the same royal personages entered the nave, in solemn procession, when the French, Spanish and Dutch flags were borne aloft, in celebration of the victory just won by the English fleet. Also before the century closed, the remains of Sir Joshua Reynolds—who had reaped harvests of fame in far other ways—were laid to rest in the crypt, at the feet of Sir Christopher Wren, with almost royal magnificence. Some provincial cathedrals witnessed other observances. Relics of mediæval pageantry lingered at Norwich, and on Guild day, in the month of June, the Corporation continued—the practice lasted until the passing of the Municipal Reform Act—to attend at the cathedral, accompanied by emblems belonging to the old Guild of St. George. An effigy of the dragon was carried to the door, and the six whifflers in bright-coloured costume waved their swords in strange fashion, as the Mayor, Aldermen and Common Council, with stately step, marched between crowds of their fellow citizens, over a carpet of rushes thickly strewn on the pavement of the nave, to hear, in the choir, morning prayer and a sermon preached by the Mayor's chaplain. Reminiscences of early religious traditions also existed at Norwich and Bradford, in the celebration of the Feast of Bishop Blaize, who through the slender link of his legendary martyrdom, by iron instruments of torture resembling combs, came to be chosen as the patron saint of the woolcombers. On the 3rd of February, no genial season for such a pageant, the effigy of this saint in the Roman calendar used to be carried through the streets in a richly-decorated chariot, accompanied by numerous shepherds and shepherdesses riding on ponies, the shepherdesses folding in their bosoms tiny lambs, while the Golden Fleece of Jason figured in the procession,—thus an ancient combination of classical mythology with the legends of the Church, kept its ground in the popular mind down to a recent period.

A remarkable exception to the use of such religious services as were established by the State, took place at Winchester just before the close of George the Second's reign. Hessian troops being quartered in the city, were allowed to worship in the cathedral, and of the service the following account is given by the Bishop's chaplain :—

"At their devotions on Sundays, in the body of the cathedral, which was a most grave and edifying sight. Their service (both of such as are Lutherans and of others that are Calvinists) is in the way of our Dissenters,—first a psalm, very long, in which every soldier bore his part ; each having a book and behaving in that, and the other parts of the service, with all possible decency and attention. I saw about 700 each time I was present. They sing very well. The psalm was set by a sergeant of grenadiers, a noble stately fellow, who had a vast pair of whiskers like birch brooms. All their grenadiers wear this distinction in their faces. When the psalm was ended, a very solemn divine (though he had no whiskers) in a black cloak gave us a sermon in their language, after a prayer which ended with the Lord's prayer. The preacher used no great action, but he had a very great voice, great earnestness, and was in a great sweat. Then followed another psalm much shorter than the first, and all was closed with a prayer, shorter also than the former. There was a collection of money, but for what purpose I know not certainly." [1]

Cathedrals in those days could number amongst their clergy not a few who united with a perfunctory discharge of their duties a life of ease and indulgence, thinking of their own aggrandizement more than the interests of that Church in which they had taken "holy orders." Owing their present position to the patronage of the Government, and hoping for future favours from the same source, their loyalty sunk into obsequiousness, and they were prepared to render support to the policy of the party in power, whatever that policy might be. Many Bishops were charge-

---

[1] Nichols' " Literary Anecdotes," vol. ix. p. 441.

able with nepotism, and the best livings in a diocese fell to the lot of the Episcopal family. Beyond cathedral precincts, practices of a similar description prevailed. Pluralities and non-residence were the order of the day, and London or Bath or Tunbridge frequently enjoyed the presence of incumbents who were rarely seen in their own parishes. Livings were bought and sold in a manner which would not be tolerated now-a-days, and a clergyman advertised for " a curacy in a good sporting country, where the duty was light and the neighbourhood convivial." [1]

Religious worship in parish churches was performed during this period in the accustomed manner. Morning and evening prayer was read in most places every Sunday; but in some agricultural districts worship did not occur more than once a week, or once a fortnight, or even once a month.[2] No doubt, clerical duties were discharged, in very many cases, after a perfunctory and even negligent fashion, and the characters of incumbents and their curates are painted by contemporary authors in no complimentary colours. It is to be observed however, that portraits of the

---

[1] Arthur Young, "Travels in France, 1789," p. 543.
[2] In an account of the Archdeaconry of Canterbury in Archbishop Herring's time (1747-57)—MSS. Lambeth Library, 1138—several churches are mentioned as having service once a month, others once a fortnight. In one case it is said of the incumbent—" He is in bad circumstances, often hides ; when he is at home he serves once a day." Generally there were services twice a day.

grosser kind, such as had been painted by Fielding and others, disappear; pictures less repulsive, though by no means exemplary, take their place. Cowper speaks of "a cassocked huntsman and a fiddling priest;" of those who taught—

> "To bow, to kneel, to sit, to stand;
> Happy to fill religion's vacant place
> With hollow form and gesture and grimace."

Also of the priest who—

> "Droning o'er his charge,
> Their fleece his pillow, and his weekly drawl
> Though short, too long, the price he pays for all."

And with delicate yet cutting satire the poet describes the purveyor of sermons :—

> "He grinds divinity of other days
> Down into modern use, transforms old print
> To zig-zag manuscript, and cheats the eyes
> Of gallery critics with a thousand arts."

In sharper tone, he tells also of those who were—

> "But loose in morals, and in meanness vain;
> In conversation frivolous, in dress
> Extreme; at once rapacious and profuse,
> Frequent in park with lady at his side
> Ambling and prattling scandal as he goes,
> But rare at home, and never at his books."

> "The things that mount the rostrum with a skip
> And then skip down again, pronounce a text,
> Cry hem! and reading what they never wrote,

Just fifteen minutes, huddle up their work,
And with a well-bred whisper close the scene."[1]

This may be thought severe; but there is no historical ground on which it can be pronounced unjust. Much more serious charges against the clergy are brought by one of their own number, who though he rebuts indiscriminate accusations poured on the profession, writes this most damaging sentence :—

"I am sorry to be obliged to confess that the serious part of mankind have long had just reason to express their abhorrence at the frequent occurrence of the *professed clerical libertine.*" "The public have long remarked with indignation that some of the most distinguished coxcombs, drunkards, debauchers, and gamesters who figure at the watering places, and all places of public resort, are young men of the sacerdotal order."[2]

It would greatly mislead the reader to leave the matter thus; and therefore I proceed to give a sketch of individual clerical characters belonging to the last forty years of the century; men who, in a literary or religious point of view, save the order from the indiscriminate and universal censures so common in many histories of the period.

In the obscure Rectory of Hatton, in Warwickshire, lived one of the most learned and able men of

---

[1] "Progress of Error," "Expostulation," "Hope," "The Timepiece."
[2] Knox's "Essays," No. 18, vol. 1. pp. 89, 90.

his age, Dr. Parr. There he settled in 1786. His Liberal politics stood in the way of promotion under a Tory Government, and the utmost preferment he obtained was a Prebendal stall in St. Paul's Cathedral. Perhaps his social peculiarities contributed to hinder his rise any further, inasmuch as, whilst benevolent and kindly to attached friends, he cherished intense antipathies to certain persons. He appears, altogether, to have been a man of immense eccentricity. His dislike to Bishop Hurd amounted almost to a mania; and to be avenged on him, for what reason is not apparent, he republished "Tracts by Warburton and a Warburtonian," though he thereby injured the reputation of the Bishop of Gloucester, whom he professed to admire. His classical learning is the foundation of his fame; and stories of his wit threw around him a brilliant halo. In this respect he is a rival to Dr. Johnson, though the circle of his acquaintance must have been much narrower, and opportunities for the display of his conversational powers less frequent. An ardent Whig, opposed to the Slave Trade and Test Act, and an advocate for Catholic Emancipation and the political rights of Dissenters, he had a strong aversion to Methodists, and betrayed a want of sympathy with efforts for the revival of spiritual religion.

In the third generation of the century, two other clerical names appear of literary renown — the brothers Joseph and Thomas Warton. Joseph was

Master of Winchester School, and wrote an "Essay on the Writings and Genius of Pope," in which he laid down a distinction between the poetry of Reason and the poetry of Fancy, maintaining a decided preference for the latter, thereby establishing a school of poetical thought which has had a powerful influence on English literature. He obtained the Rectory of Clapham, where he went to live after resigning his post at Winchester. Besides his work on Pope, he edited and translated Virgil, and proved himself an eminent Latin scholar. His brother held the Professorship of Poetry at Oxford, and distinguished himself by translations of the Greek Anthology; and by Dissertations on Bucolic Verse, prefixed to an edition of Theocritus. But these and several other classical publications are lost in the celebrity of the work entitled "History of English Poetry," which, in spite of its discursive character and tedious minuteness, remains a text-book for students on the interesting subject to which it relates. He had a small living in Oxfordshire, and another in Somersetshire, and in preaching there, as we are told, he confined himself mostly to two sermons, one of which was written by his father, Thomas Warton, who preceded his son in the Oxford professorship, and the other a printed discourse, altered here and there with the preacher's pen. He had no liking either for divinity or parochial duties; and in what we learn respecting the two brothers, we miss, even more than in the case of Parr, qualities essential to the Christian ministry. Archdeacon Cox is a literary name belonging to the same period, known in connection with a large number of works, including Political History, Travels and Discoveries, but associated with no publication, that I am aware of, immediately bearing on the duties of his sacred office.

It is difficult to connect the clerical poet, George Crabbe, with any particular spot except Alborough, in Suffolk, where he entered the world and held his first curacy, and Trowbridge, in Wilts, where he occupied his last preferment and ended his days. In the course of a singularly romantic and instructive life, he passed from place to place, a pilgrim though not a stranger on the earth. He owed no debt to either University, being a self-taught man; but his Biography furnishes an example of diligent and persevering study from beginning to end. His poetry is a faithful reflection of what he met with in his pastoral course. The village, the parish workhouse, the honest rustics, even the thieves and smugglers whom he so livingly delineates, are scenes and characters he had met with; and while they evince the gifts and cultivated taste of the poet, they indicate the kind of people amongst whom the lot of a country parish minister in those days was thrown, and the unpromising materials on which Providence sent him to execute his beneficent mission. Very gratifying is it to recognise, in this instance, a combination of literary activity with ministerial conscientiousness. Crabbe discharged his duties so as to win the respect and love of his parishioners. Gentleness and benevolence were his characteristics. He brought upon him the blessing of those that were ready to perish, and made the widow's heart to sing for joy.

A different kind of clergyman was Gilbert White, Fellow of Oriel, and Incumbent of Selborne. The sketch prefixed to his works tells his tale with appropriate simplicity :—

" Being of an unambitious temper, and strongly attached to the charms of rural scenery, he early fixed his residence in his native village, where he spent the greater part of his life in literary occupations, and especially in the study of nature. This he followed with a patient assiduity, and a mind ever open to the lessons of piety and benevolence which such a study is so well calculated to afford. Though several occasions offered of settling upon a College living, he could never persuade himself to quit the beloved spot, which was indeed a peculiarly happy situation for an observer. Thus his days passed tranquil and serene, with scarcely any other vicissitudes than those of the seasons, till they closed at a mature age on June 26th, 1793."

He undertook no parochial duties, and therefore is to be regarded as a clergyman in little more than name; but the leisure he had at command, added to his University education, enabled him to produce one of the most charming little books in the English language. We see him rambling over the chalky downs, noting the changes of the weather; remarking how " the turtle and the swallow observe the time of their coming;" verifying how "the ants are a people not strong, yet they prepare their meat in the summer;" in short, gathering from creation proofs of intelligent design and loving care: thus affording food for pious thought, and providing instruction and amusement for after generations.

These authors are well known. Names less familiar occur in literary histories, showing how much zeal members of the order manifested in intellectual pursuits, and the production of works corresponding with certain chosen lines of literary labour. But we now pass over to another class—those who devoted themselves to Biblical and theological studies—and amongst them, besides bishops and dignitaries already noticed, we meet with others not to be dismissed without some remark. Kennicott was an Oxford man—Fellow of Exeter, Canon of Christchurch, and Radcliffe Librarian. He early devoted himself to the study of Hebrew, and attained to unrivalled distinction in that department of letters. The text of the Old Testament was his chosen subject of examination. Its absolute integrity, as it then stood, idly maintained by some, he could not for a moment admit; and though he alarmed timid scholars, he boldly advanced in his path. He catalogued at first a hundred MSS., preserved in Oxford, Cambridge, and London; and then, by the aid of learned foreigners, collated besides, more than six hundred

Hebrew, and sixteen Samaritan copies. Printed Bibles and the Rabbinical writers contributed materials for his object, and the result of all this toil was his "Vetus Testamentum Hebraicum, cum variis Lectionibus, 1776–1780." It is easy for modern scholars, with accumulated advantages since his time, to find fault with this work ; but it must be remembered that Kennicott was a pioneer in new regions, that he had unparalleled difficulties to overcome, and that the confessed defects of his edition detract not from the personal merit displayed in the undertaking. Blayney was Regius Professor of Hebrew in the same University, and reached that office soon after Kennicott's death. Before that time, walking in the footsteps of his contemporary, he took pains to correct the printing of the English version issued in 1769. But his best known labours are a translation of "Jeremiah, and Lamentations, with Notes Critical, Philological, and Explanatory," and a translation of Zechariah, annotated on the same plan. His life was devoted to critical toils; and those who do not now read his books are benefited by his influence upon succeeding and more popular authors.

The theologians who claim attention are numerous. From amongst them two may be selected. Archdeacon Paley occupies the foremost rank. "My son," said his father, "is now gone to College. He'll turn out a great man, very great indeed. I'm certain of it; for he has by far the clearest head I ever met with in my life." Few parents have so correctly prognosticated their children's fortunes. After a fit of slothfulness, this young man at Cambridge out-distanced competitors, and became the senior wrangler of his year. In his parochial life as a Cumberland vicar, and in his more dignified position as Prebendary and Archdeacon, finally as Rector of Bishopwearmouth, he acted the part of a country gentleman. Farming and angling were his great amusement. In the former employment he had no success, only lost money; in the latter he was "an incorrigible disciple of Izaak Walton." In a portrait by Rodney, he appears with a fisherman's rod in his hands, and under this point of view he represented a good many contemporary clergymen; but his mind was mainly given to higher things. He is less valued and less read—less valued perhaps because less read—than he used to be; but as a writer on what are called the Evidences of Christianity, he for a long time took the lead, and his works were text-books in that department of study. His "Natural Theology" was appealed to for proofs of intelligent design in creation; his "Evidences," for proofs of the historical truthfulness of the New Testament; and his "Horæ Paulinæ," for proofs of the genuineness of St. Paul's Epistles. In the first of these, with more originality of style than of substance, he trod in the steps of Ray and Derham, leaving much to be said in the way of correcting and supplementing his arguments; for the second, he collected his materials from Lardner; but in the third, he struck out a new line of thought peculiarly his own. The age for original defences of Scripture had passed away before Paley's time. Conybeare's "Defence of Revealed Religion," Lardner's "Credibility," Leland's "Defence of Christianity," Butler's "Analogy," Sherlock and Newton "On Prophecy," and Warburton's "Divine Legation," belong to the first sixty years of the eighteenth century. But though in matter, except as author of "Horæ Paulinæ," Paley may not have much claim to originality, his manner and style are his own, and lay hold of his readers as none of his predecessors had ever done. Of his Moral Philosophy it has been well said, if he had confined himself to practical views he would have deserved universal praise; but unfortunately he laid down shallow utilitarian principles, to which grave objections have been justly taken. Another Cambridge scholar, less known, deserves to be mentioned with honour—Dr. John Hey, Norrisian Professor of Divinity. In his "Lectures," a work worth careful study, he presents what may be called orthodox opinions, together with a candid examination of difficulties, as an advocate for the Thirty-nine Articles; and a large amount of valuable information and original remark is found in his pages. He was a man of eminent culture, with considerable breadth of view, and had the art of throwing side lights, in a curious way, upon diversified topics which he handled.

The so-called orthodox Church theologians of that age had no sympathy with Puritans or with Calvinists; though it is worth remark, that Horsley takes opportunity of referring to the Genevan reformer as a critic of the highest excellence. Nor can they be said to walk in the steps of the old Anglo-Catholics. They were not followers of Laud, nor disciples of Thorndike, nor imitators of Pearson, nor were they in full accordance with Bull. They adopted the three Creeds of Christendom, though to expressions in the Athanasian symbol some of them certainly took exception. The doctrines of the Trinity, the Incarnation, and the Atonement, they upheld; but Justification by Faith in the Lutheran sense, they did not accept; or, if they did, it was in some modified way, and ideas on the subject are by no means prominent in their writings. Neither does the doctrine of Regeneration appear in their works, except as involved in the baptismal rite, whilst the work of the Holy Ghost is resolved chiefly, if not entirely, into the Inspiration of the Scriptures, and into such influences as are conceived to flow through sacramental channels. There was for the most part in the prevalent style of teaching much that is cold and hard and dry. Truths were wrought out in frost, not in fire. The writings of the period do not inspire even when they instruct; if they illuminate the intellect they often chill the heart. This undoubtedly is the case in general; yet some glow is caught in the reasonings of Horsley, and Paley, in his sermons, is not without feeling. The theological literature of the third generation is not so brilliant as that of earlier days. The judiciousness of Hooker, the golden eloquence of Jeremy Taylor, the patristic learning of Bull, the ecclesiastical lore of Bingham, the profound thoughtfulness of Butler, and the daring originality of Warburton in his younger years, found nothing to equal them during the latter decades of the eighteenth century. It was not to be expected; yet Watson and Horsley, Parr and Paley, were shining lights in the intellectual hemisphere; and besides them, there were other authors, expositors and instructors, not their equals in mental power, but their superiors in spiritual usefulness.

The transition is easy from clergymen who made themselves known by their published works, to others who made themselves known chiefly, if not entirely, by what they did in the pulpit and the parish. Of Richard Southgate, who for thirty years remained curate of St. Giles', London, it is said,—

" In this laborious curacy he continued to the time of his death, exhibiting an illustrious portraiture of a learned, pious, and most indefatigable conscientious parish priest. For many years he had no stated assistant in the discharge of his parochial duties, and he often performed in the same day the several offices of the Church belonging to the functions of a parish minister, all which, too, he ever performed with the utmost solemnity and devotion."[1]

---

[1] Life of Southgate; Nichols' " Anecdotes," vol. vi. p. 366.

Again of John Duncombe, assistant preacher of St. John's, Soho, it is remarked,—

"He was a popular and admired preacher; but he had no vanity on that account, and was equally satisfied to fulfil his duty in a country parish, and an obscure village, as in a crowded cathedral or popular church in the metropolis."[1]

We now reach a clerical division requiring particular notice. The Evangelical leaders of theology were disciples of the Puritans. They leaped back over a hundred years to get at the times of Goodwin and Owen, Baxter and Howe, Bates and Charnock, Gurnall and Flavel. The doctrines of Redemption, of Justification by Faith, of the Work of the Holy Spirit, were zealously embraced. The wells, next to those of the Bible, whence the Evangelicals drew their inspiration, were not Patristic, not Anglo-Catholic; but they were Protestant works of the sixteenth, and Nonconformist works of the seventeenth century. The Homilies were their delight. They appealed to them in proof of their own distinctive theology; certain Articles they regarded with great satisfaction, especially the Seventeenth; but several parts of the Church formularies were not quite to their taste. The Baptismal and Burial Services presented difficulties, but they found ways of bringing them into harmony with their own convictions. Let us look at the men themselves. I pass over other names

---

[1] Life of Duncombe; Nichols' "Anecdotes," vol. viii. p. 73.

and fix upon the following five: Venn, Romaine, Newton, Scott, and Cecil.

Henry Venn, Vicar of Huddersfield, and afterwards Rector of Yelling in Huntingdonshire, was descended from a line of ancestors in holy orders. His father Richard Venn, M.A., a staunch opponent of the latitudinarian Dr. Rundle, whose aspirations after a bishopric in the time of George II. were so successfully thwarted. Henry was as orthodox as his father [1] on the main points taught in the creeds, but he went beyond the creeds in the doctrines which, as a writer and a preacher, he inculcated through a long ministerial life. In early days he wrote a work which brought him into notice, and which is the corner stone of his fame as a theologian. "The Whole Duty of Man" was a favourite book with orthodox people in the latter part of the seventeenth century. Its defects, Henry Venn endeavoured to supply by publishing "The Complete Duty of Man." The title of this work is so much like that of the other that they are apt to be confounded together; and probably in course of time his book was sometimes bought in mistake for its predecessor. If so the reader would find different teaching from that with which his grandfathers and grandmothers were familiar.

---

[1] Warburton had a great dislike to him. "Don't you think Venn and Whitefield would make a proper as well as pleasant figure in a couple of bear skins." Letter to M. Desmaizeaux. Nichols' "Anecdotes," vol. v. p. 578.

The "Complete Duty of Man" inculcated evangelical truth, as well as Christian morality, and supplied powerful motives to the proper conduct of life. Passing from the one volume to the other, you cross the boundary line between the two hemispheres of Anglicanism, and Puritanism. Venn's book was by a large class denounced and ridiculed as methodistical; by another, and an increasing one, it was praised as Scriptural and edifying. The charm of the book is that it sprung from the author's heart. It was the fruit of his own spiritual experience, in this respect resembling the writings of Martin Luther and John Wesley.

William Romaine preached at St. Dunstan's, and St. George's, Hanover Square; afterwards at St. Andrew's and St. Anne's, Blackfriars. On one occasion the Earl of Northampton rebuked the parishioners for complaining of the inconvenience occasioned by the rector's popularity, observing that they bore with patience crowded ball-rooms and play-houses. "If," he said, "the power to attract be imputed as matter of admiration to Garrick, why should it be urged as a crime against Romaine? Shall excellence be considered exceptionable only in Divine things?" Romaine was strongly opposed by some who disapproved of his sentiments, and was soon turned out of St. George's Church; after this the Countess of Huntingdon made him her chaplain for awhile, in which office he preached in her drawing-room to the nobility, in her kitchen to the poor. Settled, at length, as Rector of St. Andrew's and St. Anne's, this eminent minister—of whom it has been said that he was a diamond, rough often, but very pointed, and that the more he was broken by years the more he appeared to shine—pursued uninterruptedly his edifying ministrations till the time of his death in 1795.

The ministry of John Newton cannot be understood without some reference to his personal history. His father had been educated in Spain, where he imbibed the national haughtiness of spirit and severity of character. It would seem as if paternal rigour checked the growth of affections which had begun to spring up under the tender culture of his mother's love. The discipline of a harsh schoolmaster completed the mischief. Religious impressions came and went like gleams of sunshine, till, through the reading of Shaftesbury's works, and the influence of a person who expounded and enforced their real meaning, Newton became an infidel. Other temptations, in addition to these, made him a profligate. He was of a thoroughly roving disposition, and early showed a desire for the sea—a predilection encouraged in his boyhood by voyages which he took with his father, who commanded a vessel. At twenty years of age we find him a sailor, distinguished by his ready wit, bold character, and abandoned conduct. "I not only sinned," he says, "with a high hand myself, but made it my study to tempt and seduce others upon every occasion ; nay, I eagerly sought occasion, sometimes to my own hazard and hurt." In the midst of a storm at sea, Newton was brought to his senses, and landed on the coast of Ireland a changed man. Under the influence of religious convictions he appealed to the Divine mercy through Jesus Christ, and found forgiveness. He had a wonderful dream, in which he received from a stranger a mystic ring, the pledge of safety and peace. He foolishly dropped it in the sea, through the subtle temptation of an enemy, to have it restored by one who promised thenceforth to keep it for him. Newton interpreted the ring to mean his own personal salvation, which could be secured to the end only by the gracious care of God. An experience so rich as his was not to be lost. The Church needed the benefit of his wisdom. He felt an inward call, and obeyed it. After some delay and difficulty, he chose the ministry of the Church of England ; and was ordained in 1764, being then in his thirty-ninth year. The Earl of Dartmouth presented him to the vicarage of Olney. Fifteen years afterwards, Mr. Thornton gave him the living of St. Mary Woolnoth, and St. Mary Woolchurch Haw, Lombard Street. His general usefulness as a clergyman went far beyond an ordinary degree. As a preacher, not gifted with eloquence, but full of that rare spiritual power, which through deep experience touches men's hearts, when expressed in simple straightforward language, this converted sailor and slave-dealer made an astonishing impression both on the humble townsfolk of Olney and the rich merchants of Lombard Street.

"I remember when a lad of about fifteen," says Dr. Dibdin, "being taken by my uncle to hear the well-known Mr. Newton preach his wife's funeral sermon in the church of St. Mary Woolnoth, Lombard Street. Newton was then well stricken in years, with a tremulous voice, and in the costume of the full-bottomed wig of the day. He had, and always had, the entire possession of the ears of his congregation. He spoke at first feebly and leisurely, but as he warmed, his ideas and periods seemed mutually to enlarge; the tears trickled down his cheeks, and his action and expression were at times quite out of the ordinary course of things. It was the 'mens agitans molem et magno se corpore miscens.' In fact the preacher was one with his discourse. To this day I have not forgotten his text, Hab. iii. 17, 18 : 'Although the fig tree shall not blossom, neither shall fruit be in the vines; the labour of the olive shall fail, and the fields shall yield no meat; the flock shall be cut off from the fold, and there shall be no herd in the stalls; yet I will rejoice in the Lord, I will joy in the God of my salvation.' Newton always preached extemporaneously."[1]

It is true of John Newton, and it is true of almost all the leading Evangelicals, that they were in themselves, in their personal influence, in their characters, habits, and life, more than can be fully estimated by printed copies of discourses, or by accurate reports of conversation. They were *felt* to be *spiritual*

---

[1] "Reminiscences of a Literary Life."

powers, wherever they moved. With some men we cannot talk for ten minutes without feeling their superiority. So it was with these leaders, who, though not intellectual, had a spiritual superiority which was confessed by all sorts of people who came within the circle of their influential acquaintanceship. John Newton was a great talker. Olney Vicarage, having nothing of elegance, but much of comfort, was the scene of abundant pleasurable intercourse. The gifted and gentle author of the "Task," at once so solitary and yet so social, would oft, when weighed down with sorrowful musings in his garden and summer-house, lift up the latch of the little gate which opened into the paddock adjoining the vicarage garden, to be met, as he stepped across, by the loving friend, who stood watching him, ready, with cordial grasp, to shake his hand. The subsequently laborious commentator, Thomas Scott, then a young inquisitive theologian, gradually feeling his way into the paths of truth, would every now and then drive over from his curacy at Ravenstone, sure to meet from neighbour Newton a hearty welcome, and the patient consideration of doubts and difficulties on doctrinal subjects. Bull, also, the Dissenting minister of Newport Pagnell, a man of wit and scholarship, not seldom crossed the bridge which spans the Ouse " with wearisome but needful length," to spend a few hours of edifying chat with the catholic-hearted vicar. Olney prepared Newton for London, and in his house, first at Hoxton and then in Coleman Street, he extended the conversational influence which had been felt to be so gracious to the visitors at Olney Vicarage. Dryden filled the critic's throne at Will's Coffeehouse, Russell Street; and thither came wits and poets to do him homage, and receive judgment at his lips. Johnson still more illustriously figured in the famous literary club which assembled at the Turk's Head, Soho. Though Newton's humble reunions might be scorned by many, they had a higher end and were of nobler mark. "I trust," said he, "the members are all of the royal family, and the King Himself condescends to meet with us." Numerous theological and religious books were written by Newton's pen; through his "Letters" he will speak to unborn generations, in kindly Christian tones, and by the "Olney Hymns" inspire and elevate English worship in every portion of the globe.

Thomas Scott, curate of Ravenstone, afterwards chaplain at the Lock Hospital, and at last Rector of Aston Sandford, was equally remarkable in another way. He had led a different earlier life, had sooner applied himself to study, had a stronger understanding but less imagination, and was deficient in the sensibility and sunny cheerfulness which gave a touch of grace and beauty to the rough son of Neptune. Scott speaks of himself as having been morose and proud, and it would seem that he never became a man of winning ways. He had also been very sceptical, and had, according to his own confession, adopted Socinian opinions. This account he gives of himself even when describing how he thought, after he had taken ordination vows in the Church of England. His acquaintance with Newton became the turning point of his history. He had heard of his fame, went to hear him preach, disliked the sermon, thought it was personal, went home, wrote a letter challenging his neighbour to a theological controversy, and all this ended in a victory on the part of the Olney vicar over his pugnacious brother. Scott now set himself to pray and read his Bible, aided only by two or three books which it is curious to notice :—Locke's "Essay on the Reasonableness of Christianity;" Burnet's "Pastoral Care;" Soame Jenyn's "Internal Evidences;" Dr. Clarke on "The Trinity;" and Law's "Serious Call." A strange course of reading to have helped on the effect ultimately produced. His doubts vanished, his heterodoxy came to an end; and for the rest of his life he avowed himself a staunch Evangelical. The process of his conversion is given in his "Force of Truth," the most popular of his works. Lord Lyttleton wrote a book to prove the power of Christianity in the conversion of Paul, on the ground of the extreme unlikelihood of such an event, looking at his previous circumstances and character. Something like this same kind of argument appears in Scott's volume. He had been full of prejudice, had pursued his investigations alone, had rested on Scripture, had

prayed for Divine guidance, and had been brought to
conclusions which he knew would expose himself to
contempt and ridicule ; which of all things, with his
natural disposition, he was least able to bear. After
such a course he concluded that it was impossible he
should be "delivered up to the teaching of the father
of lies." Whatever may be thought of such a story,
one thing is certain, that a man so convinced would
utter his convictions in a tone of the deepest sincerity
and earnestness. He would speak as all the most
forcible preachers of Christianity have ever done,
and that was perhaps the main recommendation
of Scott's oratory. His great power lay outside
the pulpit, and it consisted chiefly in his qualifications as a controversialist and an expositor. He
defended Evangelical opinions against the attacks of
the Bishop of Lincoln in his "Refutation of Calvinism ;" he expounded them with much clearness
in his "Essays," and in other works; but his great
work, in which these opinions luminously appear
throughout, is his "Commentary" on the Scriptures.
He was a stranger to the lights of modern criticism, he
was defective in accurate scholarship, his reading was
limited, of some important branches of critical and
theological study he was perfectly ignorant ; but his
learning, of an old-fashioned kind, has been unfairly
depreciated, and his clear *common sense* in the study
of the Bible, a rare and invaluable quality, is often
overlooked by those who pride themselves on the

riches of modern erudition. At all events he produced a "Commentary," which, next to that of Matthew Henry, was long the most popular in English literature. Ever after its publication, Evangelical clergymen, when choosing a text, turned to see what Scott had to say; and so the good man, for three-quarters of a century at least, was a guide to thought in thousands of English pulpits. It adds to the historical interest of the work to remember the difficulties amidst which it was produced. Not in an academic bower, not in a cloistered study, not surrounded by a rich library, not in correspondence with great scholars, not in wealth, or even competence; but in poverty, in a small parsonage, with scantily filled shelves, surrounded by his family, sometimes having to rock the cradle whilst he used his pen, did Thomas Scott carry on his solitary and ill-remunerated toils.

Several chapels were built in London during the latter half of the eighteenth century. Their architectural appearance did not invite strangers to enter, and the interior, if not a hindrance, certainly was no help to devotion. Built with plain brick walls, shapeless windows, ugly roofs and tasteless entrances, they presented inside deep galleries, tall pews, and a wide aisle in the middle, blocked up by rows of uncomfortable benches for the poor. There stood a pulpit with a huge sounding board, just in front of the communion table, hiding the Lord's Prayer, the Belief, and the Ten Commandments. It rose pagoda-like in distinct stories,

—three desks, one for the clerk, one for the reader, and one for the preacher. Immense brass chandeliers, studded with candles, hung from the ceiling, and the upholstery of the place was most abundant. The preacher leaned over a superb cushion, under which were violet hangings, fringed with gold, and the letters I. H. S. The hearers sat in green-lined boxes, on well-stuffed seats, with a vast apparatus of hassocks. Select corners were separated from other parts by heavy curtains, where the privileged could worship unobserved. These chapels, in fashionable quarters, were frequented by the rich and the respectable. Carriages, with stylishly-dressed ladies and gentlemen, attended by servants in livery, swept up proudly to the door; and people attracted by a popular preacher, but not entitled to sittings in the edifice, had to fee a beadle or a female attendant, who thereupon politely conducted them to a pew. St. John's, Bedford Row, was a building of this description. Richard Cecil became Incumbent of St. John's in 1780.

" I know not what to do with you," said his father to him when a youth. " I have made two experiments for your subsistence. I have offered to bring you into my own business, which at my death will be as good as an estate to you; you have rejected all my proposals. You now seem to be taking a religious turn; but I tell you plainly that if you connect yourself with Dissenters or Sectaries, I will do nothing for you, living or dying; but if you choose to go regularly into the Church, I will not only bear the expense of a university, for which you have had some education, but I will buy you a living on your entering into orders."

The youth proceeded to Oxford, and was ordained, but seems to have had no living bought for him. After having held two rectories, which together produced only £80 a year, he became minister of St. John's. By this change at first he did not much improve his circumstances, but he set resolutely to work to gather a congregation, the chapel being almost empty when he took it. He made alterations in the mode of conducting worship, so as to reduce things to greater order, and abolishing fees to pew-openers, he enjoined upon them the duty of treating strangers with marked courtesy. By these and other more efficacious means the congregation increased. There was no flow in Cecil's oratory, nothing limpid in his style; his words bubbled out in bursts; but wisdom and sagacity, conjoined with Evangelical sentiment, derived additional effect from the preacher's manly manner, his intense earnestness, and his manifest desire to save men's souls; and suffering, as he did, from delicate health, he sometimes appeared as if standing on the threshold of another world. Not merely as a preacher, but as a man of conversational power and of social influence amongst the London Evangelicals, he promoted religious objects in the city and in the neighbourhood. Bedford Row was frequented by many religious celebrities. Wilberforce might often be seen there. He took Pitt to hear the Evangelical preacher, but his doctrines were unintelligible to the great statesman. Bacon, the sculptor, was a regular attendant, whose life, written by his pastor, shows how piety and art were blended in his character. Amongst the devout women who, in Cecil's time or soon afterwards, worshipped at Bedford Row, was a lady named Hawks, eminent for her spiritual zeal; she was much visited by young clergymen and others, whom she instructed and animated by her lively religious conversation.[1] He left Bedford Row and became Rector of Chobham, and wherever he laboured, he transformed and edified numbers in his congregation, who in after life revered his name, and spoke of Richard Cecil as their "spiritual father."

Another Evangelical demands a passing notice on rather different grounds. Joseph Milner was Minister of the High Church at Hull, and Master of the Endowed Grammar School there. He had been "Orthodox" before he became "Evangelical;" and having made his way through doubts and difficulties, the opinions he embraced became indelibly burnt into his mind. His preaching was of the same stamp with that of Newton and Scott, and his memory as a

---

[1] There are many pleasant traditions of her influence amongst the Evangelical clergy. The Countess of Huntingdon has been called "St. Selina." There were other female saints of a similar order.

preacher remains with honour in the town of Kingston-upon-Hull. But as an author rather than as a clergyman did he promote the cause with which he stood identified. Through his "History of the Church," he made a deep impression upon such contemporary students as were in harmony with his religious views; by the same means he has made himself best known to posterity. He had a theological purpose in writing that work; he wished to exhibit in unbroken concatenation the existence of Evangelical sentiments, from the time of the Apostles down to the Reformation. Lovingly does he dilate on the writings of St. Augustine, St. Ambrose, and St. Bernard. Almost everything in Church History is put out of sight except this chain of testimony, and whatever in surrounding circumstances and opinions would seem to place in bolder relief the author's principles. Hence Milner's work is more a theological treatise than anything else; and it is, no doubt, this very fact which gave it such a value in the eyes of his clerical brethren and friends. It needs scarcely be said, the publication has been, and is, very differently estimated by students of a different school.

Looking at the Evangelical party of the last century from a judicial point of view, one must acknowledge their defects. They were destitute of a true appreciation of the beautiful in literature and art; they were indifferent to "some of the causes by which Evangelical religion has been rendered unacceptable to persons of cultivated taste;"[1] they had a dialect of their own, liable to be misunderstood by those not in sympathy with their convictions; they were sometimes intolerant of opinions which were not so different as they supposed; and they went so far as to question the Christianity of men devout and useful, who adopted different views, or even a different style of phraseology. There were defects in their theology. Calvinistic onesidedness pushed into the background adequate views of human responsibility, and sometimes they dangerously treated Christian experience. But what they lost in breadth they found in depth. Their convictions were full of living power, and moved their whole being, making them incisive in speech and bold in effort. They had no half-and-half ways of talking about religion, so as to leave it doubtful what they meant. Often offensive, they were never obscure. Their spirituality, zeal, love, and Gospel earnestness were as clear as day; and multitudes who did not care about literature, art, scientific theology, or ecclesiastical questions, saw the light and felt the heat of their popular ministrations. They addressed themselves not to the educated and polite but to the masses, and the common people heard them gladly. Then their disinterestedness was so conspicuous. Nobody can compare the memoirs of Bishop Newton and others with the lives of John

---

[1] See Foster's Essay on that subject.

Newton, Scott, and Cecil, without feeling the wonderful difference between the two classes in this respect. One was engrossed in hunting after Church preferment; the other did not care for it a straw. People in the eighteenth century were struck with the contrast, and were influenced accordingly. The Evangelicals were denounced by their opponents as Methodists, but it does not appear that the men just described owed their conversion to methodistical influences. They were none of them led to change their opinions and alter their lives through the preaching and writing of Wesley or Whitefield. They might receive spiritual impulses in their ministry from the lives and labours of these modern apostles—no doubt they did—and Newton and Scott were friendly with Methodists, and were not shocked at the ecclesiastical irregularities of their fellow-labourers; but Cecil and others were Churchmen to the backbone, and intensely disliked the doings of the itinerants. Conferences and Circuits found no favour in their eyes, and much of the Wesleyan preaching they deemed erroneous. Yet they had a large measure of methodistical zeal, methodistical unction, methodistical directness, methodistical activity, and the methodistical spirit of Christian fellowship.

Many respectable and worthy cathedral dignitaries, many town and country rectors and vicars and curates firmly holding Anglican or Latitudinarian opinions, looked with suspicion or with displeasure upon the writings and sermons of the men just described. They might not be wanting in charity or kindliness, but they had a supreme aversion to all *enthusiasm*. Reasonableness and moderation they admired, and the opposites of these they thought tended to excite prejudice in the learned, ridicule in the worldly, and grief in the sober-minded. Irregularity they could not tolerate; and they complained that Evangelicals, however attached to Episcopacy and the Prayer Book, went just the way that would in the end lead folks out of the enclosures of the true fold into all sorts of outlandish paths and places. These objectors decently performed their clerical duties. They attended visitations and confirmations, and read orthodox but unenthusiastic sermons with unimpeachable propriety. Many strove to do good to their parishioners, and won their affection; but, calling to mind what has been said of a large number, different language must be used. There can be no doubt that the chief matter thought of by many was the income of their office; and, as I have said already, those who had patronage at their disposal only cared to provide for relatives and friends.[1] Sinecures, pluralities and non-residence were common things. Clergymen appropriated revenues and did no duty; they held two or three

---

[1] I have heard respected prelates of the present day express themselves on this subject in much stronger terms than I have employed.

lucrative livings together, and for years an incumbent living at a distance in snugness and ease failed to pay even a hasty visit to his parish. He condemned enthusiasm respecting souls, but was very enthusiastic in seeking and keeping the good things of this life.

A few clergymen between 1774 and 1776 dissented from the Church of England, and sacrificed their preferments. Theophilus Lindsey, a man of great integrity, of pure mind, and of virtuous life was of this class. He had been educated at Cambridge, and was Incumbent of Catterick, in the county of York; but not believing in the Doctrine of our Lord's Divinity, he felt compelled to become a Nonconformist. This he did, although his prospects were brilliant, for he enjoyed the patronage of the Huntingdon and Northumberland families; nor could "the tears of a people to whom he was justly endeared, tempt him to violate the dictates of conscience."[1] He went to London, without the means of subsistence, but encouraged there by sympathetic supporters, he opened a chapel in Essex Street, where he taught Unitarian principles, and adopted a form of liturgical worship, framed on a model prepared by Dr. Samuel Clarke. A clergyman who gave Lindsey credit for sincerity and courage, argued, "If every officer in an army were to resign his com-

---

[1] Quoted in Nichols' "Lit. Hist.," vol. v. p. 415.

mission as soon as he is sensible of mal-administration therein, or even of the many intolerable grievances of State, there would never have been any instances of the most glorious and salutary revolutions."[1] If there was room for this Erasmus-like argument on the one hand, there was room for a Luther-like argument on the other, namely, that there must be an open breach with certain institutions in order to carry out thorough reforms. Even the man who wrote the above passage felt himself compelled to add, " for my own part I am heartily sick myself, and shall be glad to get out of bondage, and fully purpose to do it, and hope when free I shall be able to help others out ; but I would not have any follow my example. I have been blamed for my former resignation of my Norfolk livings." What follows is noteworthy, and throws a startling gleam over the state of things in the Church of England at that time. He remarks:—

" I am much easier now than I was,"—"for on Trinity Sunday last I made before my congregation a solemn protest against the Athanasian heresy, and desired them all to take notice of it, and that in my future ministrations, I should consider myself in no other light, in certain parts of the Offices of the Church, than as an officer of the State, exercising ministerially enjoined services, which I could not approve." This would be very surprising, if we did

---

[1] Nichols' " Lit. Hist.," vol. iv. p. 841.

not find the same person saying, "But, alas, this is but a temporary salve for a sore in itself incurable."[1]

Dr. Primatt, the writer of these odd sentences, soon after imitated the example of Lindsey. About the same time, a clergyman of the name of Jebb resigned a benefice in the Diocese of Norwich; and at the conclusion of 1776 two gentlemen threw up fellowships from dissatisfaction with the Prayer Book; another person is mentioned as having declined a family living on the same ground.[2]

On turning to the Universities we have further illustrations of the state of society, and of religion in the Church. Gibbon gives an unfavourable account of Oxford in his time (1752). He spent, he says, fourteen of the most unprofitable months of his life at Magdalen College, and he backs his statement by citing the authority of Adam Smith, who said that the greater part of the public professors had given up even the pretence of imparting instruction. Gibbon was never summoned even to attend the ceremony of a lecture, and excepting a solitary visit to his rooms, pupil and tutor lived in the same college strangers to each other. "The want of experience, of advice, and of occupation, soon betrayed me into some improprieties of conduct, ill-

---

[1] Nichols' "Lit. Hist.," vol. iv. p. 841.
[2] Lindsey's "Hist. View," p. 483; and Wakefield's "Memoirs," vol. i. p. 116.

chosen company, late hours, and inconsiderate expense; a tour to Bath, a visit into Buckinghamshire, and four excursions to London in the same winter."[1] But whatever may be the truth of Gibbon's report, it must not be inferred that Oxford, in the reign of George the Third, was destitute of eminent learning; for the very College to which Gibbon belonged could boast of Dr. George Horne, afterwards Bishop of Norwich, as its president from 1768 to 1791; and he was succeeded by one of the ripest scholars of the age, Dr. Routh, who lived far into the present century, and enriched our ecclesiastical literature by his "Reliquæ Sacræ," a work of rare erudition.

There were in the colleges men of ability and attainments, training students for high offices in Church and State; they included clergymen of intellectual and moral worth, but a circumstance occurred in 1763 which shows that a strong antipathy to "Methodism" existed in certain quarters. The spirit of the Wesleys had not died out. At the time we speak of, six pious young men were there, who not only met for devotional purposes, somewhat after the method pursued thirty years before, but also ventured publicly to preach, which the Wesleys and their companions, whilst only students, had never done. This irregularity the authorities would not tolerate, it being considered inconsistent

---

[1] Gibbon's "Autobiography."

with the Act of Uniformity, and quite contrary to University statutes. They were accused by the Vice-Chancellor, and certain Heads of Houses, for holding methodistical tenets, and taking upon them to pray, read and expound the Scriptures, and sing hymns in a private house. Reference was made to their low origin, their being illiterate, their Methodism, and their coming to Oxford for the purpose of skulking into orders. One University officer "defended the doctrines of these young men, from the Thirty-Nine Articles of the Established Church, and spoke, in the highest terms, of the piety and exemplariness of their lives; but his motion was overruled, and sentence was pronounced against them." One of the Heads of Houses, however, candidly observed that, as these six gentlemen were expelled for having too much religion, it would be proper to inquire into the conduct of some who had too little.

Wilberforce gives a sad account of Cambridge:—

"I was introduced, on the very first night of my arrival, to as licentious a set of men as can well be conceived. They drank hard, and their conversation was even worse than their lives. I lived amongst them for some time, though I never relished their society; often, indeed, I was horror-struck at their conduct, and after the first year I shook off my connection with them." He then mixed more with the fellows of St. John's, his own college, but their object he says, "seemed to be, to make and keep me idle. If ever I appeared studious they would say to me, 'Why in the world should a man of your fortune trouble himself with fagging?'"[1]

Yet at Cambridge, towards the end of the century, there was a Fellow of King's College, Charles Simeon, who became a decided Evangelical, and endeavoured to awaken serious religious conviction, according to his own ideas of gospel truth, not only in the minds of his parishioners—he was Incumbent at Trinity Church—but in the minds of University students also. He met with much discouragement and opposition. Young men who felt the value of his teaching were known to congregate in a body, lest, if going to his church alone, they should meet with insult by the way. And what seems almost incredible, when he first established Sunday evening services, in 1792, they were disturbed just in the same way as the Methodists were; gownsmen were conspicuous in these disgraceful proceedings.[2] But with boldness and humility the good man pursued his way. He listened to what objectors had to say, was willing to learn from inferiors, and manifested towards those who differed from him a catholic spirit. When not engaged in necessary duties, he devoted himself to the instruction and training of candidates for the ministry, who crowded his rooms, and looked up to him with great veneration. Diligent

---

[1] " Life of Wilberforce," vol. i. p. 10.
[2] Carus's " Life of Simeon," p. 88.

in work, he was liberal with his purse, and became at length a mighty power in the University, so that those who had once been his opponents paid him the utmost respect; and when he died, in 1836, his funeral bore witness to the truth of the text selected for his funeral sermon, "Them that honour Me, I will honour."[1] Far beyond the University his influence was felt. He travelled throughout the country as an advocate for missionary and kindred objects; and I well remember his venerable appearance, his energetic manner, and the spiritual force of his preaching in old age. His homiletic volumes gained a wide circulation, and fifty years ago numbers of clergymen betook them to "Simeon's Skeletons" for parish discourses.

An institution for promoting the interests of the Christian religion in connection with the Establishment, as it engaged the services of a number of

---

[1] It was preached by the Rev. Dr. Dealtry, Chancellor of Winchester, and from it, as the highest authority, I have drawn the above statements, sometimes in the very words he employed. A Trust, bearing Simeon's name, was instituted for the purchase of Livings in the Church of England, to be bestowed exclusively upon Evangelical preachers. Simeon prefaced the terms of the Trust with the solemn words :—" In the Name and in the Presence of Almighty God, I give the following charge to all my Trustees, and to all who shall succeed them in the Trust to the remotest ages. I implore them for the Lord Jesus Christ's sake, and I charge them also before that adorable Saviour, who will call them into judgment for their execution of this Trust."

clergymen, requires notice at the close of this chapter. The Honourable Robert Boyle founded a Lecture for the Defence of Natural and Revealed Religion, and a succession of lecturers between 1692 and 1739 delivered discourses on various subjects connected with the general theme. These were collected into three folio volumes, and published in the last mentioned year,—and respecting this collection Bishop Watson remarked, "If all other defences of religion were lost, there is solid reasoning enough (if properly weighed) in these three volumes, to remove the scruples of most unbelievers." The lectures were continued throughout the century, occasionally and at intervals, by Leonard Twells, Henry Stebbing, Ralph Heathcote, William Worthington, Henry Owen, and James Williamson. Warburton, Bishop of Gloucester, founded another Lecture for proving "the Truth of Revealed Religion in General, and of the Christian in particular, from the completion of the prophecies of the Old and New Testament, which relate to the Christian Church, and especially to the Apostacy of Papal Rome." Hurd, Bishop of Worcester, published the first course in 1772, entitled, "Introduction to the Study of the Prophecies concerning the Christian Church." Halifax, Bishop of Gloucester, followed in 1776, upon "The Prophecies, the First Establishment, and subsequent History of Christianity." Bagot, Bishop of Norwich, took up the same subject in 1780, and Dr. Apthorp discoursed on the prophecies in 1786. The Rev. John Bampton, Canon of Salisbury, bequeathed property for the endowment of eight divinity sermons, to be delivered annually at St. Mary's, Oxford, on several subjects, which he specified, and which are included in the extract from his will prefixed to the yearly publication of the discourses. The names of Bandinel, Neve, Holmes, Cobb, White, Churton, Croft, Hawkins, Shepherd, Tatham, Kett, Morres, Eveleigh, Williamson, Wintle, Veysie, Gray, Finch, Hall, and Barrow, occur in the list, which runs on from 1780, the year when the lecture commenced, to the end of the century. And these names, as well as those of the Warburton and Boyle Lectures, are given to show how slight a mark most of them have been on the theological history of the country. The majority are unknown, except to a very small class of readers. With respect to one Bampton course, that for 1783, on Mohammedism—the most popular of the series during the last century—it should be remarked that it occasioned considerable discussion on the ground of the very material, but altogether unacknowledged assistance which Dr. White, the author, received in the course of their preparation. Their composition, to a large extent, has been attributed to the Rev. Samuel Badock. Beyond all question he and Dr. Parr contributed greatly to the literary merits of the volume, yet White was really a superior Oriental scholar. The applause which the lectures received in the University was very great until the history of their origin came to be known. It may be added that scarcely any volumes of sermons by "the Orthodox clergy," besides those of Horne and Horsley, attained celebrity.

CHAPTER XX.

1760-1800.

AS the object of this history is not merely to describe great events, or to portray illustrious churchmen; it is proposed in this chapter to adduce illustrations of religious life drawn from the memoirs of well known laymen.

Habits of religious conversation can be well illustrated by reference to a man of pre-eminent power, who may be taken as a type of Orthodox churchmanship. "Dr. Johnson carried me with him," Boswell informs us, "to the Church of St. Clement Danes, where he had his seat, and his behaviour was, as I had imagined to myself, solemnly devout. I never shall forget the tremulous earnestness with which he pronounced the awful petition in the Litany, 'In the hour of death, and in the day of judgment, good Lord, deliver us.'" The spot he occupied in the north gallery, near the pulpit, is still pointed out, and one sees his shadow under circumstances which recall the most solemn moments of his earthly existence. Bolt Court was his abode during the latter part of the lexicographer's life, and it was also the scene of his death. The house is gone, and the little garden has disappeared, "which he took delight in watering;" but prints of the spot are preserved, in which we see the three circular steps leading up to the entrance, the flat projection over the doorway, the long row of windows in the roof, and the shrubs adorning the leads of a lower room, in advance of the adjoining residence. A tavern and a printing-office now occupy the chief portion of the little nook; but the name of Johnson inscribed on the entrance will be ever associated with the locality; and here it was that the moralist, one of the greatest talkers of the age, carried on many of the colloquies preserved by his admiring biographer. In Bolt Court one day occurred a remarkable interchange of thought respecting the subject of religion.

"'There are, I am afraid,' said Boswell, 'many people who have no religion at all.' 'And sensible people too,' added Mr. Seward, who happened to be present. 'Why, sir, not sensible in that respect,' rejoined Johnson. 'There must be either a natural or a moral stupidity, if one lives in a total neglect of so very important a concern.' 'I wonder that there should be people without religion,' added Seward. 'Sir,' exclaimed his host, 'you need not wonder at this, when you consider how large a proportion of almost every man's life is passed without thinking of it. I myself was for some years totally regardless of religion. It had dropped out of my mind. It was at an early period of my life. Sickness brought it back, and I hope I have never lost it since.'"[1]

---

[1] Boswell's "Life of Johnson," vol. viii. p. 210. William Seward, F.R.S., was editor of "Anecdotes," and "Literary Miscellanies."

What Johnson thought respecting two points in Christian theology he expressed when on a visit to Welwyn, the parish of which Dr. Young, author of the "Night Thoughts," had been incumbent. On Sunday after church, Johnson in a meditative mood observed,—

"With respect to original sin, the inquiry is not necessary; for whatever is the cause of human corruption, men are evidently and confessedly so corrupt, that all the laws of heaven and earth are insufficient to restrain them from crimes. Whatever difficulty there may be in the conception of vicarious punishments, it is an opinion which has had possession of mankind in all ages. There is no nation that has not used the practice of sacrifices. Whoever therefore denies the propriety of vicarious punishments, holds an opinion which the sentiments and practice of mankind have contradicted from the beginning of the world. The great sacrifice for the sins of mankind was offered at the death of the Messiah, who is called in Scripture 'The Lamb of God, that taketh away the sins of the world.' To judge of the reasonableness of the scheme of redemption, it must be considered as necessary to the government of the universe that God should make known His perpetual and irreconcilable detestation of moral evil. He might indeed punish, and punish only the offenders; but as the end of punishment is not revenge of crimes but propagation of virtue, it was more becoming the Divine clemency to find another manner of proceeding, less destructive to man, and at least equally powerful to promote goodness. The end of punishment is to reclaim and warn. *That* punishment will both reclaim and warn, which shows evidently such abhorrence of sin in God, as may deter us from it, or strike us with dread of vengeance when we have committed it." [1]

These conversations belong to the years 1781 and 1783, when Johnson was above 72 ; and it is curious to find in Cowper's correspondence a reference, in the year after the last of these dates, to the eminent critic, as having then recently passed through a great change. In writing to John Newton, the poet remarks, "We rejoice in the account you give us of Dr. Johnson. His conversion will indeed be a singular proof of the omnipotence of grace ; and the more singular the more decided." [2] This could not mean that Johnson had then begun to turn his attention to religious subjects, for he had done so for years ; but it would seem that about the time indicated, the idea was spread abroad that his convictions assumed a character more decidedly "Evangelical," and it is possible that a report respecting conversations of this kind gave rise to a rumour which gratified the Olney poet.

"For some time before his death his fears were calmed and absorbed by the prevalence of his faith and his trust in the merits and propitiation of Christ. He talked often about the necessity of faith in the sacrifice of Jesus as necessary beyond all good works whatever for the salvation of mankind." "Attend, Francis, to the salvation of your soul, which is the object of greatest importance," were among the last of his words to his faithful and favourite servant. [3]

---

[1] "Life of Johnson," vol. viii. p. 103.
[2] Cowper's Works, vol. iii. p. 109.   [3] Ibid. p. 417.

From the conversations of one literary man we proceed to the correspondence of another. In the town of Huntingdon, Cowper took up his abode with the Unwins, in an old house whose wainscoted rooms remain almost unaltered, and while there in 1766, he describes his manner of life, giving a vivid idea of the strict, methodical, unworldly habits maintained by religious people of his class.

"As to amusements, I mean what the world calls such, we have none. The place indeed swarms with them, and cards and dancing are the professed business of almost all the gentle inhabitants of Huntingdon. We refuse to take part in them, or to be accessories to this way of murdering our time, and by so doing have acquired the name of Methodists. Having told you how we do *not* spend our time, I will next say how we do. We breakfast commonly between eight and nine; till eleven we read either the Scriptures or the sermons of some faithful preacher of those holy mysteries; at eleven we attend Divine service, which is performed here twice every day; and from twelve to three we separate and amuse ourselves as we please. During that interval I either read in my own apartment, or walk or ride, or work in the garden. We seldom sit an hour after dinner, but if weather permits adjourn to the garden, where with Mrs. Unwin and her son I have generally the pleasure of religious conversation until tea time. If it rains or is too windy for walking, we either converse within doors, or sing some hymns of Martin's Collection, and by the help of Mrs. Unwin's harpsichord make up a tolerable concert, in which our hearts, I hope, are the best and most musical performers. After tea we sally forth to walk in good earnest. Mrs. Unwin is a good walker, and we have generally travelled about four miles before we see home again. When the days are short we make this excursion in the former part of the day, between church time and dinner. At night we read and converse as before till supper, and commonly finish the evening with hymns or a sermon, and last of all the family are called to prayers. I need not tell you that such a life as this is consistent with the utmost cheerfulness, accordingly we are all happy." [1]

Cowper's image is reflected in his letters; his hopes and fears, his joys and sorrows, he reveals in the confidence of friendship,—and though in some respects, especially towards the end of life, his experience became morbid, and passed beyond the limits of a sane sensibility, yet in it may be seen phases of sentiment such as he shared in common with thousands of serious Christians. In the bag of the post-boy, with "the twanging horn, crossing Olney Bridge, that with its wearisome and needful length bestrides the wintry flood,"—doubtless there might be found epistles in points of feeling similar to those of the retired poet, when he dwelt in a modest house, in the midst of the town, which so many pilgrims now love to visit. The shadows which fell over his spirit were peculiarly dark, yet his mental conflicts were not utterly unknown by other Christians in his day, any more than ours. Psychological facts of a mysterious description

---

[1] Works, vol. ii. p. 196.

form a puzzling chapter in human history, and are not to be set aside because they are unwelcome. Mental, moral, and physical causes, especially the last, have contributed to produce many-sided aspects of character; and if complete memoirs could be written of eighteenth-century Christians, particularly those of the same class as the Olney bard, it would be found that under the surface of an outwardly tranquil life often rushed angry torrents of anxiety, of terror, and even of despair. But he felt much interest in passing incidents, and charmingly pictured them in his correspondence. He lets us into petty ecclesiastical jealousies in a Buckinghamshire town, only a specimen of other English towns. "Because," he says to his friend, John Newton, after he had left the place, "we have nobody to preach the gospel at Olney, Mr. —— waits only for a barn, at present occupied by a strolling company. The moment they quit it he begins. He is disposed to think the dissatisfied of all denominations may possibly be united under his standard, and that the great work of forming a more extensive and more established interest is reserved for him." Zealous preachers, acting under an impulse of their own, did good in many of the rural districts ; but there can be no doubt that sometimes they provided an Adullam Cave for discontented members of other denominations. The catholic-hearted vicar, however, after a visit to his old cure, remarked, "There are many who have left the Church, but I hope they have not left the Lord."[1] Many sympathised with the poet in 1790, amidst the political agitation of the hour, when he wrote to Lady Hesketh :—

"For my sentiments on the subject of the Test Act, I cannot do better than refer them to my poem entitled and called 'Expostulation.' I have there expressed myself not much in its favour, considering it in a religious view; and in a political one I like it not a jot the better. I am neither Tory or High Churchman, but an old Whig, as my father was before me; and an enemy to all tyrannical impositions."[2] Cowper was lukewarm in reference to ecclesiastical reform. "As to the reformation of the Church, I want none unless by a better provision for the inferior clergy; and if that could be brought about by emaciating a little some of our too corpulent dignitaries, I should be well contented. The Dissenters, I think, Catholics and others, have also a right to the privileges of all other Englishmen, because to deprive them is persecution, and persecution on any account, but especially on a religious one, is an abomination. But after all, *valeat respublica*, I love my country, I love my king, and I wish peace and prosperity to old England."[3]

If Cowper's correspondence embalms much of the popular religious sentiment in reference to ecclesiastical politics, one of Cowper's friends may be here introduced as an example of the liberality which in a few instances might be found in the Evangelical section of the Church :—

---

[1] Southey's Cowper, vol. i. p. 249. [2] Ibid. vol. iv. p. 115.
[3] Ibid. vol. iv. p. 295.

"John Thornton, by living with great simplicity of intention and conduct, in the practice of a Christian life, more than by any superiority of understanding or of knowledge, rendered his name illustrious in the view of all the more respectable of his contemporaries. He had a country house in London, and a handsome villa at Clapham. His personal habits were remarkably simple. His dinner-hour was two o'clock. He generally attended public worship at some church or Episcopalian chapel several evenings in the week, and would often sit up to a late hour in his own study, at the top of the house, engaged in religious exercises."[1]

He was one of a class, rather numerous at that time, who while conscientiously attached to the Establishment, were exceedingly Low Churchmen, and attached more importance to evangelical principles than to any political or ecclesiastical questions. Hence they lived on the confines of Dissent, so far in a kind of borderland, which instead of being a district disturbed by war, was a region full of peace, where Episcopalians and Nonconformists dwelt together in love and concord.

"Cowper," Southey informs us, "was supplied by this excellent man with a sum for charitable distribution; Mr. Thornton having been informed how little his means for relieving the distressed were commensurate with his will." At the same time John Newton, as curate of Olney, receiving not more than eighty pounds a year, derived material assistance in the shape of "bank notes" from his merchant

---

[1] "Wilberforce's Life," by his sons, vol. i. p. 283.

friend. "Be hospitable," he said, "and keep open house for such as are worthy of an entertainment; help the poor and needy; I will statedly allow you two hundred pounds a year, and readily send whatever you have occasion to draw for more." [1]

Of all forms of Christian effort maintained by the laity, none can surpass, if even it can equal, that which was begun on a large scale and in a lasting way, by Robert Raikes, of Gloucester, about 1783. He has given an account of the origin of his undertaking:—

" Some business leading me one morning into the suburbs of the city, where the lowest of the people (who are principally employed in the pin manufactory) chiefly reside, I was struck with concern at seeing a group of children, wretchedly ragged, at play in the streets. I asked an inhabitant whether those children belonged to that part of the town, and lamented their misery and idleness. 'Ah! sir,' said the woman to whom I was speaking, ' could you take a view of this part of the town on a Sunday, you would be shocked indeed; for then the street is filled with multitudes of these wretches, who, released that day from employment, spend their time in noise and riot, playing at ' chuck,' and cursing and swearing in a manner so horrid as to convey to any serious mind an idea of hell rather than any other place. We have a worthy clergyman (said she), curate of our parish, who has put some of them to school; but upon the Sabbath they are all given up to follow their own inclinations without restraint, as their parents, totally abandoned themselves, have no idea of instilling into the

---

[1] " Life of Cowper," vol. i. p. 168.

minds of their children principles to which they themselves are entire strangers.' This conversation suggested to me that it would be at least a harmless attempt, if it were productive of no good, should some little plan be formed to check the deplorable profanation of the Sabbath. I then inquired of the woman if there were any decent, well-disposed women of the neighbourhood, who kept schools for teaching to read. I presently was directed to four; to them I applied, and made an agreement with them to receive as many children as I should send upon the Sunday, whom they were to instruct in reading and in the Church Catechism. For this I engaged to pay them each a shilling for their day's employment. The women seemed pleased with the proposal. I then waited on the clergyman before mentioned, and imparted to him my plan. He was so much satisfied with the idea, that he engaged to lend his assistance, by going round to the schools on a Sunday afternoon, to examine the progress that was made, and to enforce order and decorum among such a set of little heathens." [1]

Thus commenced a movement which soon inspired the sympathy of religious people in general and led to the establishment of schools, at first in many instances imperfectly conducted, but which improved as they multiplied, and ultimately took the form now so familiar to English Christians of every name.

Another Christian lay worker in the Church of England was William Wilberforce, who combined within himself powers of conversation and correspondence akin to those of Johnson and Cowper, whilst

---

[1] Quoted in Gloucestershire Tracts, No. XIX., Robert Raikes.

he emulated the charity of Thornton and the activity of Raikes. In early life he had reverently perused the Scriptures and formed habits of devotion, and when at the University of Cambridge had refused to sign the Articles; after he had attained his majority he became immersed in the dissipation of fashionable society, and for a while he was addicted to gambling. A great spiritual change passed upon his character and life when about twenty-five, referring to which in after days, he remarked—" By degrees the promises and offers of the Gospel produced in me something of a settled peace of conscience. I devoted myself, for whatever might be the term of my future life, to the service of my God and Saviour, and, with many infirmities and deficiencies, through His help I continue to this day."[1] He had not long felt the results of such a renewal when he engaged in efforts for reviving religion and reforming social manners, procuring a Royal Proclamation against vice and immorality, and establishing a Society for the promotion of his objects. His purpose is explained as supplementing the labours of John Wesley. Wesley's mission was to the poor; but there was needed some reformer who should raise his voice in high places, and do, within the Church and near the throne, what Wesley had accomplished in the humble meeting-house and amongst the vulgar

---

[1] " Wilberforce's Life," by his sons, vol. i. p. 112.

multitude.[1] Associations for the "better observance of the Sabbath day" were included in Wilberforce's plans, so were religious schools and the erection of chapels of ease ; and to provide for the advocacy of Evangelical principles, which he firmly embraced, he engaged in establishing the "Christian Observer." The exercise of church patronage largely occupied his thoughts ; and to throw light on the theological views which guided him in the selection of clergymen, he explicitly stated—

"It is my fixed opinion, formed on much reading, consideration, and experience, that there has been for many years, among the majority of our clergy, a fatal and melancholy departure from the true principles of Christianity, and of the Church of England; from those principles which prevail throughout her Articles, her Liturgy, the writings of her venerable martyrs, and of many of her brightest ornaments."[2]

At the close of the century he commenced his career as an Abolitionist, in connection with Henry Thornton ; and, with the assistance of Thomas Clarkson, Zachary Macaulay, and James Stephens, he carried his work through early as well as later stages. From first to last he met with opposition ; but Chris-

---

[1] "Life," vol. i. p. 130. The Biographers, who had little sympathy with Wesley, remark that "his measures, even from the very first, were such as fostered a sectarian spirit."

[2] Ibid., vol. ii. p. 290.

tian faith was the talisman of all his success as well as of all his happiness.[1]

The most important instance of Wilberforce's activity in connection with Evangelical sentiments, was the publication of his " Practical View."

" ' 1793, Saturday, August 3rd,' he says in his Journal, ' I laid the first timbers of my Tract.' In 1797 the tract had increased to a volume, and when launched it was hailed in most religious circles as a good vessel. It was translated into French, Italian, Spanish, Dutch, and German; and its influence corresponded with its diffusion. ' It may be affirmed,' say his biographers, ' beyond all question, that it gave the first general impulse to that warmer and more earnest spring of piety which, amongst all its many evils, has happily distinguished the last half-century.' " [2]

Wilberforce, as a man, attracted much attention. A favourite at Court, a leading Member of Parliament, the friend of William Pitt, and a popular advocate of philanthropic measures, his *conversion* excited inquiry, and the book was intended to explain what to many seemed a riddle.[3] The author laid open that faith which had produced the change, and

---

[1] " Life," vol. v. p. 378.
[2] Ibid., vol. ii. p. 205.
[3] In 1818 the work had reached the thirteenth edition ; and I have now a copy of it before me with his autograph, " To the Athenæum, this Book is respectfully presented by W. Wilberforce." In this presentation he showed his desire to promote the circulation of the volume amongst literary men.

he felt sure that what had transformed him could transform others. He wrote, not for literary fame, but for religious usefulness. The work is open to criticism; yet criticism is disarmed by its tone and temper. Devotional rather than argumentative, it is not so much designed to convince the sceptic as to contrast defective views of religion with what the author apprehended to be real Christianity. In short, it is a Lay sermon on Evangelical piety, in which the social position of the preacher commands the widest audience, and his unprofessional character gives additional weight to his appeals. He dwells upon the corruption of human nature, upon inadequate views with regard to our Lord Jesus Christ and the Holy Spirit, upon the terms of acceptance with God, and the nature of practical Christianity. Defects in this respect he seeks to supply according to his own convictions. He deeply laments that Christianity has been reduced to a system of ethics, which he describes as a reaction against the extremes of Puritanical theology, whilst he praises Owen, Howe, and Flavel, and mentions that " most useful book, 'The Rise and Progress of Religion in the Soul,' by Dr. Doddridge," to which he was greatly indebted for his own spiritual change. He deplores the scepticism of contemporary literary men, and refutes the allegation that the world could not go on if his system of religion prevailed. A mild genial tone pervades the Treatise, with little or nothing to offend, although he insists that the time in which he lived was no time for half-measures. The steel glove Wilberforce wore was covered as well as lined with velvet. He did not follow the fashion of previous reformers, and therefore he did not please all Evangelicals. Some called him "legal," others "a man of rigid Calvinism;" such counter opinions being the best tribute that could be paid to a work which united the spiritual and practical sides of religion.

Before leaving the subject of lay activity for improving the condition of society, it is pertinent to notice the condition of the lower classes. Southey, in his "Life of Wesley," referring to the middle of the last century, speaks of the rudeness of the peasantry, the brutality of the town population, the prevalence of drunkenness, the growth of impiety, and the general deadness to religion. The picture of these times may be rather overcharged with dark colouring; but, beyond all doubt, England was then in a much more deplorable state than it is now. Old-fashioned burglaries, with the robberies and rogueries of the highway, were still perpetrated. A walk out of London after dark was by no means safe, and therefore, at the end of a bill of entertainment at Belsize House, in the Hampstead Road, St. John's Wood, there was this postscript—" For the security of the guests, there are twelve stout fellows, completely armed, to patrol between London and Belsize, to prevent the insults of highwaymen and footpads who infest the road."

To cross Hounslow Heath or Finchley Common after sunset was a daring enterprise, nor did travellers venture on it without being armed; and even ball-proof carriages were used by some. At Kensington and other places in the vicinity of London, it was customary on Sunday evenings to ring a bell at intervals, to summon those who were returning to town, to form themselves into a band, affording mutual protection as they wended their way homewards. Town itself did not afford security, for George IV. and the Duke of York, when very young men, were stopped one night in a hackney-coach, and robbed on Hay Hill, Berkeley Square. The state of the police, as these facts indicate, was most inefficient; but when the law seized on its transgressors it was merciless in the penalty inflicted. Long trains of prisoners, chained together, might be seen marching through the streets on the way to jail, where the treatment they received, cruel in the extreme, was much more calculated to harden than to correct. The number of executions almost exceeds belief; and every approach to London exhibited a gibbet, with some miserable creature hanging in chains. These public spectacles missed their professed object, and frequent executions did anything but check the commission of crime. The lowest classes, who assembled to witness such spectacles, regarded them generally as mere matters of amusement, or as affording opportunities for the indulgence of vice. Distinct facts of this nature tell more than sweeping generalities, and they suffice to indicate the state of things amidst which Christian workers of the last century pursued their self-denying efforts.

CHAPTER XXI.

1760-1800.

DURING ten years of the period now under consideration Whitefield pursued his work with unwearied assiduity. From one end to the other of the United Kingdom he travelled and preached "through evil report,"—mocked on the stage, abused in pamphlets, and spoken of even by the benevolent Jonas Hanway as "demeaning himself like an inhabitant of Bedlam;" and "through good report,"— cheered, not only by the sympathy of Methodist friends, but by the warm commendations of the Houses of Assembly and the Governor-general of Georgia, where, in his transatlantic visits, he had established his famous Orphanage. He persevered with steady determination and unfaltering courage,[1] and just before his death, his zeal was burning with the same ardour as ever. In a letter dated April 1st, 1769, is found the following passage, a fair specimen of his style of correspondence, and illustrating his satisfaction at the acceptance given to his labours in fashionable circles :—

---

[1] Tyerman's " Life of Whitefield," vol. ii. pp. 449, 481.

"Blessed be His name, we have been favoured with delightful Passover feasts. The shout of the King of Kings is still heard in the midst of our Methodist camps, and the shout of 'Grace, Grace!' resounds from many quarters. Our Almighty Jesus knows how to build His temple in troublous times. His work prospers in the hands of the Elect Countess, who is gone to Bath much recovered from her late indisposition, and worthy Lady Fanny Shirley proposes soon to follow, in order to reside there. Some more coronets, I hear, are likely to be laid at the Redeemer's feet. They glitter gloriously when set in and surrounded by a crown of thorns—

> "Subjects of the Lord, be bold;
> Jesus will His kingdom hold;
> Wheels encircling wheels must run,
> Each in course to bring it on." [1]

This style of expression is characteristic of the man. It violated rules of taste, and savoured of conventional phraseology liable to be misapprehended; but of Whitefield's perfect sincerity there cannot be a doubt. His zeal knew no affectation, whatever may be thought of certain expressions to which he was fondly attached. The letters of his last year are full of exclamations, such as "Grace, Grace!" "Ebenezer, Ebenezer!" "Hallelujah!" "Abba Father!" and the like, which it would be insufferable to read, if Whitefield had been an ease-loving, self-indulgent man. He wished to die in harness, to fall in the field

---

[1] "Whitefield's Letters," vol. iii. p. 384.

of conflict, to finish amidst the blaze of battle. He ever was going to and fro on his Master's behests —"a floating pilgrim," to use his own expression. He liked to revisit spots where he had been before, doing, as he said, his work thoroughly, "cross-ploughing the ground again." He could never rest. When the weather might have drawn him into winter quarters, he was out in the fields amidst frost and snow. Sickness did not repress his zeal, and when another man would have been nursed in his chamber he was standing up in the pulpit. His death, which occurred in America during his seventh visit, was worthy of his life.

" While at supper in Newbury Port, the pavement in front of the house, and even its hall, were crowded with people impatient to hear a few words from his eloquent lips ; but he was exhausted, and rising from the table, said to one of the clergymen who were with him—' Brother, you must speak to these dear people, I cannot say a word.' Taking a candle, he hastened towards his bedroom ; but before reaching it, he was arrested by the suggestion of his own generous heart, that he ought not thus to desert the anxious crowd hungering for the Bread of Life from his hands. He paused on the stairs to address them. He had preached his last sermon ; this was to be his last exhortation. It would seem that some pensive misgiving, some vague presentiment touched his soul with the saddening apprehension that the moments were too precious to be lost in rest; he lingered on the stairway whilst the crowd gazed up at him with tearful eyes, as Elisha at the ascending prophet. His voice . . .

flowed on until the candle, which he held in his hand, burnt away, and went out in its socket. The next morning he was not." [1]

He ended not his ministry until the last moment; and went on talking sacred words until he was caught away and carried home.

Moorfields Tabernacle and Tottenham Court Chapel—places where Whitefield most frequently preached—were huge edifices of no architectural character whatever. The red brick walls were as plain as possible, perforated by small, mean-looking windows, cut up into tiny panes. The doors were little better than barn doors; and, on entering, the worshipper found himself in a vast area, overshadowed by four deep galleries resting on heavy columns. The floor was for the most part covered with rude benches; a cluster of pews, lined with green baize, stretched out a little way in front of the pulpit. After Whitefield's death, the pulpits continued to be supplied by clergymen and Nonconformists; and at length an energetic man, named Matthew Wilks, took the oversight of both congregations, assisted by pastors from different parts of the country. He pro-

---

[1] Stevens's " History of Methodism," p. 360. This incident is not found in any memoir of Whitefield, except Tyerman's (vol. ii. p. 598), where it is abridged from Stevens. It is gratifying to find this statement in Mr. Tyerman's Preface—" As a matter of fact, I have felt bound to show that the friendship between Whitefield and the Wesleys was much more loving and constant than it has been represented by previous biographers" (p. 5).

longed his labours for many years during the present century. Of singular appearance, with what might be called a *knowing face*, above which rested a curious little wig, he possessed a voice very inharmonious, a style and manner very odd. His thoughts were ingenious and striking, his language quaint, pointed, and easy to be remembered. His sermons abounded in racy remarks, which rendered it difficult for his audience to sleep; and whilst common people were attracted by his knowledge of human nature and Divine truth, the educated were not repelled by his extreme homeliness.[1]

The most remarkable of Whitefield's disciples was Rowland Hill. When a boy at Eton he held prayer meetings, and used for that purpose to go to a poor woman's cottage, which he reached across the College fields, leaping over a ditch by the help of a pole. At Cambridge, his religious decision struck everybody, and while there he came under the influence of George Whitefield. At Hawkston, the domain of his father—"which for extent, natural diversified beauty, and landscape gardening, surpasses everything in Shropshire"—he began to preach at an early age, uniting in this irregular proceeding with his brother Richard, much to the concern and trouble of their venerable parent.

---

[1] A friend of mine, a good classical scholar and man of refined taste, often went to hear him in his young days, and found his sermons instructive and edifying.

Rowland Hill had an expressive countenance, eloquent eyes, an imperial nose, a powerful voice, an erect gait, and a very commanding appearance altogether.[1] He was the perfect gentleman, full of wit and humour, yet intent on religious usefulness. Not learned, not logical in the scholastic sense of the term, but rambling, disconnected, diffuse, he nevertheless produced great effect by his pointed, piercing, and practical homilies. Sheridan used to say, "I go to hear Rowland Hill because his ideas come red-hot from the heart." And Milner, the Dean of Carlisle, told him, "Mr. Hill, I felt to-day 'tis this *slap-dash* preaching, say what they will, that does all the good."

His having preached as a student, and his having avowed a determination never to confine himself to the pulpits of the Establishment, prevented for some time his obtaining Holy Orders. He was refused by six bishops; but at length, in 1773, he received ordination, "without any promise or condition whatever," from the Bishop of Bath and Wells. But it should be remembered, that whilst he used these words, by taking Orders and by subscription, he subjected

---

[1] Mr. Hill was a friend of my wife's family, and I have often heard that he liked to have the Eton boys to hear him when he preached at the Dissenters' Chapel at Windsor. At the hymn which concludes with the line, "When rolling years shall cease to move," they would chime in with the words, "When Rowland Hill shall cease to move."

himself to Episcopal control, and to the authority of the Church canons.

Throughout life, he continued to preach all over the country. When he could, he obtained admission to parish pulpits; but in meeting-houses, barns, and the open air, he was ready to engage in his sacred employment.

Amidst his wanderings, there were two places which he regarded as his home,—Wotton-under-Edge and Surrey Chapel. The former is situated in one of the most beautiful districts in Gloucestershire, and is famous as the scene of Whitefield's preaching: there Hill built a modest country house, and a place of worship in the Whitefield style, called the *Tabernacle*. Opposite stretched an amphitheatre of hills, covered with hanging woods, and enclosing a fertile valley. About half an hour before the service, the preacher might be seen, watching through a telescope his scattered flock, as they descended the valley, and making remarks to those near him on the seriousness or levity of their manners. The first stone of Surrey Chapel was laid in 1782, and the notorious Lord George Gordon contributed towards it fifty pounds. In June, 1783, it was opened for worship, when Rowland Hill selected for his text, "But we preach Christ crucified, unto the Jews a stumbling-block, and unto the Greeks foolishness; but unto them which are called, both Jews and Greeks, Christ the power of God, and the wisdom of God."[1] The

---

[1] 1 Cor. i. 23, 24.

building was vested in trustees, but its care was entrusted to the occupant of the pulpit "As long as he should preach agreeably to the doctrinal articles of the Church of England, and did not give the use of the pulpit to any one who was known to preach otherwise." Out of the income of the place he received only three hundred pounds per annum, the remaining receipts being devoted to charitable institutions connected with the chapel, which were further supported munificently by himself.

It has been often said that Whitefield was a mere preacher, and instituted no kind of organization for perpetuating the influence of his life work; but a distinguished personage once more claims our attention, who co-operated with him most energetically whilst he was living, and who supplied his lack of service in point of ecclesiastical leadership after he was dead. In 1760, Selina, Countess of Huntingdon, had attained the age of fifty-three, and, as we have seen, had long been known as a patroness of the Methodist movement. Numbers of the nobility had then for twenty years been in the habit of crowding her Drawing Rooms to listen to Whitefield's preaching, and during that period she had earnestly endeavoured to impress the minds of her friends with the importance of religious subjects. Turning back to gather up a few facts, we find the proud Sarah, Duchess of Marlborough, telling her in a letter,—

"The Duchess of Ancaster, Lady Townsend, and Lady

Cobham were exceedingly pleased with many observations in Mr. Whitefield's sermon in St. Sepulchre's Church, which has made me lament ever since that I did not hear it, as it might have been the means of doing me some good—for good, alas, I do want, but where among the corrupt sons and daughters of Adam am I to find it? Your Ladyship must direct me."[1] This would awaken hope respecting her illustrious friend, but a different impression would be made upon her sanguine mind, when she opened a note from another woman, prouder even than Queen Sarah. "I thank your Ladyship," said the Duchess of Buckingham, "for the information concerning the Methodist preachers; their doctrines are most repulsive and strongly tinctured with impertinence, and disrespect towards their superiors, in perpetually endeavouring to level all ranks and do away with all distinctions. It is monstrous to be told that you have a heart as sinful as the common wretches that crawl on the earth. This is highly offensive and insulting, and I cannot but wonder that your Ladyship should relish any sentiments so much at variance with high rank and good breeding."[2]

The Countess of Suffolk, the "Mrs. Howard" of the poet Pope, "more remarkable for beauty than understanding," carried her hatred to the spiritually levelling principle still further than her imperious contemporary, and after hearing Whitefield at the Countess's house, flew into a passion, denounced the sermon as a personal attack, and rushed out of

---

[1] "Life and Times of the Countess of Huntingdon," vol. i. p. 25. Letter dated 1739.
[2] Ibid., vol. i. p. 27. Letter dated 1739.

the room. Several, no doubt, were much affected by Whitefield's preaching; but it is to be feared, that as it had become a fashion to hear the orator, too many listened without real benefit, and the goodness of some who were touched by his appeals was as the "morning cloud."

Lady Huntingdon found more to encourage and repay her religious zeal in other classes of society. Amongst them in later life her efforts for the conversion of sinners were chiefly carried on; and in her earlier days she had indicated signs of preparation for the singular post she ultimately occupied, as the "Elect Lady," presiding over the Calvinistic followers of her popular friend and chaplain. In 1741, she had distinctly patronized lay preaching in the neighbourhood of Donnington Park, where she resided; and it was to lay preaching, at least to that which Anglican Churchmen regarded as such, that Lady Huntingdon was at last mainly indebted for the perpetuation and success of her missionary plans. In 1749 a striking incident occurred, marking her out as an ecclesiastical leader. In that year Whitefield told Lady Fanny Shirley, the Countess's relative, that they two were to be to him a Dorcas and a Phœbe, female helpers in the Church. He opened the subject to the Countess herself, and received from her in reply a letter, which he read to the congregation in the Tabernacle, after which "thousands heartily joined in singing the following verses:—

"'Gladly we join to pray for those,
　Who rich with worldly honours shine,
　Who dare to own a Saviour's cause,
　And in that hated cause to join.
　Yes, we would praise Thee, that a few
　Love Thee, though rich and noble too.
　Uphold this star in Thy right hand,
　Crown her endeavours with success;
　Among the great ones may she stand,
　A witness of Thy righteousness,
　Till many nobles join Thy train,
　And triumph in the Lamb that's slain.'"

A hymn so full of exultation that at least one titled lady had identified herself with them, would inspire the sympathies of the Tabernacle congregation, and raise their voices to a loftier pitch than usual; and when the service had concluded, the preacher wrote to his noble friend: "A leader is wanting. This however has been put upon your ladyship by the Great Head of the Church, an honour conferred on few, but an earnest of one to be put upon your ladyship before men and angels when time shall be no more." [1] In ecclesiastical history we read of men suddenly raised to bishoprics—Ambrose at Milan, for example, by the consentaneous shout of an assembled multitude; but never before had there been an election like this at the Moorfields Tabernacle in 1749. From that time may be dated Lady Huntingdon's intimate connexion with the body of Calvinistic Methodists.

---

[1] "Life and Times of the Countess of Huntingdon," vol. i. p. 117.

Another preparation for her office may be found in the interest she manifested about the year 1750, respecting the education of young men for the ministry. Notwithstanding her countenance of religious efforts unconnected with the Episcopal Church, to that Church, however inconsistent it may appear, she continued to cling with fond tenacity. Like Wesley, like Whitefield, she disavowed all enmity to its ministers and principles; and strove, as she thought, to strengthen it by infusing new life into its drooping condition. Whilst she failed to understand the objections of Bishops and others, they failed to appreciate her revivalistic zeal. Difference of religious sentiment, and of theological conviction, even more than of ecclesiastical rules and forms, separated the two parties from one another. Union between them, however conducive to the strength of the Established Church, and the moral welfare of the country, now appears to us, looking calmly across the breadth of a century and more, as a thing really impossible under the circumstances of the period. The ruling powers of the State Church went on their way, and the Countess of Huntingdon went on hers, until the divergence issued in entire separation.

Her Ladyship's *Connexion*, as it is called, was gradually formed. Though never very definite, it had something about it distinctive—not as a new form of Episcopalianism, or of Presbyterianism, or of Independency; ecclesiastical distinctiveness it had none. Its distinctiveness lay in the very absence of specific Church legislation, and in one absorbing purpose to secure places of worship where evangelical preaching should be maintained, either by Episcopally ordained clergymen, or ministers of another order; the doctrinal articles of the Church of England being the standard of faith, and the Common Prayer of the Church the standard of worship. The security of chapels for these general purposes, seem to have been the object of the Connexion.

Brighthelmstone, as it was then called, was only beginning to rise into importance about 1750, when attention was drawn to it as a bathing place, and the former fishing village became a town of fashionable resort. There distinguished people from London were wont to congregate, and the Countess of Huntingdon saw how favourable a spot it presented for one of her chapels. Whitefield visited Brighton, in 1759, and first preached under a tree in a field behind the the White Lion Inn. Lady Huntingdon took a house in North Street, and built a chapel near it, the expense being defrayed by the sale of her jewels to the amount of nearly seven hundred pounds. It was opened in 1761. Bath was much earlier in its renown than Brighton. Fashionable society had been accustomed to assemble there in the early part of the century. Bishops and other dignitaries " drank the waters," and in the beautiful city on a hill, sought rest and recreation. It was just the place for her Ladyship's efforts, and she distinguished it above others by the chapel she built in 1765, in the "Vineyards." Horace Walpole heard John Wesley preach there.

"They have (says he) boys and girls with charming voices that sing hymns in parts. The chapel is very neat, with *true* Gothic windows. I was glad to see that luxury is creeping in upon them before persecution. They have very neat mahogany stands for branches, and brackets of the same in taste. At the upper end is a broad *haut-pas* of four steps, advancing in the middle; at each end of the broadest part are two eagles with red cushions for the parson and the clerk. Behind them rise three more steps, in the midst of which is a third eagle for a pulpit. Scarlet arm-chairs to all three. On either hand a balcony for elect ladies. The rest of the congregation sit on forms. Behind the pit, in a dark niche, is a plain table within rails; so you see the throne is for the apostle. Wesley is a clean elderly man, fresh coloured, his hair smoothly combed, but with a little *soupçon* of curl at the ends. Wondrous clever, but as evidently an actor as Garrick. He spoke his sermon, but so fast, and with so little accent, that I am sure he has often uttered it, for it was like a lesson. There were parts and eloquence in it; but towards the end he exalted his voice, and acted very vulgar enthusiasm."[1]

Tonbridge Wells was, in the middle of the last century, a more favourite resort than Bath or Brighton. Card parties, balls, assemblies, and masquerades were the fashionable amusements, and above seventy coaches sometimes drew up at the door of the

---

[1] "Life and Times of the Countess of Huntingdon," vol. i., p. 477.

Assembly Rooms. There might be seen Dr. Johnson, in snuff-coloured suit, bag wig and cocked hat; and Dr. Gilbert, Bishop of Salisbury, in his black gown and garter, blue ribbon and badge; and William Whiston, lean and spare, in clerical dress, and a pair of bands;—Garrick, the Earl of Chatham, Speaker Onslow, and the Duchess of Kingston were among the visitors. After preachings, promoted by the Countess, in the little Presbyterian meeting-house, she determined, on one of her visits to Tonbridge Wells, in 1769, to erect a new place of worship, "a quaint structure of weather-board and tiles," which, after being several times enlarged, was taken down in 1870. Whitefield preached at the opening, one of his wonderful sermons, from the words: "How dreadful is this place! this is none other but the House of God, and this is the gate of Heaven." The dramatic power with which he painted Christ's agony in the Garden, and appealed to the people, to look and listen as if the scene had been before them, was long talked of among the people at the Wells. Lady Huntingdon did not neglect the metropolis; the place of worship most commonly identified with her name there is *Spa Fields Chapel*, once a pantheon in the midst of pleasure gardens. Difficulties existed in the way of her obtaining the property, and devoting it to sacred uses, but at length these were overcome and the building was opened in 1775.

It has already been noticed how unwilling she was

to separate from the Establishment, and on this account, as well as from personal partiality, she secured the services of Episcopalian clergymen. Wesley and Whitefield were especially welcome in her pulpits on this ground as well as others. So were Romaine and Venn, who often officiated for her. The same may be said of other less-known clergymen. There were two not yet named, who threw themselves into the Methodist enterprise, and were willing to officiate in the Countess's chapels and in similar places of worship. Martin Madan, founder and first chaplain of the Lock Hospital, was one of them. Being at a coffee-house one evening he was asked to go and hear John Wesley, and then to return and imitate the manner of the preacher; for Madan was a great mimic. When he listened to the text, "Prepare to meet thy God," he was awestruck; and on coming back to his gay companions, as they enquired "if he had taken off the old Methodist," "No gentlemen," he replied, "but he has taken me off." Being a man of ability and education, he entered into holy orders, and acquired a leading position among Methodist clergymen. John Berridge, Vicar of Everton, was another of the same class in point of doctrine, but very eccentric both in his character and preaching. On being summoned to appear before his Diocesan, to account for certain irregularities, his Lordship noticing that he did not seem to be sufficiently deferential, asked, "Do you know who I am?" "Yes," he replied, "poor sinful dust and ashes like myself." There were two other clergymen who also assisted the Countess, Dr. Haweis, Rector of All Saints', Aldwinkle, Northamptonshire, and a clergyman named Glascott. The former of these preached at the opening of Spa Fields Chapel, and the latter officiated in the same place. William Sellon, who, with several other pieces of preferment, held the living of St. James', Clerkenwell, was a bitter opponent of Methodism, and he determined to put a stop to the ministration of his brethren in unconsecrated and unlicensed edifices. He first endeavoured to get Spa Fields Chapel entirely in his own hands, to nominate the ministers and to officiate himself, whenever he pleased. Failing to accomplish this, he instituted a suit in the Consistorial Court of the Bishop of London, against the clergymen who had preached there. Lady Huntingdon imagined that, as a peeress, she had a right to employ her own chaplains where she pleased; and as she invested these clergymen with that office, and attached Spa Fields to her own residence, she claimed on that ground exemption from the operation of the ecclesiastical law. But in this she failed. The ecclesiastical suit against Haweis and Glascott was successful; and they were prohibited from officiating any more at Spa Fields. Clergymen being thus excluded from the pulpit, no course remained for her, determined as she was to have worship carried on according to her own views, but to employ Dissenting ministers, and to place them and the building under the shield of the Toleration Act, and so she was compelled at last, most reluctantly, to become an avowed Dissenter. To perpetuate her *Connexion*, she had long seen that ministers, not Episcopally ordained, must be employed in her chapels, and that, therefore, the education of young men for the purpose was of vital importance.

Some years before, as early as 1767, she founded a College at Trevecca, South Wales, and appointed as president an able and pious clergyman, John William Fletcher, Vicar of Madeley, whose early history, character, and parochial zeal were most remarkable. He was from a boy decidedly of an intellectual turn; and when at school in Geneva he would pursue his studies all day, and then carry them far into the night. His friends hoped he would be a clergyman, but he made up his mind to enter the army, and accepted a captain's commission in the service of the King of Portugal. Circumstances prevented him from carrying out his purpose, and he came to England on a visit; it proved to be his permanent residence. During his employment as tutor in a gentleman's family in Shropshire, he passed through a process of experience not uncommon. He was brought to see that the religion he possessed lacked vitality—it was not rooted in gospel faith. Consciousness of the need of abundant prayer seems to have been one of the first pulsations of his spiritual life. "I shall wonder," said the lady in whose family he lived, "if our tutor does not turn Methodist by-and-by." "Methodist, madam?" asked he; "what is that?" "Why," she replied, with contemptuous exaggeration, "the Methodists are a people that do nothing but pray—they are praying all day and all night." "Are they?" said he; "then, by the help of God, I will find them out, if they be above ground." "About the time of my entering into the ministry" (he was ordained a clergyman of the Church of England in 1757), he says, "I one evening wandered into a wood, musing on the importance of the office I was going to undertake. I then began to pour out my soul in prayer, when such a feeling sense of the justice of God fell upon me, and such a discovery of His displeasure at sin, as absorbed all my powers, and filled my soul with an agony of prayer for poor lost sinners, and I continued there till the dawn of day."

A young man called on the eccentric John Berridge. "Who are you?" he enquired. "A Swiss from the Canton of Berne," was the reply. "From Berne, then probably you can give me some account of a young countryman of yours, one John Fletcher, who has lately preached a few times for the Wesleys, and of whose talents, learning, and piety, they both speak in terms of high eulogy. Do you know him?" "Yes, sir, I know him intimately; and did those gentlemen know him as well, they would not speak of him in such terms, for which he is more obliged to their partial friendship than to his own merits." "You surprise me," said Mr. Berridge, "in speaking so coldly of a countryman, in whose praise they are so warm." "I have the best reason," he rejoined, "for speaking of him as I do,—I am John Fletcher." "If you are John Fletcher," replied his host, "you must do me the favour to take my pulpit to-morrow; and when we are better acquainted, without implicitly receiving your statement, or that of your friends, I shall be able to judge for myself." Thus commenced an intimacy with Mr. Berridge, which subsequent controversy could not destroy.

Madeley Church, in the county of Shropshire, was the scene of Fletcher's apostolic preaching, and in the plain-looking vicarage hard by he lived and studied, wrote and prayed; whilst the parish—containing a degraded, ignorant, and vicious population, employed in mines and iron-works—became under his diligent Christian culture, a thoroughly different place. His public discourses, his pastoral conversations, his catechizing of the young, his reproofs to the wicked, his encouragements to the penitent, his accessibility at all hours, his readiness to go out in the coldest night and the deepest snow to see the sick or the sorrowing, his establishment of schools, and his personal efforts in promoting their prosperity—in short, his almost unrivalled efforts in all kinds of ministerial activity—have thrown around

Madeley beautiful associations, not to be matched by the hills and hanging woods which environ and adorn that hive of industry. This extraordinary man travelled as often as possible from Madeley to Trevecca, that he might discharge his duties as superintendent of the Countess's college. The college was established on a principle in harmony with his pious judgment. None were to be admitted as students but such as "were truly converted to God and fully dedicated to His service." They were to stay three years—to have their education gratis, with all the necessaries of life, and "a new suit of clothes every year. On the completion of their studies, they were allowed to minister either in the Established Church, or in some other Protestant denomination. Fletcher was no pluralist, for he did his work at Trevecca without fee or reward, from the sole motive of being useful." Mr. Benson, at the time an Oxford student, afterwards an eminent Wesleyan preacher, was associated with Fletcher in the instruction of the students, and he delighted to bear witness to the saintly character of his friend and colleague.[1]

But like Wesley, Fletcher and Benson differed from Lady Huntingdon and her clerical friends on the subject of the Divine Decrees. Wesley and his

---

[1] See Benson's "Life of Fletcher," for most of the statements now made.

coadjutors were Evangelical Arminians, and believed in what was called the doctrine of Universal Redemption. Lady Huntingdon and her Connexion were Calvinists, and connecting the atonement with the Divine Decrees, considered that it was really made only for the elect. In consequence of this diversity of opinion, Fletcher and Benson retired from the College at Trevecca.

Personal feeling mixed itself up with this controversy, as it affected Lady Huntingdon and John Wesley. Both had spirits made to rule. Without adopting the unhistorical and unreasonable theory, that spiritual ambition was the mainspring of their religious activities, there can be no doubt that, with pure motives, each valued power, and exercised it, as the means of accomplishing their ends. Indeed, if each had not exercised an unusual amount of authority under exceptional circumstances, it is impossible to understand how they could have accomplished what they did. Neither of them can be regarded as perfect, and it is no wonder that each saw a good deal of egotism in the other. "Trevecca," Wesley wrote to Benson, "is much more, than Kingswood," alluding to his favourite school near Bristol, "is to *me*. 'I' mixes with everything. It is *my* college, *my* masters, *my* students. I could not speak so of this school." Rowland Hill also detected something of the same thing in the admirable lady; and on the other hand, she and her friends thought they discovered too great an assumption of importance and power on the part of the founder of the Conference. Each was unconscious of what the other discerned.

In 1783 a decisive step was taken which severed almost the last link between the Countess's Connexion and the Episcopal Church of England. An ordination service was held at Spa Fields Chapel on the 9th of March in that year. Two clergymen took part in the service; one called the congregation to witness how the ecclesiastical courts had harassed the clergy officiating in that chapel, and stated that they were therefore compelled to secede from the Establishment; the other clergyman delivered a discourse and offered up prayer. Each took a Bible from the communion table, and then gave it to one of the two candidates, who knelt together according to seniority; hands were laid upon their heads successively, and these words were repeated, "Take thou authority to preach the Word of God, and administer His appointed ordinances, in the name of the Father, and of the Son, and of the Holy Ghost." The service lasted five hours.

As Dr. Haweis still identified himself with the Connexion without the surrender of his living, it shows that the decision of the ecclesiastical courts respecting the Spa Fields case was not regarded as settling the more important question, as to whether co-operation with the Countess affected the legal position of an English incumbent? At all events,

Dr. Haweis, his wife, Lady Erskine, and a lay gentleman, named Lloyd, were appointed by the Countess's will trustees of her chapels, houses, and other effects, and they were to appoint successors. So the line of trustees was to go on applying the produce of her estate, to such uses, and for such purposes, as they in their discretion should think proper. The Connexion became not a fixed ecclesiastical body with certain officers, but simply a number of congregations worshipping in certain buildings, secured for the purpose by her Ladyship's last Will and Testament.[1]

Lady Huntingdon died at the age of eighty-four, in the Chapel House, Spa Fields, June 17th, 1791, and was interred at Ashby de la Zouch, the burial place of her husband. "I am encircled in the arms of love and mercy." "I long to be at home. I shall go to my Father; can He forget to be gracious? Is there any end of His loving kindness? My work is done, I have nothing to do but to go to my Father,"—were amongst her last words.

After her death the college was removed from Trevecca to Cheshunt.

---

[1] "Life and Times of the Countess," vol. ii. p. 524.

CHAPTER XXII.

1760-1800.

DURING the forty years embraced within our present general review of Methodism, its development in organization and its increase in numbers are manifest and wonderful. It is also plain, and by no means surprising, that with all the desire manifested by the founder to remain in fellowship with the Established Church, Methodism loosened itself from its original moorings, and drifted into the open sea. It has been often imagined, how Methodism might have retained an intimate connection with the Episcopalian system; how preachers might have become a distinct but friendly order of agencies within its bounds, and under its authority; but this could only have happened through the existence of thorough sympathy between the clergy and laity of the Church on the one hand, and the promoters of the great revival on the other. The supposition however of such a state of things is scarcely compatible with the possibility of a strain of spiritual excitement, such as Methodism obviously was, and that from the very necessity of its nature. If the Church could have been Methodistical in spirit, organised Methodism would have had no reason for its existence. As it was, antagonism came to be its inevitable condition of progress. It gained strength by drawing away members from the mother Church of England. Its advance involved the disintegration of the community out of which it sprang.[1]

Another fact, which marks the history of Methodism, is equally natural. It was not to be expected that such a religious awakening would be unattended by fanatical excitement. Two instances of that excitement meet us at the outset of this chapter. One of the early Methodist preachers, named James Wheatley, brought great discredit upon the cause by his disgraceful conduct. After a few years spent in zeal and activity, he fell into an immoral course of life; and then, whilst at the same time professing penitence and extenuating his faults, he traduced his brethren. Wesley expelled him from all ministerial fellowship, an early act of the kind in the history of the founder; but Wheatley found friends and followers, and gave great trouble to his former associates. He went to Norwich in 1751, preached out of doors,

---

[1] "Conventicles are innocuous to the Church, only when the latter rests upon a very energetic and active community of feeling. Thus in Lutheranism, when the Church, in this respect, fell so far short of what was required of it, the pietistic conventicles could only act in a disintegrating and destructive way, against that whereby the members of the Church as such were still held together."—Ritsche's "Crit. Hist. of Scriptural Doctrine of Justification," p. 330.

gathered large congregations, united two thousand people into a society, erected a building in imitation of Whitefield's Tabernacles, and raised a commotion in the city, which provoked riots of an extraordinary description. The mob made a coffin, kindled a bonfire, and buried the preacher in effigy amidst the flames. Horrid blasphemies were connected with these acts, yet the wretched rioters shouted in the streets, "Church and King, down with the meetings." Wheatley afterwards became more popular than ever, but again he disgraced himself by his immoralities, was convicted in the ecclesiastical court, had to leave the kingdom, and at last died suddenly at Bristol.[1]

Another cause of offence occurred in 1762. Two preachers entertained extraordinary and almost unintelligible opinions, amounting to the grossest Antinomianism, with which they blended pretensions to supernatural inspiration, and boasted that they were oracles of divine truth. Smitten with the fascination of prophetic forecast, so perilous to minds of a certain order, they foolishly proclaimed in January, 1763, "that the end of the world would be on the 28th of February following." In this case there was enthusiasm, but no practical immorality, and the grievance ended by the secession of the two leaders, with about 170 members.

The Conference of 1765 showed that ninety-two

---

[1] Tyerman's "Wesley," vol. ii. p. 123.

itinerant preachers were then in Connexion; and that the circuits in two years had increased in England from twenty to twenty-five; in Ireland from seven to eight; and in Scotland from two to four. At this Conference, one of the minor peculiarities of the system became definitely fixed. Tickets had been used from an early period as tokens of fellowship, but they varied in form and appearance; now—in accordance with Wesley's minute, as well as comprehensive legislation for the body, which he saw growing larger year by year—uniformity was established in this instance of detail. A small card was prepared with a border, and a text of Scripture printed in the middle; the month and year at the top, and at the bottom the member's name written by the preacher. Tickets were renewed every quarter, the preachers meeting the classes for that purpose. The Methodist communion thus became more definite and compact than ever, and at the same Conference in which this arrangement was fixed, Wesley recorded a characteristic account of the rise and progress of his great work.

"In 1729, my brother and I read the Bible; saw inward and outward *holiness* therein; followed after it, and incited others so to do. In 1737, we saw, 'this holiness comes by *faith*.' In 1738, we saw 'we must be *justified* before we are sanctified.' But still holiness was our point, inward and outward holiness. God then thrust us out, utterly against our will, to raise a *holy* people. When Satan could no wise prevent this, he threw *Calvinism* in our way; and then *Antinomianism*, which struck at the root both of inward and outward *holiness*. Then many Methodists grew *rich*, and thereby *lovers* of this present *world*. Next they married unawakened or half-awakened wives, and conversed with *their relations*. Hence worldly *prudence, maxims, customs*, crept back upon us, producing more and more *conformity to the world*. There followed gross neglect of *relative duties*, especially education of children. This is not cured by the preachers. Either they have not *light* or not *weight* enough. But the want of these may be in some measure supplied by publicly reading the sermons everywhere, especially the fourth volume, which supplies them with remedies suited to the disease."[1]

The founder of Methodism now asserted authority over the Connexion, which he had drawn together. Preachers had joined him voluntarily; he accepted their services, and superintended their work. People had come to him for spiritual counsel and help; he had arranged them in classes, and over them he maintained religious discipline. Everything was freely done on both sides. It was a mutual compact, nobody was enslaved; and those who did not like the arrangements were free to retire from the body. To keep things together a controlling power was necessary; this fell on Wesley as a burden, it was not sought by him as a privilege. So he argued; and knowing what he was, we have no reason to believe that he was influenced by ambition in what he did,

---

[1] Smith's " Hist. of Methodism," vol. i. p. 322.

that he assumed power for any other purpose than the edification of the people; but, then, it must be remembered, many ecclesiastics have been quite as *honest* in claiming influence of a more despotic kind, and it is moreover important to notice that the founder of Methodism rested his case upon expediency, and never appealed to Scripture or ecclesiastical history for the sanction of his sagacious plans.

As the ramifications of the system spread in all directions, Wesley felt solicitous for its permanence. He had sought help from fifty or sixty clergymen, and he despondingly records the result.[1] After suggesting some prudential steps to be taken after his death, he characteristically prepared a succinct declaration to be signed by the preachers as a bond of union.

"I. To devote ourselves entirely to God denying ourselves, taking up our cross daily, steadily aiming at one thing,—to save our own souls and them that hear us.

II. To preach the old Methodist doctrine, and no other contained in the 'Minutes of the Conference.'

III. To observe and enforce the whole Methodist discipline laid down in the said 'Minutes.'"[2]

He, from the beginning, had been anxious to bring as many clergymen as possible into co-operation with himself. Several of them appeared at the early Con-

---

[1] Smith's History, vol. i. p. 355.
[2] Ibid., vol. i. p. 356.

ferences, but they dropped off, and few remained as his pledged coadjutors. One proved remarkably faithful. William Grimshaw, of Haworth, "was as much a Methodist as Wesley was, with this difference —the former had a church, the latter not." With wonderful ardour he preached from twelve to thirty sermons a week. Round the neighbouring hamlets, over the bleak moors, up the hills, and down the valleys, this self-denying shepherd sought the wanderers, and brought them into the fold. Weather mattered not to him; amidst rain and hail and snow and frost, with his one coat on his back, and his one pair of shoes on his feet, and a crust of bread in his pocket, he would go out for days and days on his preaching expeditions, sleeping wherever he could find shelter, and on his return home, spend the night in his own hayloft, to leave room in his parsonage for the entertainment of strangers. As one of Wesley's "assistants" he visited the Methodist classes, held Methodist love feasts, attended Methodist quarterly meetings, and allowed Methodist itinerants to preach in his kitchen.

In 1770 Minutes of Conference were framed as a protest against Antinomianism, as an assertion of the paramount claims of practical religion, and as a censure of minute theological terms, which make a distinction where there is little or no difference. But, in avoiding evils and mistakes of this kind, Wesley fell into a style of expression which it is extremely difficult to harmonise with his habitual mode of teaching the doctrine of Justification. Upon this point his Calvinistic friends immediately fastened; and they did so in a manner which laid them open to grave censure. Instead of asking for an explanation, they pronounced the doctrines taught in the Minutes as "*a dreadful heresy*," and injurious to the fundamental principles of Christianity; they insisted upon a formal recantation, and threatened, if this were refused, to publish a protest against what had been done. These charges and declarations were conveyed in a letter to the clergy throughout the three kingdoms, announcing that Lady Huntingdon and other Christian friends, real "Protestants,' were to have a meeting at Bristol, in August, 1771, when the Methodist Conference was to assemble, and that they meant to go in a body to lay their demands before the brethren. A more unwise proceeding can scarcely be imagined. But the issue of the meeting, which took place according to the determination expressed, was far better than might have been expected. It was acknowledged that the circular was hastily drawn up, and for the offensive expressions an apology was offered. Wesley, on the other hand, declared his constant and unwavering belief in the old doctrine of Justification by Faith, and contended that the language he had employed was not inconsistent with it. He does not, however, appear to have acknowledged that some of the propositions he had laid down were open to misconstruction, and therefore required revision. This is to be regretted, and also that he should have mixed up what was personal with what was theological, by saying that he had received ill-treatment from persons who had been under obligations to him, and that the present opposition was not to the Minutes but to him. This threw fresh fuel on the fire; and the charge was met by a simple denial. But, as an exception to what generally occurs in ecclesiastical councils, the two parties on this occasion came to an amicable arrangement; Wesley and the preachers, with one exception, signed a declaration, that they did not believe in Justification by Works, and the Calvinistic friends, represented by the Rev. Mr. Shirley, acknowledged that they had misapprehended the Minutes, and that they were satisfied with the Declaration. But the controversy did not end there. After private correspondence and negotiation—which is differently represented by the two parties, and upon which it would be tedious and unprofitable to enter—Fletcher of Madeley felt it to be his duty, in the interests of truth, to write what he entitled "Checks to Antinomianism." His first check vindicated the evangelical orthodoxy of the Minutes; defended the doctrine of Justification by Works at the day of judgment; asserted the principle of free will, and dwelt upon the evil consequences of Antinomianism. One "Check" after another appeared in consequence of letters written by Richard Hill. The "Checks" amounted to five, and covered a considerable portion of debateable ground between Calvinists and Anti-Calvinists. The extremely high Calvinistic doctrines of Dr. Crisp came under the merited lash of Fletcher; and he took care to show how they were condemned by Flavel and other Puritan authors. Into the merits of the controversy it is impossible to enter; but respecting it a general remark may be allowed. The combatants are entitled on both sides to a charitable construction of their motives. Fletcher was jealous for the interests of Christian morality, and at the same time maintained the freeness of Divine grace in the salvation of men; and his opponent was jealous for the doctrines of Divine sovereignty, and the unmerited love of God, whilst he shrunk from giving any countenance to practical ungodliness. Each saw evils to be avoided, and good to be accomplished, and became absorbed in the contemplation of the subject from his own special point of view, without being able to estimate the force of what could fairly be advanced on the other side. Neither party always did justice to views in a direction opposite to his own. Fletcher dwelt too much upon the monstrous principles of Crisp, as if they were approved by his antagonist; and his antagonist put meanings upon Fletcher's words, which he repudiated; and with the main points at issue minor ones were mixed up, which only tended to complicate and encumber the dispute.

Whatever may be the theological opinions of any one who has studied the controversy, he must needs admit that Fletcher has the advantage in precision of thought, in skilful reasoning, and in eloquence of expression. Without justifying all his conclusions, whilst demurring to several of his arguments, I must bear witness to the high moral tone and sweet Christian temper of these productions, and not forget to remark that he could and did rise to an elevation above one-sided views, and brought together what in other parts of the discussion were too often torn asunder. He beautifully observes :—

"If friendship brings the greatest monarch down from his throne, and makes him sit on the same couch with his favourites, may not brotherly love, much more powerful than natural friendship,—may not humility excited by the example of Christ washing His disciples' feet,—may not a deep regard for that precept, 'He that will be greatest among you, let him be the least of all,' sink the true Christian in the dust, and make him lie in spirit at the feet of every one?"[1]

The dispute unhappily fell into other forms. Toplady published a treatise upon absolute predestination, translated out of Zanchius; and Wesley, for the purpose of illustrating the absurdity of the argu-

---

[1] "Five Checks to Antinomianism," p. 133.

ment, reduced the substance of it to this form; appending to it Toplady's initials, as if Toplady acknowledged the caricature. " The sum of all is this—one in twenty (suppose) of mankind are elected; nineteen out of twenty are reprobated. The elect shall be saved, do what they will; the reprobate shall be damned, do what they can. Reader, believe this or be damned. Witness my hand, A. T."[1] That so good and wise a man as Wesley should go such a length, shows the perils of theological controversy, and how a strong man may be carried off his feet by the rushing tide of polemic thought. These conclusions, of course, his opponents would not admit; and it is one of the vices of controversy for any body to charge on another person doctrines which, however logically they may seem to follow from certain premises, are expressly repudiated by those to whom they are attributed. It was easy, but it only made the fire hotter than before, for Toplady to push, as he did, the other side of the question to an extreme, by striving to make Arminius responsible for Pelagianism, and even Atheism. Nor did he mend the matter by his counter charge. " In almost any other case, a similar forgery would transmit the criminal to Virginia, or Maryland, if not to Tyburn. The satanic guilt of the person who could

---

[1] Wesley defended himself in his little tract entitled "The Consequences Proved."

excogitate and publish to the world, a position like that, baffles all power of description, and is only to be exceeded (if exceedable) by the satanic shamelessness which dares to lay the black position at the door of other men." To charge Wesley with forgery was absurd, as everybody must know he did not pretend to give Toplady's signature, but only to indicate, in the strongest manner, that this was the consequence to which he believed his antagonist was led by the doctrines he upheld. Toplady afterwards descended to the vulgarest abuse; and seriously damaged his fame by his scurrilous pamphlet entitled "An Old Fox Tarred and Feathered."[1]

Fletcher continued to co-operate with Wesley, more or less, during the remainder of his life. In 1781 he preached before the Conference at Leeds, and assisted Wesley, with other clergymen, in administering the Lord's Supper in a parish church; his name appears in the Minutes on the preachers' list at different times; and, in 1784, he rose and said, "I have built a chapel in Madeley Wood, and I hope, sir, you will continue to supply it, and that Madeley may still be a part of the

---

[1] Rowland Hill lamented some things that he had said in this controversy. (Sydney's Life of Hill, p. 529, etc.) Rowland Hill was as much opposed to Antinomianism as any man could be. In the name of himself and his brother Calvinists, he said, "We are making it the subject of almost every discourse, that without holiness, personal and universal holiness, no man shall see the Lord." (p. 115.)

circuit. If you please I should be glad to be put down on the Minutes as a supernumerary." At this Wesley was deeply affected. Several preachers burst into tears. Wesley had hoped Fletcher would succeed him as President of the Conference, but the sands of the good man's life ran out the following year.

Before Fletcher's death, another coadjutor came forward to assist John Wesley, and thoroughly to identify himself with Methodism. Thomas Coke was a Welsh gentleman of property, " naturally ambitious and aspiring," educated at Oxford, and there infected with infidel principles. His faith was established by the writings of Sherlock and other divines ; and after ordination, he became curate at South Petherton, in Somersetshire. He met with Wesley, who told him to attend to his parish duties, but he wished for a larger sphere, and soon formed a sort of Methodist circuit in his own neighbourhood, Addicted to ecclesiastical irregularities, his character and zeal provoked such opposition on the part of his parishioners, that they rung the bells on his removal from the place. He joined the Methodists ; through their teaching became " converted " as he had not been before ; and entering the Connexion in 1777, took a prominent part in subsequent characteristic measures. Another accession to the Wesleyan forces in 1782, appeared in

---

[1] Moore, in his "Life of Wesley," gives a full account of Coke. See vol. ii. p. 310, etc.

an Irish convert, Adam Clarke. His mother took him to a class-meeting and he became a Methodist; his experience afterwards he thus records :—

"It was necessary that I should have hard travail. God was preparing me for an important work. I must emphatically sell all to get the pearl of great price. If I had lightly come by the consolations of the Gospel, I might have let them go as lightly. It was good that I bore the yoke in my youth. The experience that I learned in my long tribulation was none of the least of my qualifications as a minister of the Gospel." [1]

Such language as a youth, indicated spiritual precocity; but his religious judgments at the beginning were confirmed at the end of a long and learned life. Clarke became as remarkable, after he entered the Methodist ministry in 1782, for his exemplary discharge of pulpit and pastoral duties, as for the attainment of vast stores of learning. Of the labours and privations of preachers at that time he gives copious details in his reminiscences. With miserable accommodation in the residences attached to the chapels, with long wearisome journeys performed on foot, with hard fare and mean shelter, but a warm welcome, in the cottages of the poor, Clarke went on his way, like the humblest of his brethren, attending to the details of discipline; yet at the same time reading to such an enormous extent, and acquiring a knowledge of so

---

[1] Moore's "Life of Wesley."

many languages, ancient and modern, as to lead any one to suppose that he could have had nothing else to do, and that the library, as well as the seclusion of a college, had been at his command.[1]

Three incidents appear in connection with the period between Coke's joining the Methodists, in 1776, and the year 1784, just after Clarke became a Methodist preacher. The first was the building of what may be called the temple or cathedral of Methodism, in City Road. Plain and spacious, with deep galleries and studded all over with pews, it remains much the same as it ever was, only that from time to time it has gathered round it memories respecting conferences, debates, meetings, and men, of unspeakable influence throughout the Methodist world. Nor was the cost of the building a trifle in 1776, when the resolution was formed that it should take the place of the old Foundry. Six thousand pounds could be raised by Methodists then, only by riches of Corinthian liberality abounding in the depths of Corinthian poverty. However, the chapel was completed in 1778, and opened by John Wesley, who preached two sermons, one on part of Solomon's prayer, and another on the hundred and forty and four thousand standing with the Lamb on Mount Zion.

A second incident belonging to the year 1777, was the publication of a monthly magazine, first

---

[1] See Dr. Adam Clarke's "Memoirs."

known as *The Arminian*, then as *The Methodist*, and afterwards as *The Wesleyan Methodist Magazine*. It laid strong hold on the whole denomination, especially when periodicals were rare, and Methodist habits of reading, save in exceptional cases like Adam Clarke's, were very limited. Its sermons, essays, and anecdotes had a wonderful charm for readers, old and young. It was the Methodist household book, studied in private and read aloud on Sundays to the children and servants of the family. Nor did the excellent Founder by any means leave this publication to sink or swim, according to its own merits; but enjoined its circulation, sometimes in very dictatorial style.[1]

A third incident pertaining to 1783 and 1784 is still more important. Then was framed the Magna Charta of Wesleyanism, "The Deed of Declaration," about which there has been no little debate. The first chapel built for preaching was put in trust according to Presbyterian form; but it was objected, that if the trustees were allowed to name the preacher, they might object to Wesley himself entering the pulpit. The Deed was cancelled, and the power of appointing preachers became legally entrusted in the Founder's

---

[1] These statements rest on my own personal recollections. When a child, my father, who was a sort of Church Methodist, used diligently to read the magazine aloud on Sundays; and it is not long since, that I was favoured with a sight of an autograph letter of the Founder, in which he very peremptorily requires a Preacher to look after the selling of the periodical.

hands. Wesley was identified with the Conference. The Conference was identified with Wesley.[1]

Wesley saw that something more definite was needed for the security of chapel property than had yet been arranged, that according to his own practice and theory—for out of his practice had arisen a theory, the merits of which I shall not discuss—care must be taken to prevent the power of appointing preachers from slipping into the hands of trustees; and that the legal holding of so many buildings could not be wisely left to an indefinite company of preachers, but needed some restriction as to numbers. "My first thought," he says, "was to name a very few, suppose ten or twelve persons—Count Zinzendorff named only six—who were to preside over the community after my decease. But on second thoughts, I believed there would be more safety in a greater number of counsellors, and therefore decided on having one hundred." Hence "the legal hundred" appointed by Deed enrolled in Chancery, for holding the estates of the Wesleyan Connexion, and selecting preachers to preach in the chapels and to travel in the circuits. This measure created great agitation; and the controversy which arose out of it, and which has been renewed again and again at intervals, cannot be dis-

---

[1] Smith's "History of Methodism," vol. i. p. 482. He is the chief authority for the account given here of the progress of Methodism.

cussed in a work like this. First, to determine the point of view from which the controversy is to be considered, and then to enter into an examination of arguments on both sides—which is the only equitable mode of proceeding—would require a volume, and lead us completely out of the path of history. Any sweeping assertion would be an idle piece of assumption.

The same year which saw the Wesleyan Magna Charta, witnessed another important event. The American branch of the communion had rapidly grown; the members numbered about fifteen thousand, yet the sacraments were not administered among them, because of the prevalent idea that Episcopal ordination was required for that purpose. The American Methodists wished for the supply of this defect, and, unable to procure such ordination as they desired in any other way, they turned their thoughts to the Father and Founder, with the hope that he would set apart some ministers, whom they might welcome as administrators of the Lord's Supper. He proceeded in a peculiar way, and his conduct led to a great deal of controversy. On the 2nd of September, 1784, he signed a document containing the following passage:—

"I have appointed Dr. Coke and Mr. Francis Asbury to be joint superintendents over our brethren in North America, as also Richard Whatcoat and Thomas Vasey, to act as elders among them, by baptizing and administering the Lord's Supper. And I have prepared a Liturgy, little differing from that of the Church of England, (I think the best constituted national Church in the world,) which I advise all the travelling preachers to use on the Lord's day in all the congregations, reading the Litany only on Wednesdays and Fridays, and praying extempore on all other days. I also advise the elders to administer the Supper of the Lord on every Lord's day."[1]

Coke reached New York in November, and the next month held a Conference at Baltimore, when he and Asbury were by unanimous vote elected general superintendents. Afterwards Coke, assisted by a German clergyman, "set apart" on three successive days, "by imposition of hands and prayer," this same Mr. Asbury, first as deacon, then as elder, then as superintendent. Early in the following year, Charles Wesley wrote to an Episcopal minister a letter full of lamentations, on account of what had been done. "Lord Mansfield," he adds, "told me last year, that ordination was separation. This my brother does not and will not see; or that he has renounced the principles and practices of his whole life; that he has acted contrary to all his declarations, protestations and writings; robbed his friends of their boastings, realized the Nag's Head ordination (consecration?) and left an indelible blot on his name as long as it shall be remembered." In the following August, Charles Wesley addressed to his brother a strong letter to the

---

[1] Smith, vol. i. p. 513.

same effect, which elicited a reply in which John concluded that he was now no more separated from the Church of England than he had been before, that he submitted still (though sometimes with a doubting conscience) to "wicked infidels." These are his words. Yet he admitted that he varied from the Church "in some points of doctrine, and in some points of discipline," "but not a hair's breadth further than he deemed it his bounden duty."[1]

It should be observed that John Wesley did not speak of consecrating bishops. Not a word occurs as to any diocese or see which Coke and Asbury were to occupy. The language throughout is singularly guarded, they were set apart simply as *superintendents*. At the same time no one can feel surprised that Charles Wesley and others should have regarded it in the light of a consecration; and it is a little remarkable, that when his brother saw how it was regarded, he should not have repudiated an idea which his previously careful phraseology was insufficient to warrant. It must also be confessed that there was something anomalous in his first setting Dr. Coke apart as a superintendent by the imposition of hands; and then in Dr. Coke's being elected in America afterwards to that office; more anomalous still was Wesley's appointment of Asbury to be joint super-

---

[1] Smith, vol. i. p. 521.

intendent with Coke, and the subsequent setting apart by Coke of Asbury, in the course of three days, to be first a deacon, then a presbyter, and then a superintendent in the Methodist Episcopal Church. Coke assumed the title of Bishop, which Wesley had not given him. Thus he went beyond his commission, and his assumption of episcopal dignity displeased the simple-minded Founder, whose moral greatness comes out in strong contrast with the small ambition of his well-meaning friend.[1]

When Wesley had gone so far, it was only consistent to ordain others in a similar way, for different spheres of service. Accordingly we find him recording in his journal respecting the Conference of 1785, " Having with a few select friends weighed the matter thoroughly, I yielded to their judgment, *and set apart* three of our well-tried preachers." Here again, though the act performed was what is always meant by *ordination*, the Founder avoids using the word.[2] The Methodists in England, becoming more and more desirous for the administration of sacraments by their own ministers, he set apart in 1787, by im-

---

[1] The ambition of Dr. Coke in early life is noticed by Methodist writers (Moore's " Life of Wesley," vol. ii. p. 310, and Smith's " Methodism," vol. i. p. 398, and Tyerman, in his "Life of Wesley," vol. iii. p. 44).

[2] Pawson, in a letter after Wesley's death, says, " he ordained Mr. Mather and Dr. Coke Bishops." MS. letter in Smith, vol. ii. p. 98. The statement might be accepted in a certain sense; but it was not made in Wesley's characteristic phraseology.

position of hands and prayer, Alexander Mather, Thomas Rankin, and Henry Moore, three men who were to be leaders when Wesley was gone, for the service of Methodism in England. Mr. Mather he afterwards made a superintendent.[1]

According to the Anglican theory, which both the Wesleys adopted in their early days, and which Charles retained to the last, this setting apart of ministers by the imposition of hands was altogether unjustifiable; but John Wesley, as he distinctly states, had given up that theory, and had adopted the idea held by Lord King, and in substance by all Presbyterians and Independents, even by many Low Churchmen also, that Bishops and Presbyters were, in the beginning, but one order. Wesley considered that an episcopal mode of government—presbyters, with an *episcopus primus inter pares*, is not inconsistent with Scripture, is in full harmony with early practice, and is an arrangement conducive to the order and welfare of a Church; with this conviction, his proceeding in setting men apart by the imposition of hands to the work of the ministry was perfectly consistent. The consistency of his conduct in reference to Coke, is another question.

The course thus pursued in his last days, led Churchmen more generally and more decidedly than ever to pronounce John Wesley a Dissenter. He

---

[1] Smith, vol i. p. 547.

ways disliked to be so regarded, seeing that the latter were decidedly condemned by all authorities in the Church. When what may be called the last, long step of his great ecclesiastical life was taken, he became *practically* a Dissenter, however he might be regarded before.

In 1787, November 3rd, he writes in his journal,—

"I had a long conversation with Mr. Clulow, an attorney, on the execrable Act, called the Conventicle Act. After consulting the Act of Toleration, with that of the tenth of Anne, we were both clearly convinced that it was the safest way to license all our chapels, and all our travelling preachers; and no justice or bench of justices has any authority to refuse licensing either the houses or the preachers."

In other words, he placed the chapels and ministers of Methodism under the protection of "an Act for exempting their Majesties' Protestant subjects, *dissenting* from the Church of England, from the penalties of certain laws." [1]

This important determination placed Methodism in a new position. Rude interruptions of worship continued. Congregations were sometimes disturbed at evening service by young men bringing birds into a chapel and letting them fly, so that their fluttering wings might extinguish the tallow candles which

---

[1] The language of the Act throughout accords with the title. It is for "Dissenting Protestants," people "dissenting from the Church of England."

served to make darkness visible. Poverty remained. Preachers were treated in some circuits, even by their friends, after the humblest fashion. A room over a gateway served for lodgings; the furniture was of the meanest description, and thongs of leather attached to a chest of drawers were the only means of opening them.[1] But, amidst a lingering fight of affliction, and the scantiest pecuniary resources, the era of violent conflict and almost utter destitution came to an end; the record of this circumstance, therefore, offers a convenient place for noticing the lives and labours of men, amongst the most extraordinary the Church of Christ in England has ever seen.

On turning to "The Early Methodist Preachers,"[2] one of the first things noticeable, is the singularly excitable temperament of some amongst them—a fact which accounts for much of the extravagance with which they are charged. Thomas Olivers, before his conversion, seems to have lived in an atmosphere of strong passions, swept along by a current of profanity. In the parish where he resided, Tregonan, in Wales, he was accustomed to vent most extraordinary outflowings of indignation against all kinds of objects, cursing with the fury of a maniac the winds as they blew,

---

[1] Traditions of Norwich Methodism about the year 1780.
[2] Their lives are comprised in six volumes, edited by the Rev. Thomas Jackson, one of the most remarkable collections I ever read.

the cattle as they rested in the fields, the trees in the hedges, and the doors of his neighbours' dwellings. He, for a long time before he knew anything of Methodism, was completely beside himself.[1] And this man lived to write the favourite hymn, so full of power and pathos, which Henry Martyn repeated to himself as he saw the shores of England disappearing on his way to India.[2] Another, John Haime, speaks as having been, in his early days, before he knew anything of religion, in a state of conscious slavery to the evil one. He wandered by the river side, through woods and wild solitary places, looking up to heaven with a broken heart, the devil constantly telling him that no hope was left. He was terrified asleep and awake, thinking that the world was at an end, and that he saw it wrapped in flames. "I wept bitterly," he says, "I moaned like a dove, I chattered like a swallow."[3] George Storey was excitable in another and gentler way. When as a boy he heard the burial service read by a clergyman, he was awe-struck with the prospect of eternity; and so tender was his nature, that, having killed a bird, he was filled with remorse, and lay awake for nights, praying with tears the great Creator to forgive his cruelty. He took to all kinds of books—devouring

---

[1] "Lives of Early Methodist Preachers," vol. ii. p. 49.
[2] The hymn begins with the words—
  "The God of Abraham praise."
[3] "Lives of Early Methodist Preachers," vol. i. p. 271.

them with amazing eagerness—and states that he recollected reading over three hundred volumes, some of them folios, before he was sixteen. His "passion" in this respect, "was insatiable."[1] The effect which Methodism had on these men was to tame rather than increase the violence of their natural excitability, to deliver them from their tormenting fears, and to inspire them with a peace which often rose superior to their fiery temperament or their constitutional melancholy.

The force of imagination in some of them was surprising, and took at times poetical forms. Thomas Payne, a native of Gloucestershire, fancied that he saw wild creatures crossing his path. He did not sleep one whole night for thirteen months, without dreadful dreams, but beauty blended itself with terror. "I thought I saw myself standing on the summit of a frightful precipice, whence I was suddenly hurled down headlong through the air, expecting every moment to be dashed in pieces, *when I was turned into a white dove and flew up again.*"[2] In the case of Thomas Olivers, the poet, what might be a natural phenomenon, was transformed into a blessed pledge of peace, like what Bunyan's pilgrim saw.—

"As I returned home, just as I came to the bottom of

---

[1] "Lives of Early Methodist Preachers," vol. v. p. 223.
[2] Ibid., vol. ii. p. 285.

the hill, at the entrance of the town, a ray of light resembling the shining of a star, descended through a small opening in the heavens, and instantly shone upon me. In that instant my burden fell off, and I was so elevated that I felt as if I could literally fly away to heaven. This was the more surprising to me as I had always been (what I still am) so prejudiced in favour of rational religion, as not to regard visions or revelations, perhaps, as much as I ought to do. But this light was so clear, and the sweetness and other effects attending it were so great, that though it happened about twenty-seven years ago, the several circumstances thereof are as fresh in my remembrance as if they had happened but yesterday." [1]

Men who could dream such dreams, and so interpret nature, had a gift which, like Bunyan's, must have mightily helped them in the pulpit and in the preaching fields.

Some had been military men and passed through strange scenes. Payne enlisted in the service of the East India Company; met men of war and frigates in his passage out; passed through hurricanes; saw one mate fall overboard, another dashed to pieces by a fall from the mast, a third bitten in two by a shark; and then, after a strange, wandering, adventurous life, he settled down into a Methodist preacher, on grounds anything but enthusiastic, even in the estimation of the soberest people. "I desired to join with the people called Methodists." "I saw, to

---

[1] "Lives of Early Methodist Preachers," vol. ii. p. 60.

begin with smaller things, that wherever they came they promoted cleanliness, industry, frugality, and economy, loyalty, conscientious subjection to the king and all that are in authority, and real vital religion, which was well-nigh banished from the earth." [1]

The miserable pecuniary support and the multiform self-denial of these men seem almost incredible. One example will suffice, and it had better be given in the man's own words. Thomas Taylor, a noted preacher, upon whose death Montgomery wrote his beautiful hymn,—

> "Servant of Christ, well done,
> Rest from thy loved employ;
> The battle's fought, the victory's won,
> Enter thy Master's joy."

thus tells his tale of poverty:

"I set out for London, and from thence into Wales. Here my work was rugged and disagreeable enough. I had no quarterage, no travelling expenses, but now and then a shilling or half a crown was put into my hands. Sometimes I was obliged to dine and lodge at an inn, and to pay both for my horse and myself. In this manner I passed the year, preaching as I could, sometimes under cover, and often in the open air, even throughout the winter, which some may remember was very severe. Some time before the Conference, I made an excursion into Caermarthenshire and Pembrokeshire, counties in which none of our preachers

---

[1] "Lives of Early Methodist Preachers," vol. ii. p. 288.

had ever set foot. It appeared to me that in Pembrokeshire there was a probability of doing good, as I preached several times in Pembroke town, and in various other places." " I was sent from Leeds Conference back to Pembrokeshire, where everything was quite new; nor had I one shilling given me, either for the expense of my journey thither, or for my support when I got thither. But it may be said, 'How did you live?' I lived upon my own stock, till Providence raised me friends. I formed a circuit, including about two hundred and fifty persons, by Christmas; and at the end of the year I went to the London Conference, but still at my own expense, except some small matters which a friend here and there might give me, which could not amount to much, as the people were generally poor. From the Conference at London I was appointed for Castlebar, in Ireland. Here for the first time I received thirty shillings from Conference, for my expenses on the way. Fifteen shillings I paid for a place on the outside of the coach to Bristol, besides the expenses on the road, twenty-seven shillings I paid the captain for my passage to Dublin, besides provision, mate, sailors, etc. When I got to Dublin, I had about a hundred miles to travel to Castlebar, and even there my allowance was very short. I think when I left Wales, my stock was about thirty pounds. It was considerably reduced by the time I got to Castlebar. I stayed two years in Ireland; and from Limerick I came to the Manchester Conference. My stock of money was now reduced to about fifteen guineas. It was thought there was a probability of raising a society in Glasgow, and I was appointed to make trial; and out of my fifteen guineas I gave nine pounds for a horse, saddle, etc. I received from the Conference three guineas to take me to Glasgow, a place where we had no society, no place to receive me, no place to preach in, strong prejudices to oppose, and a long, cold dark winter before me." [1]

The adventures of these men were most remarkable. They met with hair-breadth escapes from drowning, from perishing amidst storms and pitfalls in wintry journeys, and especially from the murderous violence of mobs, when the preachers resembled the Apostle Paul who fought with beasts at Ephesus.

Their circumstances in many places wonderfully changed as time rolled on. A perfect contrast is presented between the stories told by some of them at the beginning and at the close of their career. Thomas Taylor, speaking of his young days, relates how a preacher at Bristol said to him,—

"'You seem pretty well dressed, and will hold out well enough for a year, but must expect nothing to buy any more clothes when those are worn out.' I went on till after Christmas, and endured a good deal of hardship from hunger and cold, especially in passing those dreadful mountains from Neath to Brecon, which are nearly forty miles over, and have a most dismal aspect in winter. On these I travelled a long way, and saw neither house nor field, hedge nor tree; nor yet any living creature, excepting here and there a poor sheep or two, nor scarcely any visible track to know my way by."

It is touching to find him telling a very different

---

[1] "Lives of Early Methodist Preachers," vol. v. pp. 82–84.

story in his old age, as he records a journey amongst the Cornish Methodists.

"There would be no great cross in itinerating in this manner, where in every place all things we wish for are made ready to one's hand. Groups of kind friends waiting in every place to receive one, and crowds assembling to hear, are exceedingly pleasing; and all the company in every friend's house looking up to one as to a superior species of being."[1]

In perusing the lives of these men, we meet with sensational excitement, with boisterous expressions of feeling, with ascriptions of sin to Satanic agency, when we might more truly trace it home to the human heart, and with ideas of special judgments and of special favour in daily events. But we must take into account the conflicts through which these preachers passed, such as we in these days amidst home comforts can scarcely imagine; the persecutions they encountered, their consequent absorption in one thing, which narrowed whilst it elevated their range of vision; and, above all, the heated religious atmosphere in which they travelled and laboured. Nor let it be overlooked that where fanaticism existed it took the side of morality, not immorality; of practical religion, not Antinomianism; of unworldliness, not fashion and self-indulgence; of spiritual faith, not earthly ambition. Minds might mistake their own

---

[1] "Lives of Early Methodist Preachers," vol. v. pp. 18, 94.

imaginings for Divine revelations, they might misinterpret the grammatical meaning of Holy Scripture; but a conviction that the things not seen are eternal, and that Christ is the same yesterday, to-day, and for ever, had in their minds supreme, habitual, all-mastering power, and "e'en the light that led astray was light from heaven."

Amongst such men, John Wesley, Fellow of Lincoln, a classical scholar, a learned divine, a man of accomplishments, spent the years of a long life on terms of intimate friendship, and whilst ruling them as their superior, he treated them as his brothers, or as his sons. Stories used to be told, sixty years ago, how in venerable age he walked the streets, accompanied by a couple of these worthies; how he would take them to the houses of poor old women, and with the consideration of a gentleman, put up with little inconveniences, sometimes too much for his humbler companions; how he would ride with them by day and occasionally share the same bed at night, and all for the spiritual good of his fellow-creatures.[1] The grandfather of the present Sir Robert Peel, when residing at Bury, in

---

[1] I remember hearing, when I was a child at Norwich, of his once having presented to him, by a humble Christian woman, as he and another preacher sat on the side of a bedstead, a basin of broth sweetened with sugar. Wesley's companion did not know how to swallow such a mess. "Brother," said he, "if you refuse, it will hurt her feelings. I have eaten mine." Again, he lay down one night with a travelling preacher, who thought what a privilege it would be to hear his conversation, and began

Lancashire, invited Mr. Wesley to breakfast with him. He agreed, on condition that he might bring *some of his children* with him. This was granted, and he went to the manufacturer's home with six-and-thirty of his itinerants.[1]

His appearance in latter days must have been singularly impressive, judging from portraits and traditions. Whilst the associations which gathered round him for years before his death made him a sight worth seeing; his cheerful countenance, his winning smile, his long grey locks, and his blended dignity and gentleness made him an object of special love and admiration to the young.

Southey once said to a Methodist preacher,—

" I was in a house in Bristol where he was, when a mere child. On running down stairs before him, with a beautiful little sister of my own, whose ringlets were floating over her shoulders, he overtook us on the landing, when he took my sister in his arms and kissed her. Placing her on her feet again, he then put his hand upon my head, and blessed me; and I feel," continued the bard, highly impassioned,—his eyes glistening with tears, yet in a tone of grateful and tender recollection,—" I feel as though I had the blessing of that good man upon me at the present moment."[2]

---

to put questions. " Brother," said Wesley, " I came to bed to sleep, not to talk."

[1] Tyerman's " Life of Wesley," vol. iii. p. 499.

[2] Everett's " Life of Dr. Clarke," vol. i. p. 259. My own mother often boasted of having, when a child, been taken up in the old man's arms and kissed by him.

Few men have lived like John Wesley, and few have died like him. In a small house beside the yard in front of City Road Chapel, he took his departure out of the world.

We are told that he dozed and wandered, but in his wanderings was always preaching or meeting classes. He seldom spoke; but once, in a wakeful interval, said,—

"There is no way into the holiest but by the blood of Jesus. 'Ye know the grace of our Lord Jesus Christ, that though He was rich, yet for your sakes He became poor, that ye through His poverty might be rich.' That is the foundation, the only foundation, there is no other."

After a restless night, being asked if he suffered pain, he answered, "No," and began singing,—

"'All glory to God in the sky.
And peace upon earth be restored !
O Jesus, exalted on high,
Appear our Omnipotent Lord.
Who, meanly in Bethlehem born,
Didst stoop to redeem a lost race,
Once more to Thy people return,
And reign in Thy kingdom of grace.

"' Oh, wouldst Thou again be made known,
Again in the Spirit descend ;
And set up in each of Thy own
A kingdom that never shall end !
Thou only art able to bless,
And make the glad nations obey,
And bid the dire enmity cease,
And bow the whole world to Thy sway.'

"I want to write," he said. A pen was put into his hand.

"I cannot," he exclaimed. "Let me write for you. Tell me what you wish to say," said Miss Ritchie. "Nothing," he replied, "but that God is with us. The best of all is, God is with us." Lifting up his dying arm in token of victory, and raising his feeble voice he again repeated the heart-reviving words, "The best of all is, God is with us." "Pray and praise," again and again he repeated. "Farewell, farewell," he uttered, as he shook hands with all around his dying bed. "The clouds drop fatness," he went on to say, as he felt heavenly strength shed upon him, "as showers that water the earth." After a pause came the watchwords, "The Lord of Hosts is with us, the God of Jacob is our refuge." Scores of times he strove to say, "I'll praise, I'll praise;" but nature failed. "Farewell," was the last word on his lips, as he passed away "in the presence of his brethren," Wednesday, March 2nd, 1791,[1] between three and four months before the Countess of Huntingdon.

His corpse was carried into City Road Chapel the day before the funeral; his face, even in death, beaming with a heavenly smile. The crowds who came to see him as he lay there were so great that, to prevent any accident, it was arranged that he should be buried at between five and six the next morning, and that the hour should not be known till late that night. Nevertheless, hundreds attended at that early hour, and as the Burial Service was read, and the word *father* was substituted for the word *brother*, the congregation burst out into loud weeping.

Before we leave Wesley in his last earthly resting-

---

[1] Moore's "Life," vol. ii. pp. 388-394; Tyerman, vol. iii. p. 652.

place, one more word may be said as to the character of his preaching. It was very popular, much more so than is generally supposed. His fame in one respect has eclipsed his fame in another; but there is reason to believe, if he had never organized the Methodist body, he would have made an ineffaceable impression on the mind of England by his living voice. History, tradition, and a stream of invisible influence would have preserved his name as the most illustrious of preachers, next to one whom we have already described. But he was of a different order from Whitefield.

There is an eloquence which has in it nothing rhetorical; with no dramatic power, no melting pathos, and yet it penetrates, subdues, and leads away captive. The calm, strong, deliberate, invincible conviction expressed by every sentence uttered, evokes sympathy. Wesley's eloquence must have been exactly of that description.

The fortunes of Methodism after Wesley's death were exceedingly critical. At the Conference in 1791, it must have been very affecting to see the chair so long occupied by the Founder left vacant, and to have for the first time to elect a successor to the post of President. The honour and responsibility fell to the lot of a preacher of reputed experience, judgment, and sagacity, named Thompson. At this Conference it was determined, "for the preservation of our whole economy as the Rev. Mr. Wesley left it,—

"That the three kingdoms should be divided into districts: England into nineteen, Scotland into two, and Ireland into six; and that district meetings should be held, consisting of preachers in full connection, who were to choose a chairman, and to act as an authoritative committee, having a power of final decision in any case of ecclesiastical dispute, until the meeting of the next Conference."

This completed the machinery of Methodism, which began with class-meetings and expanded into circuits. Soon the question arose about ordination and the administering of sacraments; and it was found, that after the presiding spirit had been withdrawn, elements of division previously in existence began to develop in two distinct and powerful parties—one for continuing things as they were, another for alterations in harmony with the Founder's latest measures. It is manifest that his earlier policy had been to avoid separation from the Church of England; but latterly his conduct, in spite of his professions, had leaned on the side of Dissent; at any rate he had ordained ministers outside of the Establishment, whom he appointed to administer the sacraments. Hence, some followers were anxious to maintain his earlier conservatism; whilst others were anxious to complete and perfect his organizations, though at the expense of real separation from the Church. The matter of ordination was settled in 1792, by the rule, that ordination should not take place without the consent of Conference, and that a breach of this rule should entail exclusion from the Connexion.[1]

The question as to administering sacraments was not so easily solved. Here two distinct parties made their appearance. The first consisted chiefly of leading laymen, trustees of chapels, who retained a good deal of old-fashioned Episcopalian feeling, and wished Wesleyanism to be, "if not a pillar inside, at least a buttress outside the Church of the nation." They preferred to receive the Lord's Supper at the hands of episcopally ordained clergymen, and so to keep up a connection with the parish churches. The strong expressions of attachment to the national Establishment so often employed by their venerated spiritual Father of course formed the stronghold of their cause. The second of these parties consisted chiefly of preachers and a large body of the people—the commonalty of Methodism—who preferred receiving the Lord's Supper at the hands of those whom they regarded as their spiritual guides, and who, moreover, in numerous cases, shrank from approaching the parish altars, where they found many an immoral communicant, and also perhaps a clergyman who did not command their respect. The contest between the two sections became strong, and the feeling was increased by a suspicion in some quarters that a few preachers were aiming to establish

---

[1] Minutes for 1792; and Smith's "Methodism," vol. ii. p. 18.

a Methodist hierarchy. But an amicable termination of the dispute was reached at the Conference of 1795.

A plan of pacification was devised to this effect —that the Sacrament of the Lord's Supper should not be administered in any chapel, except the majority of the trustees of that chapel on the one hand, and the majority of the stewards and leaders on the other, should allow it. Nevertheless, that the consent of the Conference should be obtained. It was also provided that, wherever the Communion had been already "peacefully administered," the administration of it should be continued. It is remarkable that a compromise which does not rest upon any deep ecclesiastical principle should have brought peace; but it shows how strong must have been the bonds of sympathy which could keep so large a community together, under arrangements so frail, and so likely, without love, to burst asunder. It was in this one particular, brotherly love, that the old Methodists were so mighty and invincible.

A painful personal dispute arose, however, in connection with the sacrament controversy, and tended to intensify the excitement. A young minister, named Alexander Kilham, advocated what he considered to be plans of reform, but which were regarded by elder brethren as involving a revolution. Here again comes up a question of domestic ecclesiastical polity, the settlement of which depends on the point of view adopted for its examination. Methodists and those who are not Methodists can scarcely be expected to reach the same conclusion on a point of this nature. I therefore pass it over; but the personal element of the controversy requires a remark. Alexander Kilham was a man of ability, of great zeal, of honest purpose; but he was rash, and did not go the way to work to accomplish what he attempted. He reflected, to some extent, on the character of John Wesley, and to a much greater extent on the character of some of his brethren. When thousands of hearts were bleeding with sorrow for an irreparable loss, even slight reflections on what was regarded as almost unexampled excellence, were likely to exasperate. At the same time the way in which he spoke of some of his brethren was calculated to provoke unfriendly feeling, and to disturb the connexion to which he belonged. At first he was censured at the Conference in 1792, yet allowed to remain on the preachers' list; but he afterwards issued anonymously certain offensive circulars, about the origin of which there could be no doubt; and in them he brought grave charges against Methodist preachers. At the Conference in 1796, he was accused of having stated what was not true; and the trial ended in his expulsion from the body. He laid the basis of what is called the New Connexion; a highly respectable body, well known in the religious world of after times.

It is gratifying to add, on closing the record of Methodism in the eighteenth century, that the controversies raised after the death of Wesley do not seem to have interrupted the spiritual work which he commenced. A great revival in Yorkshire was reported in 1794; and a visit by Joseph Benson into Cornwall is described as producing a powerful religious impression. Thirty-six years afterwards it is referred to by one living in the neighbourhood as "deep and hallowed beyond example."[1]

"If Methodism," says the author of "Wesley's Life and Times," "does not exist in Palestine, Asia Minor, Arabia, Greece, or Egypt, it exists in Britain, France, Germany, Switzerland, Italy, Spain, Denmark, Norway, Sweden, and Africa; and, passing to other regions which the Romans never trod, it has long since entered India and Ceylon; it has already won its triumphs in the flowery land of the Chinese; it has a vast multitude of adherents in Australia and the islands of the Pacific Ocean; and in the West Indies its converts are numbered by tens of thousands; while in America it has diffused its blessings from the most remote settlements of Canada in the north, to the Gulf of Mexico in the south, and from Nova Scotia in the east to California in the west."

"We must make a total of more than twelve millions of persons receiving Methodist instruction, and, from week to week, meeting together in Methodist buildings for the purpose of worshipping Almighty God. The statement is

---

[1] Smith, vol. ii. p. 44.

startling, but the statistics given entitle it to the fullest consideration."[1]

The rise and progress of Methodism may be regarded as the most important ecclesiastical fact of modern times, and requires to be studied in relation to the Established Church of England, the old Nonconformist bodies, and the missionary interests of Christianity throughout the world, by every one who would understand the religious history of the last hundred years.

In another respect the history of Methodism is important and suggestive. Methodism, like Puritanism, might have been, at least to a large extent, preserved as so much vital force within the national Church; but neither were allowed a place within its precincts. By a hard, narrow, unsympathetic, and exclusive policy, both these parties were forced into a position outside; and the same policy which ejected so many clergymen at the Restoration, and threw off the Wesleyan revivalists, also increased these sections of Dissent in point of numbers. At the same time this policy strengthened and developed the principles which the two sections embodied. At last it placed their followers in an attitude towards the Establishment far beyond what the leaders had ever contemplated. Of course that policy was meant to strengthen and preserve the Church, but it had an

---

[1] Tyerman's "Wesley," vol. i. pp. 3, 9.

opposite effect. It perpetuated and promoted Nonconformity. What was employed as a means of union and consolidation operated as a solvent, and separated from the rest the most active elements of the Church's religion. This might have been foreseen in 1662: they must have been blind indeed who did not perceive it a century afterwards.

CHAPTER XXIII.

1760–1800.

THE name of Presbyterian came to be more loosely applied than ever during the last half of the eighteenth century; and no wonder, since Presbyterians and Independents were closely associated, and, in some cases, a minister of the one denomination took the oversight of a congregation belonging to the other. The clergy who retained the Presbyterian name were independent in ecclesiastical action, perhaps even more so than their brethren; and this arose from the fact, that the people in the one case had less power than the people in the other. An Independent Church, worked on its own distinctive principle, was very much of a democracy. The people were the source and the agents of power. They had their Church meetings, where they discussed questions respecting their affairs, and determined the result by popular vote. The admission of members and the exercise of discipline rested with the community; the pastor, of course, having much influence in the spiritual republic. But a Presbyterian congregation claimed and exercised no such republican rights. The people chose their pastor, and when they had done so, they left the management of Church business very much in his hands. They did not hold meetings for discussion, or to admit and suspend communicants.

The relinquishment of congregational power has been assigned as a reason for ministerial deviations from orthodoxy. The circumstance, perhaps, may account for it thus far; that guidance being implicitly left to the man of their choice, he had free scope for his theological inquiries, and plenty of room for the sway of his opinions. When heterodox sentiments appeared, they sprang from the pulpit rather than from the pew. The congregation did not innovate upon old creeds and customs; the pastor was left to take the lead. He started what they might think novelties, but by respectful attention to his arguments they came by-and-by to adopt his conclusions. The shepherd went before, the flock followed. No despotism was claimed on the one hand, or admitted on the other. A Presbyterian minister did not impose his beliefs, but appealed to the understanding and judgment of his hearers. Free inquiry was the watchword; liberty of thought was extolled; necessarily however, under the circumstances, the persuasive influence of a learned and beloved instructor would be very great.

There is a marked difference between Presbyterians and the members of an Episcopalian establishment. The former attached no authority to the teaching of other days, nor did they care for uniformity of belief, whereas the latter did, and that most decidedly. Not that Presbyterians were destitute of reverence for the past. They never threw overboard old traditions; but their reverence was restricted to the character, spirit, and temper of Reformers and Puritans; it extended not to their opinions. They paid no attention to Westminster Confessions and Catechisms, to Declarations of Faith, and Articles of Agreement; but they had a profound respect for the Westminster Assembly, and for Puritan confessors under the Stuart dynasty. They valued them, more for what they had thrown off, than for what they had preserved. With a strong, one-sided tendency, they exalted the memory of their fathers, as pioneers of free inquiry. Could those fathers have risen from the grave, they would scarcely have accepted the kind of admiration sometimes bestowed on them by their sons.

Unlike Episcopalians, the Presbyterian body did not aim at uniformity, either in faith or in practice, though there was more of uniformity in worship and methods of government than in opinions respecting points of divinity. Their love of free inquiry prevented them from attaching much importance to any consentaneous maintenance of religious sentiment. They thought of errors which ought to be exploded, more than of truths remaining to be learnt. Throwing off the checks of the past, they fancied there was no limit to future discoveries. Full of hope, they were as daring as they were sanguine. They launched their barks on perilous waters, and whither they were drifted, we shall see as we proceed.

One of the first things which arrests the student during the second forty or fifty years of the last century, is the remarkable degree and extent of mental culture in the Presbyterian denomination. In accordance with their love of inquiry, was their diligence in education. Presbyterian names for about half a century are conspicuous in English literature and science. We have already referred to Price, Priestley, and Chandler. Dr. Kippis was also one of the Presbyterian *literati*, well known as the editor of the "Biographia Britannica," and as a large contributor to the historical and philological pages of a once popular work, "The New Annual Register." Another of the same period, little known to fame, but, if report be true, a very extraordinary man, was George Walker, educated at Newcastle, in the same school as Lord Eldon and his brother Lord Stowell. He settled at Durham, Leeds, and Yarmouth, and then removed to Warrington, where he became tutor in the Presbyterian Academy. In 1775 he published an extraordinary book, entitled, "The Doctrine of the Sphere." His mathematical attainments are reported to have been wonderful; and some of his hymns are still remembered. He was an antiquary and a man of taste; and, at Manchester, the Literary and Philosophical Society elected him as President. Though he published little, he was one of those men whose names, when they are gone, gather round them a nimbus of intellectual glory.[1] All these five, Price, Priestley, Chandler, Kippis, and Walker, were Fellows of the Royal Society.

Dr. Taylor, the Presbyterian minister at Norwich, and afterwards tutor at Warrington, who died in 1761, was distinguished not only by his numerous works on controversial and practical divinity, but by his attainments as an Oriental scholar, of which his Hebrew-English Concordance is a proof. Dr. Furneaux, a learned London Presbyterian, author of "Letters to Blackstone," respecting certain positions in his "Commentaries," may be added to the list; and also the accomplished Dr. Aiken, first classical, and then theological tutor at the Warrington Academy. Gilbert Wakefield, another literary name, is also connected with the Presbyterianism of Warrington and Hackney; inasmuch as, after his secession from the Church of England, he became a teacher at both places. In the course of a life filled with strange adventures, he published a number of classical works, marred, no doubt, as in Priestley's case, by the rapidity of production; indeed, a want of careful accuracy

---

[1] Notices of Mr. Walker are found in the *Monthly Repository*, Oct. 1810; "Perlustration of Great Yarmouth," (a repository of all kinds of curious information), vol. ii. p. 132; and Dr. Halley's "Lancashire," vol. ii. p. 394.

was not uncommon in this school of authors. Dr. Enfield belongs to the literary succession, and we may add the name of William Taylor, of Norwich, friend of Robert Southey, and father of English-German literature.

But the taste cultivated by the Presbyterians spread far beyond this range of authorship. In certain cities and towns there are fondly preserved traditions of literary Presbyterian circles in pleasant brightness three or four generations ago. If I may here venture to intrude my own recollections, let me mention the Taylors, the Martineaus, and the Aldersons of Norwich, at the beginning of the present century, descendants of eminent Presbyterians whose memories they reverently cherished.

Next to their culture, was their advocacy of freedom. They, more than the Independents, were the "political Dissenters" of the age. Price and Priestley we have already seen in that capacity. They were esteemed by Burke and others as leaders in the vanguard of progress, or rather, as such critics thought, of revolution and ruin. They hailed the beginning of the French Revolution as the dawn of European freedom; and though they did not condemn a limited monarchy, but prized the liberties of the English Constitution, they hoped to see them more fully developed. Especially did they desire an equality of political rights, and earnestly did they contend for what has been since obtained, the repeal of the

Corporation and Test Acts. That which in one age is resisted as an extravagant demand, is in another paid as a righteous debt.

Kippis laid aside his huge folios to write "A Vindication of the Protestant Dissenting Ministers, with regard to their late Application to Parliament," and this brought him into controversy with Dr. Josiah Tucker, Dean of Gloucester. It is pleasant to witness the courtesies of literature observed in the midst of this new discussion, unlike the personal animosity which so often mingles in such conflicts. "Dr. Tucker is the ablest apologist for the Church of England," says Dr. Kippis. "You, sir," replies the latter, "appear to me in the light of a very able advocate for your cause; and, what is much better, but which, alas! can be said of a very few controversial writers, in the light of an honest man; you are on the whole a candid and impartial searcher after truth."[1] Dr. Furneaux, already mentioned, was another zealous champion on the side of civil and religious liberty; and in that capacity his name appears in the minutes of the Deputies of the three denominations. When, in 1767, the important cause between the elected Sheriff Evans and the Corporation of London came on for hearing, and Lord Mansfield delivered his famous judgment, Dr. Furneaux was present, and brought home *memoriter* the whole

---

[1] "Letters to the Rev. Dr. Kippis," by J. Tucker, D.D., p. 5.

speech; and that with such accuracy, that when the report was submitted to his lordship, he found only two or three trifling errors to correct.[1] Dr. Amory, pastor of the Old Jewry congregation, is particularly noticed for his disapproval of subscription to human formularies.[2]

A community so devoted to intellectual pursuits, and to the interests of free inquiry, would be sure to provide for the education of their families and of the rising ministry. They supported an Academy, under Dr. David Jennings, who presided over it eighteen years, and was assisted by Dr. Savage, who delivered lectures at his residence in Wellclose Square. When Dr. Jennings died, in 1762, the seminary was provided for in the village of Hoxton, and Dr. Savage became theological teacher and principal. With him, Dr. Kippis and Dr. Rees were associated. The tutors were of different theological opinions, and Independents and Presbyterians were united in the support as well as in the administration of the establishment; soon differences arose, and after a time the whole scheme of education was abandoned.

The Hoxton Academy being dissolved, another was framed at Hackney; and at that place we find Dr. Kippis engaged as principal tutor in 1786. Gilbert

---

[1] " Proceedings of the Deputies," p. 31; Wilson's " Dissenting Churches," vol. i. p. 119.

[2] " Brit. Biog.," vol. i. pp. 175–77; written by Kippis, a friend of Amory.

Wakefield, just now mentioned, a man of advanced opinions, was associated with him; also the Rev. Thomas Belsham, who had been both student and professor in the academy of Dr. Doddridge. Belsham had been instructed in Calvinistic principles, afterwards he forsook the faith of his fathers, and embraced views of a widely different character.

From London we turn to the provinces, and proceed to the Academy at Warrington. Lancashire had been the stronghold of Presbyterianism during the Civil Wars and the Commonwealth; and its name and traditions were widely cherished among the Nonconformists of that part of England. They determined to have an institution for educating their ministers, such as should surpass all others; and resolved to elect "tutors of known ability and good character in theology; moral philosophy, including logic and metaphysics; natural philosophy, including mathematics; and in the languages and polite literature." They elected the claimant of the Willoughby title and barony as their President, and John Holt, the representative of the Worsleys, an old and honourable Nonconformist family, as their Vice-president. Great credit for public spirit is due to those who commenced the enterprise. The first professor they elected was Dr. Taylor of Norwich, the Hebraist, with whom was associated a tutor in mathematics and natural philosophy: the person invited to the chair of languages and elegant literature, declined the invitation. The number of pupils at first was only three, one alone engaged in divinity studies: then we read of five—but altogether, during its whole continuance, the Warrington Academy received nearly four hundred young men. Dr. Taylor was not successful in the administration of affairs. The trustees turned out more troublesome than the students; nor did the principal get on well with his colleague. Dr. Taylor died suddenly in 1761, worn out, it was thought, by the troubles of his latter days, and Dr. Aiken succeeded him as president; the classical chair was occupied by Priestley.

After other changes, the Institution was dissolved in 1783. Of nearly four hundred students, several became eminent in the medical and legal profession, but only about six "rendered any service to the Presbyterian interest of the country." Another Academy arose in 1786, at Manchester, and was afterwards transferred to York.[1]

An Academy existed at Carmarthen in Wales, whither, after other migrations, it had been finally transferred from Gloucestershire. Being under the care of a succession of ministers who had lived in different

---

[1] For information respecting Warrington and Manchester, I am chiefly indebted to Dr. Halley, who made himself well acquainted with the subject. See "Lancashire, its Puritanism and Nonconformity," vol. ii. pp. 395-410. An account of these Academies is also given by Bogue and Bennett in their "History of Dissenters," vol. ii. pp. 531-535.

places, it had followed them from one abode to another. Dr. Jenkyn Jenkins conducted it at Carmarthen, until he removed to London, in 1779; Robert Gentleman succeeded him in 1780; but changes in the religious opinions of the teacher alienated the Independents who had joined in its support, and it now fell entirely into Presbyterian hands.

As might be expected from their disregard of uniformity in opinion, and their zeal for freedom of thought, great diversities of judgment existed among Presbyterians. Orthodoxy of the old-fashioned type did not totally disappear. Dr. Langford is "said to have been, in the latter part of his life, the only Presbyterian minister in London who retained the faith of the [earlier] Nonconformists." Whether this statement be correct or not, it shows that at least one metropolitan pastor of the denomination held substantially the same doctrine as his Puritan predecessors. It is stated by Dr. Gibbons, in a Funeral Sermon for him, that his views of the doctrines of the Gospel were what are generally termed Calvinistical; not that he called any man master on earth, but the sentiments which appeared to him to be contained in the Bible, and which he deduced thence, agreed on the whole with the tenets of the Genevan Reformer.[1] Finally Langford is seen at the Independent Meeting, King's Weigh-house, Little Eastcheap, first as

---

[1] Gibbons' Funeral Sermon for Langford, pp. 18-31.

colleague, and next as sole pastor.¹ He lived on the debatable ecclesiastical ground between Presbyterianism and Independency; and perhaps his ultimate identification with the latter may be attributed to his disapproval of latitudinarian tendencies, manifested by the former. Be that as it may, certainly he was orthodox whilst occupying a Presbyterian pulpit in Silver Street; and probably other examples might be found in provincial Churches.

In Shrewsbury there occurs an instance closely approaching to that now cited. Job Orton has made a mark on the old Salopian town, almost as deep as that of Baxter on Kidderminster, and that of Doddridge on Northampton. The visitor is reminded by the Guide Book, that Job Orton was born there. The chapel connected with the Presbyterian Church, of which he was pastor, is pointed out in High Street, where Coleridge once preached, and Hazlitt walked from Wern to hear his eloquent friend; and amongst the monuments in old St. Chad's, one—recently modernized and carefully preserved, in perpetuation of his memory—claims, in the estimation of local antiquaries, particular notice. Job Orton was a favourite student in Dr. Doddridge's Academy; and the interesting memoirs which he wrote of his master show how much he loved him, and how greatly he admired his

---

[1] Wilson's "History of Dissenting Churches," vol. i. p. 183; see also vol. iii. p. 68.

character and work. Orton's name is now almost inseparably entwined around Doddridge's; and in piety, candour, and moderation he strongly resembled him. Also with Baxter he has been brought into connection by Dr. Kippis, who says, Orton had a considerable resemblance in certain respects, to that famous divine. But it has been justly remarked, that there was a formality in Orton, to which no resemblance can be detected in Baxter; that the one was as calm as the other was impassioned; "that the souls of the two men were cast in totally different moulds;" and that "Baxter would have set the world on fire while Orton was lighting a match."[2] Theologically however, there existed a similarity between Orton and Doddridge, and between Orton and Baxter. Neither Doddridge nor Baxter were one-sided in their investigations, and in the results at which they arrived. They looked at religious truth under various aspects, and at the relation in which one principle stands to another. They sought to harmonize what appeared contradictory, and to employ reason in the explanation of religion. Job Orton attempted to do the same; but he was less doctrinal in his reflections and lessons than either of his predecessors. He did not strive to disentangle metaphysical webs, like Baxter; or to set out in array dogmas

---

[1] "Biog. Brit.," art. "Orton."
[2] Orme's "Life of Baxter," p. 772.

and difficulties, like Doddridge. He confined himself very much to the plainest truths and most practical precepts. His sermons, expositions, and other writings are pervaded by a tone of reverence, faith, conscientiousness, candour and charity; but there lacks that "evangelical unction" which touches our hearts as we peruse the pages of Doddridge—still more when we read the works of Baxter.

The first example of a marked divergence occurs in Dr. Taylor's "Scripture Doctrine of Original Sin."

Taylor's standpoint was a Pelagian one. He had no patience with Augustine's theology. He did not believe that men came into the world with a sinful nature; he believed that the moral evil of their lives may be accounted for by the influence of example, the state of society, and the like; that if the innocent Adam in paradise, not surrounded by corrupting influences, yielded to temptation and fell, no wonder that individuals, encompassed by the wickedness of others, should yield to the power of temptation; and that no native corruption is necessary to account for this. As to the "death" spoken of by Paul in the 5th of Romans, Taylor understands it to mean simply temporal death, as inflicted on Adam; and he maintains that there was no federal relationship between him and his posterity, no such connection as Augustine and others have taught, but that human beings are treated as individuals, according to their personal acts; and that physical death and other afflictions and sorrows, though they be consequences of our first parents' transgression, are also arrangements made by a merciful Providence for the chastisement of mankind with a view to their amendment. They are not punitive, but remedial.

He grants the degeneracy of mankind as undeniable; but maintains that men have still power to do their duty; and that, taking the Gospel into account, our condition is happier than Adam's. He objects strongly to the "federal headship" of our first parent, and contends against the doctrine of original righteousness, as held by some divines.

It would be turning this history into a polemical treatise to criticise such a theory; the reader is referred to the elaborate reply written by the renowned American metaphysician, Jonathan Edwards, where will be found ideas as Augustinian as Taylor's are Pelagian. But I may remark, from the historical point of view, that whilst Taylor diverged widely from earlier Presbyterian opinions on this mysterious subject, he still regarded the condition of mankind as powerfully affected by the conduct of Adam; he still believed that death and sorrow had entered our world through his "primary fault." In these latter respects he upheld a theology since abandoned by those who have adopted and followed his tendencies; and also, it should be noticed, that in arriving at what Evangelical divines will regard as erroneous results, he reached them by orthodox lines of inquiry, for he professed only to follow Scripture. He did not set up his philosophy against the authority of St. Paul, but acknowledged his inspiration, and contended that the Apostle's teaching is opposed to principles which since his time crept into the Church. Edwards, and others, denied his conclusions, and contended that they were based upon "misapprehension of the Epistle to the Romans;" but no controversy arose between Taylor and Edwards or anybody else, as to the existence of a Divine Revelation in the New Testament, and the obligation of Christians to bow to the apostolic oracles.

Dr. Price, in a similar spirit, combined with reverence for Scripture, proceeded upon a track of investigation different from that chosen by Taylor. Price devoted himself, not to the study of that which rendered the Gospel necessary, but to the contents of the Gospel itself. He reached conclusions of a peculiar kind.

His idea was, that the core of the Gospel may be found in the words, "*Eternal life is the gift of God, through Jesus Christ our Lord and Saviour;*" and with that he remained "perfectly easy, with respect to the contrary opinions which are entertained about the dignity of Christ; about His Nature, Person, and Offices, and the manner in which He saves." Theories, Trinitarian or Anti-trinitarian, Calvinistic or Arminian, Augustinian or Pelagian, he deemed matters of such subordinate importance, that whichever might be adopted, it need not imperil the simple faith, that "Christ did rise from the dead, and will raise us from the dead ; and that all righteous penitents will, through God's grace in Him, be accepted and made happy for ever." But Price had a theory of his own respecting the points in dispute between different schools of theology; he called it the middle scheme between Calvinism and Socinianism.

As for himself, he believed that Christ was more than a

human being; that His conception was miraculous; that His character was immaculate; that He existed in the glory of the Father before His incarnation; that He exchanged that glory for the condition of a man, to encounter the difficulties of human life, and to suffer and die on the cross; that He was God's Minister in creation, and thus sustained a particular relation to those whom, by His future gracious agency, He was to create anew. He also said that the "doctrine of Christ's simple Humanity, when viewed in common with the Scripture account of His exaltation, implies an inconsistency and improbability which falls little short of an impossibility." He strongly objected to the Socinian scheme, without adopting any Arian hypothesis.

As to the manner in which Jesus Christ accomplished the salvation of the world, Price did not believe that He was merely a teacher. " Our race," he says, " as sinful and mortal creatures, required more than instruction. Instruction could only bring us repentance. It could not make repentance the means of remission, or an exemption from the effects of guilt. It could not create a fitness that offenders should be favoured, as if they had never offended. It could not raise from death, or restore to a new life." He explicitly declares that the language of St. Paul signifies more than that our Lord died to seal the covenant of grace, and to assure us of pardon. " Their obvious meaning seems to be, that as the sacrifices under the law of Moses expiated guilt, and procured remission, so Christ's shedding His blood, and offering up His life, was the means of remission and favour to penitent sinners." Dr. Price refused to say anything of *Substitution* or *Satisfaction*, or of any theological explanation as to the *manner* in which we are redeemed. Some of these explanations he deemed absurd, and he was persuaded that his interest in this redemption depended, not on the justness of his conceptions respecting it, but on the sincerity of his heart.[1]

Dr. Price was a decided advocate of the doctrine of Free-will, and shrunk from any theory of Predestination resembling that of Augustine or Jonathan Edwards. And a strong aversion to Calvinism constituted a main characteristic generally of the liberal school of Presbyterian thought. ' Dr. Kippis, for example, expresses his invincible objection to the doctrine of Divine Decrees, as taught by theologians of the Genevan order; and curiously enough informs us that a once famous book — Coles on "God's Sovereignty"—intended to support a Supralapsarian scheme of divinity, was the cause of his utterly rejecting it.[2] But it is a still more striking example of the curiosities of theological literature, that the famous Dr. Priestley, who outstripped all his Presbyterian competitors in the race of free inquiry, should have interwoven the doctrine of philosophical necessity into the web of his peculiar speculations. Priestley attempted to distinguish between his own views on this subject and the Calvinistic doctrine of Predestination; but it comes so near to the latter, that no wonder theologians who adhered to the Genevan Reformer rejoiced to see the advocate of philosophical inquiry approaching their own position.

---

[1] See Price's "Sermons," vols. iv. and v., and Appendix.
[2] "Biog. Brit.," vol. iv. p. 3.

Toplady was delighted when he read Priestley's lucubrations, and wrote to him in the following strain,—
"Every Christian Necessitarian is so far a Calvinist. Have a care, therefore, Dr. Priestley, lest, having set your foot in the Lemaine Lake, you plunge in, *quantus quantus;* a catastrophe which, for my own part, and for your own sake, I sincerely wish may come to pass, and of which I do not wholly despair."[1] Priestley never made that plunge, and, by the way in which he treated Toplady's letter, highly displeased the Calvinistic divine.

Steering in an opposite direction to that of his brethren, as it regards the doctrine of Necessity, Priestley proceeded in their wake as it regards the doctrines of Christ's Divinity and Atonement, reaching points much farther removed from the old Presbyterian orthodoxy than those at which his principal contemporaries had arrived. He believed in the simple humanity of our Lord, and denied altogether the doctrine of the Atonement.[2]

Priestley represents a theological school, proceeding as far as possible in the extreme of liberal inquiry, whilst still retaining a hold upon the authority of Scripture. He was no Intuitionalist. He was a disciple of John Locke, and believed that knowledge, truth, and wisdom, flow into the spirit of man from springs which lie beyond himself. As other

---

[1] Priestley's "Works," vol. i. p. 260.   [2] Ibid., p. 257.

knowledge, in Priestley's estimation, proceeds from the external world, so he regarded spiritual knowledge as proceeding from Divine instruction. He reached the *ne plus ultra* of religious rationalism in that path of inquiry which suited the constitution of his mind. But another order of thought was beginning even then to make its appearance amongst Presbyterians. Breaking loose from what is termed the *authority* of Scripture, and relying upon the spiritual faculties of the soul, they sought for truth in that direction, without denying the aid to be derived from prophets and apostles, especially from the Lord Jesus. Not rejecting miracles, they gave them a place in the system of evidence, but different from that assigned by Price and Priestley; and whilst far from denying Inspiration, they nevertheless weakened the distinctive force of it in Scripture, by relegating it to an operation so wide and vast as to comprise all genius, all mental and spiritual power whatever, whether possessed by poet or by sage, by artist or by legislator. At the same time more scope was given to the affections. Religion had become with many of the Presbyterians more an intellectual exercise than anything else. Free inquiry had been idolized, and certain hard dogmas reached by that process had been raised to the highest point of veneration. Only one side of human nature had been provided for; the emotional part had been sadly neglected. But fervour of soul was enkindled in the new school; some glow began to appear in worship, and spiritual sentiment gained a place which had been monopolized by speculative ratiocination. Of this complex habit, which produced an immense effect on theological belief, some examples appear at the end of the eighteenth century; perhaps Mrs. Barbauld may be taken as a representative. Her writings are of a different cast from those of Price and Priestley. She pleaded for the emotional element in Christian piety. She saw the perils of mere intellectual inquisitiveness. She vindicated faith as well as reason; admitted that too critical a spirit is the bane of everything great and pathetic, and recommended that free scope should be given to the language of the affections and the outflow of a devotion.[1]

But the chief leaders in this path must be sought in writers of later date—Channing and Tayler,[2] not to mention others who are still living.

The Presbyterianism which yielded theological results such as I have endeavoured to specify, was remarkable in many instances for its social respectability. If congregations were not very large, if they did not include many of the poor, they consisted of well-to-do people of the middle class, with several of

---

[1] See Mrs. Barbauld's "Thoughts on Devotional Taste," etc. —Works, vol. ii. p. 232 *et seq.* Also her "Remarks on Gilbert Wakefield's Inquiry into the Expediency and Propriety of Public or Social Worship."—Works, vol. ii. p. 413 *et seq.*

[2] See J. J. Tayler's "Retrospect," etc.

the rich and prosperous who sought intelligence and culture. Take an example from East Anglia.

The Octagon Chapel at Norwich is a renowned Presbyterian place of worship; and must have been indeed a wonder in 1756, when it was opened; for it cost above £5000, a rare sum to have been expended for the purpose in those days, and manifesting the large resources and the rising taste of the congregation which erected it. It has a portico supported by Ionic columns, approached by a spacious front area; the domed roof is sustained by arches on eight fluted Corinthian pillars; and the original mahogany and oak fittings were of a description very unusual in Dissenting meeting-houses. Dr. John Taylor, already noticed, was pastor at the time; and amongst his successors came Robert Alderson, who afterwards went to the bar and obtained the Recordership of Yarmouth; George Cadozan Morgan, a writer mentioned before in these pages; Dr. Enfield, who had been tutor at Warrington; and Pendlebury Houghton, a man of superior abilities and attainments. Such a remarkable succession of ministers indicates well the extent and status of the congregation. Few cities in the kingdom could present so much literary and artistic society as did the East Anglian capital, during the latter part of the eighteenth and the early part of the present century. Men and women were there rising up to take a leading position in literature and art, most of whom belonged to the Presbyterian body. John Taylor, the German scholar Edward Taylor, the Gresham professor of music; Dr. Alderson and his accomplished daughter, afterwards Mrs. Opie; the family of the Martineaus, rich in literary fame; and the family of the Starks, connected with the Norwich school of painting; not to mention others, whose celebrity was confined to their native place—all these persons were wont to attend the Octagon Chapel.

In winding up what has been said respecting English Presbyterianism, it is sufficient to add, that with all the ability of its ministers, all the respectability of its congregations, all the culture of its society, and all the services which it rendered to science, literature, and liberty, it did not advance in numbers or in power. So far from it, its history for fifty years was one of decline. The causes are obvious. A dry, hard, cold method of preaching generally marked the pulpit; warm, vigorous, spiritual life appeared not in the pews. No greater contrast can be imagined, than between the Methodist and the Presbyterian preacher, the Methodists and the Presbyterian people. The unction, the fire, the moral force, so visible in the one case, is absent in the other. Methodism laid hold on the conscience of England; Presbyterianism did not. The sympathy elicited there, is found wanting here; and no culture, no intellectual power, no respectability of position, could make up for the lack of earnest gospel preaching and warm-hearted spiritual life.

Scotch Presbyterianism in England must be distinguished from that just described. No imputation has ever been cast on the orthodoxy of the former. Dr. Hunter was one of its great ornaments in the City of London.

But Westminster was the chief seat of the denomination. The Meeting-house in Crown Court, under the shadow of Drury Lane Theatre, was erected in 1718; and a band of brethren from the north of the Tweed might be found, before 1710, worshipping in Glasshouse Street, whence they removed to Swallow Street. The last is described as having been "a place of considerable resort for people of the Scotch nation;" and there, no doubt, in the last century, stately coaches were driven up to the door, containing the families of Scotch noblemen and thrifty merchants. A congregation of seceders comes dimly into view more than a hundred years ago, somewhere in the parish of St. Thomas the Apostle, which migrated, about 1807, to Oxenden Street Chapel, which had been built by good Margaret Baxter for the use of her illustrious husband Richard. Much more distinctly, and carrying with it more importance and effect, a Secession Church in Wells Street, especially when under the pastoral care of Dr. Waugh, comes under historical notice towards the end of the century. Educated in Scotland, imbued with the principles of moderate Calvinism, commanding in person, of a wonderfully genial and loving temper, eminently devout, excelling in what is called "the gift of prayer," the Scotch clergyman became a prominent centre of social influence soon after his arrival in London, and continued so for about thirty years.

In the north of England were congregations composed of Scotch Presbyterians. They were found in Lancashire, where "Burghers, Antiburghers, Relief Men, and Kirkfolk harmoniously worshipped together." "The Covenanters were the only Presbyterians who absolutely refused all religious association with their countrymen. After the three communities in Scotland, the Burghers, the Antiburghers, and the Relief became the United Presbyterians, their union in England followed of course, and the old distinctions were soon forgotten."[1] And in Northumberland, Presbyterianism naturally presented the Scotch form of faith and discipline. In the title deeds of chapels was inserted a provision that no one should be elected as minister, unless he subscribed a declaration of belief in the Westminster Confession.[2] The learned Roman antiquary, Horsley, presided over a Presbyterian Church at Morpeth; and Dr. Harle, or Harlen, of Alnwick, also was an eminent Presbyterian clergyman; and Dr. Young was an eminent minister at Whitby. For a long time the only connection traceable between the border counties or any other part of England,

---

[1] Halley's "Lancashire," vol. ii. p. 492.
[2] M'Crie's "Annals of English Presbyterianism," p. 318.

and the Established Church or the Secession bodies of Scotland, is to be found in the supply of English vacancies by the transference of probationers, or already ordained clergymen from the north of the Tweed. Scotland sent no missionaries to England, nor did it organize any scheme for extending its own discipline and worship beyond its national borders. All existing Scotch Churches in our country a century old, are of English foundation, and from the first, invited ministers from amongst their northern brethren.[1]

---

[1] For this information I am indebted to the Rev. Dr. Lorimer.

CHAPTER XXIV.

1760–1800.

THE relinquishment of orthodox opinions by Presbyterian divines has been put down to the account of their ecclesiastical discipline, and the contrast between that and the strict ecclesiastical system of Independency has been urged as manifest evidence of its superiority in preserving Evangelical truth. It is certainly a fact, that Independent Churches generally adhered to Calvinistic theology, with such modifications as would be produced by the spirit of the day and by individual idiosyncrasies. This may be largely attributed to the prominence given to old Evangelical beliefs in their Church Confessions and Covenants, as they were termed, and still more to the traditions as well as to the spirit kept alive in these communities. But it is a remarkable fact, that in the Academies supported by Independents, there really originated very considerable divergencies, which Independents afterwards deplored.[1] Little or no inquiry arose respecting spiritual character in the case of those intended for the ministry; they mingled with lay pupils, and no test, religious

---

[1] Halley's "Lancashire," vol. ii. p. 380.

or theological, seems to have been applied to any of them. When Dr. Doddridge died, his Academy was removed to Daventry, and placed under the care of Dr. Ashworth, his friend and favourite. Little can be gathered respecting him, beyond a general impression of ability, learning, and piety. He died in 1775, in his fifty-fifth year, after having occupied his post from 1751, the period of Doddridge's death.[1] The literary reputation of the Seminary stood as high as ever under Ashworth's presidency, and in this respect it certainly appears superior to others of a similar description; but, whatever may have been the measure of free thought allowed under the administration of his predecessor, he suffered a tendency of that order to proceed to a very much greater length. Students were about equally divided between Trinitarianism and Arianism, the latter being the extreme of existing departures from the creed of the Puritan divines.

Ashworth was succeeded by Thomas Robins, a man remarkable "for delicacy of taste and elegance of diction," to whom Robert Hall owed his first perception of these qualities when listening to a sermon preached at Northampton. No imputation of heterodoxy could be cast on the name of this excellent

---

[1] There is a Funeral Sermon for Ashworth, by Mr. Palmer, who says scarcely anything respecting him of a personal nature. I have seen two Sermons by Ashworth, one on the death of Dr. Watts, the other on the death of Mr. Clarke; both are decidedly Evangelical.

man; but Thomas Belsham, already mentioned, who had been his assistant and who became his successor, after being educated a Calvinist, proceeded to adopt Socinian views. Being a gentleman of honour, when he felt his convictions were at variance with his position he relinquished office; but his influence, before his resignation, could not but have been in favour of that unlimited inquiry which predominated in Presbyterian circles. After his removal, John Horsey, of Northampton, took charge of the students, and he is said to have made it difficult for any one to ascertain what opinions he held on controverted points; nevertheless, he, shortly before his death, declared, "Whenever the summons shall arrive to call me from time to eternity, I wish to leave the world in the character of a penitent believer, lying at the foot of the Cross, imploring Divine mercy through the merit and mediation of Christ, the great Redeemer and Saviour of the lost."[1] It is difficult to ascertain, in this and other cases, what, after all, exactly was the method of teaching adopted, because statements made by different parties received a colouring from their individual tendencies.[2]

---

[1] Article in *Monthly Repository*, and Coward Trust Papers, and Traditions.

[2] I make these statements respecting Mr. Horsey, on the authority of letters amongst the Coward Trust Papers, Traditions preserved by early friends, and an Article in the *Monthly Repository*.

The academic vessel appears to have been drifting into conflicting currents, which imperilled its safety, and at length those who were responsible for its support felt it necessary to do something to guide its course. But before that was done, another Educational Institution was found drifting away from the orthodox creed. Dr. Savage, a distinguished tutor in those days, fixed his residence at Hoxton, and there the students lodged under his roof; but whatever might be his personal influence, it does not seem to have checked the tendencies inspired by his Presbyterian colleagues. When questions arose as to individuals of heterodox or doubtful inclination, he leaned in favour of a charitable and comprehensive construction; and such a course was supported by the opinions of eminent lawyers, who were consulted on the subject in reference to certain trusts involved.[1] In 1785, the old Hoxton Academy came to an end. Another Academy was then established by the Coward Trustees, which, after many years' continuance at Wymondley, was removed to Torrington Square, London. The Fund Board and the King's Head Society have been already mentioned. A formal union between these two bodies took place in 1754.[2] A plan was arranged by which the Fund

---

[1] Coward Trust documents.

[2] The Academy, or College, in 1851, was united with the Highbury and Homerton Institutions for educating Independent Ministers, under the name of New College, St. John's Wood.

Board, according to its original constitution, supported only those who were engaged in theological studies, while the King's Head Society took under its patronage youths occupied in the acquisition of elementary learning. Premises were secured at Mile End, by a Committee, not by the tutors, the former taking the management of affairs entirely into their own keeping. Dr. Gibbons and Dr. Conder, two Independent celebrities, had charge of this Institution, the former in full-bottomed wig and clerical dress, appearing the very type of an eighteenth-century professor.[1] The Academy was afterwards removed to the College of Homerton, according to the migratory fashion set in earlier times.

The last Academic Institution in the neighbourhood of London commenced in 1778. It originated with the Evangelical Society, as it was called, composed of persons who had caught the fire of Whitefield's ministry, and who deplored the coldness existing in Independent Churches; it was intended to supply the spiritual needs of village congregations, the projectors intending their little bark, with a few hard rowers, to run beside larger vessels ably manned. It prospered at Hoxton, under the care of Dr. Simpson, who succeeded Dr. Addington in 1791; and of the former it may be remarked, that while there are many who can enlighten and persuade, there are few

---

[1] See Portrait at New College, St. John's Wood.

that can inspire, but this rare power was possessed by the principal at Hoxton, who, to his fervour of spirit and orthodoxy of opinion, added an acquaintance with the Hebrew Scriptures rather uncommon in those days.[1] The Institution owed much of its success to the indefatigable exertions of the treasurer, Thomas Wilson, a London merchant of singular simplicity and force of character.

The same spirit which produced an Academy at Hoxton, also originated one at Newport Pagnell; but in the former case Dissenters were its patrons and supporters, whereas in the latter, Churchmen and Dissenters united on its behalf. The tutor was William Bull, whom his friend, William Cowper, thus describes: "A Dissenter, but a liberal one; a man of letters and of genius; a master of a fine imagination, or rather, not master of it—an imagination which, when he finds himself in the company he loves and can confide in, runs away with him into such fields of speculation as amuse and enliven every other imagination that has the happiness to be of the party; at other times he has a tender and delicate sort of melancholy in his disposition, not less agreeable in its way."[2]

Bull was an intimate friend of John Thornton, who at length took the entire support of the Seminary on

---

[1] Traditions amongst his students.
[2] Cowper's "Life," vol. i. p. 261.

himself, and by his will determined that it should be carried on in the same way after his death.

Turning to the north of England, we find an Academy at Heckmondwike in 1756, under the care of James Scott, who repaid the devout solicitude of the founders; "under him were educated about sixty ministers, who laboured in the northern counties with great fidelity and success; and could an entire record of their influence be recovered from oblivion, it would be found that many a Church existing in this part of the kingdom has received an inspiration for good from the pupils of the venerable man who was placed at the spring-head of the waters." Another educational movement in Yorkshire led to the establishment of Rotherham Academy, placed under the presidency of Dr. Williams, whose character as a theologian will be described in a later portion of this chapter; again, we find a second provision of a similar nature at a village in the same county, named Idle, afterwards called Airedale.

Passing from Academies, subsequently called Colleges it is appropriate to notice the literary culture of the Independent ministry. It must be confessed that, taken generally, in this respect, Independents were not equal to Presbyterians. They had no Hebrew scholar to be compared with Dr. Taylor of Warrington; or any one versed in general literature equal to Dr. Aiken and Dr. Enfield; not one amongst them could think of competing with Dr.

Price in a genius for calculation, or with Dr. Priestley in scientific discovery. But Independency numbered many men of highly respectable attainments, and a few stand out as proficients in certain departments of theological study.

Many readers are familiar with the name, if not with the writings, of Thomas Harmer, author of a work on "Solomon's Song," and of "Observations on Scripture," the best known of any of his publications. He took the lead in a new department of Biblical learning. There had not been wanting writers upon the grammatical meaning of Hebrew and Greek sentences; and attention had been also paid to the subject of various readings, and to the critical determination of the original text. But the elucidation of difficulties arising out of the obscurity of certain allusions in the Old and New Testament, and the illustration of narratives and parables, of prophecies, psalms, and epistles, by a knowledge of Oriental scenery, habits, and customs, had been little heeded. The enormous amount of charming literature of this description, which enables the untravelled to read the sacred volume through the eyes of observant explorers, accomplished archeologists, and scientific investigators, had not then begun to exist. Harmer was a meritorious pioneer in this neglected field. He struck out an early path across it, and deserves to be acknowledged with honour by those who are walking in his steps. His "Observations" now have lost much of their primitive value, being superseded by later and more comprehensive publications; but they remain a monument of the pursuit of knowledge under difficulties, and of the ingenious working out of an original idea. He lived in the village of Wattisfield, in Suffolk, still the same rural spot it was a hundred years ago, with its church, its rectory, its blacksmith's shop; there, within a snug Nonconformist parsonage, not yet pulled down, he collected all the books he could procure bearing on his subject, and wrote to learned friends in every direction, seeking such assistance as they could render. His name lingers in the locality; and he is counted amongst the celebrities of the Eastern Counties. In country lanes, running by pleasant homesteads, one can picture this retired student of the Bible, and of nature as its expository hand-book, taking his daily walk, botanizing and musing on Scripture plants, flowers, and trees,—and trying to find resemblances to them in Suffolk hedgerows and gardens. A few of Mr. Harmer's letters have been published, and they exhibit him as an antiquary, describing coins, and rejoicing in a coronation medal of Charles I., which he had purchased for the sum of one shilling—a fact which may inspire envy in the breasts of modern collectors. His merits as a student do not seem to have been appreciated by his village congregation, nor were his "Observations" at first duly estimated by some of his friends. "I thought, sir," said a lady, "you would have published a *good* book." His Biographer,[1] who spent much of his time at Wattisfield, says, he never heard him speak of his own production, and when at a distance first learned that his friend was an author. Little was known of him except at home until after his death,—"By strangers honoured, and by strangers mourned."

His preaching was not, as some imagined, cold, critical, and uninteresting. For fifty years he addressed a flourishing congregation in a quaint, old-fashioned meeting-house; and fathers, with their sons, daughters, and grandchildren, learned to look up to their learned pastor with respect and love for his personal virtues and the exemplary discharge of his ministrations.

He wrote a treatise on "The Ancient and Present State of the Congregational Churches of Norfolk and Suffolk," published in 1777; and this work manifests not only an intimate acquaintance with the past and contemporaneous usages of his denomination, but also with ecclesiastical antiquities of more comprehensive range and earlier date. He was zealous in maintaining the Congregational practices of a former period, and lamented modern inno-

---

[1] The late William Youngman, of Norwich, who edited Harmer's "Miscellaneous Works," and wrote a sketch of his life, was one of the most intelligent, inquisitive, and sagacious men I ever knew, and a great ornament to Nonconformist society in Norwich, where he lived and died.

vations, endeavouring, with a reverence for the past worthy of his Episcopalian friends, to point out the correspondence of customs amongst Dissenters with precedents set by the primitive Churches. Earnestly did he contend for the imposition of hands in the rite of ordination; and for the value and importance of united fellowship and action between Church and Church; at the same time, when he received to communion any one who had been a communicant in the Establishment, he informed the parish clergyman of the circumstance. For Methodists the good man appears to have had no liking, on account of their irregularities; and much did they displease him when they received one of his flock into their fold, without taking any notice either of him or of them.

Less known perhaps, though not unnoticed in the history of Biblical Literature, is the name of Dr. Benjamin Boothroyd, a Hebrew scholar, born in 1763, of very humble origin. An Independent minister, residing successively at Pontefract and Leeds, he felt it necessary, owing to his limited income in the first of these places, to unite the business of printer and bookseller with the ministerial vocation. At Pontefract, under the shadow of the ruined feudal castle, crowning the heights of the pleasantly situated town, he searched its records, and threw light upon its history, in a carefully compiled volume of local interest; and there too he published his "Biblia Hebraica," or Hebrew Scriptures without points, after the text of Kennicott. Various readings are given, selected not only from the collation of that Hebraist, but from De Rossi, and also from ancient versions. Dr. Boothroyd was at once annotator, editor, and printer; and the work, though not perfectly accurate, has been praised by competent critics. A new Family Bible afterwards appeared under the editorship of the same person. These works were not published until after the commencement of the present century; but this industrious and struggling scholar busied himself in preparatory studies immediately after his ordination in the Church at Pontefract, in 1794.[1]

The most distinguished theologian among the Independents at that time was Dr. Edward Williams, who, after holding a pastorate in Birmingham, became, as we have seen, president of the Rotherham Academy, in 1795. He possessed metaphysical powers of extraordinary subtlety and acuteness, and was competent to walk by the side of the renowned Jonathan Edwards, whose system he critically studied, and whose works he edited with elaborate notes, containing strictures and expansions indicative of great ability, and exceedingly useful to the thoughtful reader of the American Calvinist; perhaps Williams' analytical genius is there seen, in a scholastic form, to the greatest advantage, but his

---

[1] Miall's "Congregationalism in Yorkshire," p. 193.

essay on "Divine Equity and Sovereignty" is the most famous of his works.

Defining *Equity* to mean "a supreme disposition and right to give unto all their own," and Sovereignty to mean "a supreme right to will and to do whatever is not inconsistent with universal equity," he endeavoured to show how these attributes are displayed in the government of the universe ; and how, by a careful observation of what distinguishes the one from the other, perplexities may be removed out of the way of theological inquirers. It was a fundamental part of his theory, that sin originates not in God, nor in chance, nor in a self-determining power of the will, but "in a principle of defectibility in a free agent, the operation of which, nevertheless, the all-sufficient source of good is always able to prevent." He attributed all the moral excellence in the world to the influence of sovereign grace ; and all its moral evil to the fallen nature of man, as the result of inherent defectibility,—in the permission, the repression, and the punishment of which, there is a constant display of unimpeachable justice.

He thought that in this theory he held a key sufficient to unlock a good many mysteries, and in his ingenious Dissertations he made very extensive use of it; but critical readers of this critical divine will, in many instances, question the potency of his reasonings, perceiving the inadequacy of logical formularies to explain the comprehensive scheme of the Divine government. Whilst he sagaciously diminishes some difficulties, he leaves others just where they were, without seeming himself to apprehend their nature and position. What he thinks he has swept away altogether, he has only lifted from a lower to a higher shelf. There it remains, as formidable as before. The wise maxim of Butler is overlooked, that the Divine ways are a scheme but imperfectly understood, and there is no adequate recognition of the dense rim of darkness round the circle of revealed light. Yet, with these and other defects, Dr. Williams made some valuable contributions to theological science; bringing distinctly into view the responsibility of man, in connection with the Divine righteousness, as well as the salvation of man, in connection with Divine grace. His object was to check Calvinistic extremes, and to establish the reasonableness of Evangelical religion.[1]

To men of learning we must add those of pastoral efficiency, whose labours, connected with the condition of their flocks, will repay attention. A distinction may, with advantage, be drawn, especially in reference to the metropolis, between the old Independency and the new Congregationalism. By the old Independency, I mean that government and order, and those traditions and sentiments, which had been in existence from the Commonwealth times; and by the new Congregationalism, that modified polity and discipline, and those inspirations and sympathies,

---

[1] "Equity and Sovereignty," pp. xxiii., xxv., xxviii., xxxvii., and 60, 80, 108.

which characterized communities fundamentally independent of each other, self-governed and self-controlled, yet powerfully influenced, in their modes of operation, by the great Methodistic movement.

Independency in the first generation of the eighteenth century was not so strong in London as Presbyterianism; but, during the last thirty or forty years of that period, the relative position of the two bodies materially changed—Presbyterianism declined, Independency advanced. This was the case with regard to numbers; probably it was also the case with regard to worldly respectability and social influence. It is true, that at the close of the hundred years, people of title, and celebrities descended from Cromwell's aristocracy, could not be found in London meeting-houses; but the rank and file of congregations had then risen to a better social position. The quiet habits, the inexpensive mode of living, the industrial energy, and the self-reliance of a staunch Independent could not but be conducive to his worldly prosperity, in spite of prejudices incurred by his peculiar opinions. By economy and diligence, the people who chiefly filled the modest buildings set apart for worship got on in the world beyond many of their neighbours. Their well-managed shops secured customers; their mercantile ledgers exhibited pretty good balances at the end of the year; and the result was visible in their comfortable appearance, and their superior dress on a Sunday morning in their well-filled pews. With the increase of pecuniary resources, ministerial incomes would correspond, supplemented, in some cases, by advantageous marriages on the part of ministers presiding over prosperous congregations. Divine services were carried on under George the Third much after the same fashion as under Queen Anne; for the influence of tradition, even among extreme Dissenters, bears with it immense power. Not a single London building used by Independents in the last century now remains, but several of them preserved their original form and appearance, with slight alteration, down to a date within my own remembrance; and the children or grandchildren of merchants, bankers, and prosperous tradesmen, were then occupying the same parlour-like pews, lined with green baize, as did their ancestors to whom they owed their fortunes.

In some instances an old building gave place to a new one. This was the case with the King's Weigh-house, Little Eastcheap; and perhaps I cannot select a better example of an old-fashioned congregation in the first half of the reign of George III. I am not sure but what something of a Presbyterian element at first found room at the Weigh-house; but if so, it gradually disappeared, until it was quite lost. Samuel Palmer, the Nonconformist Historian, was assistant minister from 1763 to 1766; and Dr. Samuel Wilton was pastor from 1766 to 1768,—a short term of labour, but one sufficient, it would seem, to make a decided mark in the history of the congregation. His portrait presents him as a good-looking young man, with a handsome powdered wig, not so full and massive as those worn by his predecessors, with ample bands on his neck, and wearing a coat very similar to that of a dean or an archdeacon of the present day, when arrayed in full dress. So Dr. Wilton appeared in the meeting house built over the King's Weigh-house, to which people ascended by a flight of stairs ; and from the account given of his attainments and character—for we are told he had "a mind richly furnished both with knowledge and piety"—it may be inferred that the London citizens who gathered round his ministry did not attend in vain. He was diligent as a student, acceptable as a preacher, and exemplary in the discharge of pastoral work, catechising the children, and visiting the poor. He distinguished himself as an advocate for the removal of Dissenters' grievances; and we read, "If in anything the zeal of Dr. Wilton seemed to carry him beyond the bounds of moderation, it was in the glorious cause of civil and religious liberty." His piety appears by no means to have been of that calm and cool description, so much admired by some of his contemporaries ; it burnt with an almost superhuman glow as the young man approached his end. To him succeeded John Clayton, whose long ministry over the Weigh-house congregation is a beautiful memory, still lingering in the minds of London Independents, who reckon him and his sons among the ornaments of their denomination. He lived to extreme old age, and I well recollect his dignified appearance, his urbanity of demeanour, his conversational power, and his pulpit ability. Under him the Weigh-house congregation increased ; and in 1795, the old building was taken down, and a new one erected. Though an Independent in Church polity, and one who might be said to represent its old-fashioned type—for he became a decided Dissenter from reading Towgood's Letters—his education and spirit allied him in some measure to the Methodist movement. For he had been a student in the Countess of Huntingdon's College at Trevecca, and he used to preach at the Tabernacle. His Calvinism stood out in a pronounced form ; and, unlike his predecessor, Wilton, who was an unmistakable Whig, Clayton appeared an unmistakable Tory.

This leads me briefly to mention the new form of Congregationalism which appeared in London side by side with the old-fashioned Independency. Of Calvinistic-Methodist origin, it settled down into something like the old-fashioned ecclesiastical polity. The lay officers might not be called deacons, but they performed diaconal duties. Church meetings might not be formally held, but gatherings took place very much of that nature. In some places Church prayers were read ; but extempore devotion formed a main part of worship, being much more popular than a liturgical service. No submission to diocesan control, or to synodical government could be detected. The Tabernacle in Moorfields, Tottenham Court Road Chapel, and Orange Street Chapel, all noticed in former chapters, were of this description.

In the country several Churches were noticeable on different accounts. Bideford, in Devonshire, could boast of Samuel Lavington, pastor there from 1752 to 1807; a man of pulpit power, as local traditions asserts and as his published Discourses testify. His Discourses to the Young are of an uncommon character; the introductions to some of them afford singular examples of bold and startling eloquence, somewhat of the French type, calculated to arrest attention, and inspire curiosity in reference to what might follow; nor is the substance or the peroration unworthy of the commencement. Not that the composition is a model of smooth and elegant style, resembling that of the Scotch preacher, Dr. Blair, whose sermons were in such repute a hundred years ago. Lavington was abrupt in his method, incisive in his appeals, and often colloquial in his forms of expression. Other volumes of Discourses addressed to adults, published after his death, are of a like order, and they sustain his fame as one of the impressive preachers of his day.[1] His personal virtues

---

[1] It is remarked in a funeral sermon for him, by Mr. Rooker, of Tavistock, that when young he was a frequent hearer of the

have been eulogized, as much as his pulpit addresses. The evenness of his temper, the gentleness of his disposition, and the devoutness of his life, are canonized in the language of admiring brethren, who officiated at the funeral ; and it is worth mention that his namesake, the Bishop of Exeter, the relentless enemy of Methodism, treated the Bideford pastor with kindness, would have been glad to number him amongst the Devonshire clergy, and promised him preferment if he were willing to conform.

Congregationalism, at the same period, in the town of Bedford is conspicuous on another ground. The philanthropist, John Howard, was a member of the Church originally formed by John Bunyan, consisting of both Independents and Baptists. But after a time, a secession, in which Howard was included, took place, and a Church was formed upon the Pædobaptist principle. That secession was conducted in a most conciliatory and friendly manner, and Howard offered to build a parsonage for the pastor of the old Church, an offer which was delicately declined.

The pastor's daughter often spoke of Howard's Sunday morning calls, and told how the children used to watch his knock, and walk to meeting by his side. He and the minister were wont to ride out together on horseback, when the former would decoy him to

---

celebrated Dr. Grosvenor ; "and that valuable as Dr. Grosvenor's sermons are, they are surpassed by those of Mr. Lavington."

Cardington, and persuade him to remain to dinner. "My father," the lady related, "has often said those were some of the most delightful hours of his life, for that Mr. Howard would then completely unbend himself, and give the most entertaining accounts of his past travels; open up to him all his future plans, all his trials and sorrows, in short, every feeling of his heart in the most free and confidential manner." In a room at the corner of Mill Street, Bedford, Howard partook a slender repast, between the Sunday morning and afternoon services. He is chiefly known to the world as the great prison philanthropist, and some have insinuated that his public enterprises spoiled his home charity, and interfered with his domestic duties. This notion is utterly at variance with manifold and long remembered proofs of considerate beneficence in the neighbourhood where he lived. His pew in the meeting-house as it used to be shown I well remember; and I have been told that he often stood up with his arm round the waist of his little son—who lived to give him so much pain—holding the hymn-book before the boy's eyes, and helping him to spell out easy words of Divine praise. No less a village than a world reformer, he inspected the cottages at Cardington, and set the people to work, bidding the women wash their floors, and setting them to make linen, while he employed the men in hedging, ditching, draining, and building. He founded schools for the use of all denominations;

but required the children to attend some place of worship. He also made a similar stipulation with his tenants, and fitted up one of his cottages as a preaching station. His marked profile, his commanding presence, his neat wig, his cocked hat, his pigtail and other outward signs, were familiar enough in Bedford and Cardington a century ago, as he went to and fro between his own home and the house of God. Nor can we help picturing by his side during the week, in the earliest and happiest days of his Bedfordshire life, the handsome Henrietta Leeds, his second wife, tripping over the grass to train some wayward flowers, as her husband laid out new walks; or selling her jewels for the relief of the poor; or saying, when a pleasure trip was suggested, "What a pretty cottage might be built with the money." The private life of the philanthropist as a Dissenting country gentleman is too tempting a theme to be lightly passed over, possessing, as I happen to do, some local traditionary information on the subject, gathered long ago from the descendants of Howard's servants and friends. It is only appropriate to add, that religious principle, developed in simple and unostentatious, perhaps one might say, in somewhat puritanical forms, constituted the strength and inspiration of Howard's world-known character.

Another town remarkable in the annals of Independency is Kettering, in Northamptonshire. It rose in this respect to high renown, chiefly through the ministry of Thomas Toller, who inspired on the part of his people such an amount of admiration, that it bordered upon idolatry. And the impression he made upon particular occasions in other places corresponded with the reputation in which he was held by his own flock. Referring to a sermon by Toller, preached at Bedford, one of the greatest of orators described the effect as being what he never witnessed before or since. "All other emotions were absorbed in devotional feeling," says Robert Hall. "It seemed to us as though we were permitted for a short space to look into eternity, and every sublunary object vanished before the powers of the world to come. It will always be considered by those who witnessed it, as affording as high a specimen as can easily be conceived of the power of a preacher over his audience, the habitual, or even the frequent recurrence of which would create an epoch in the religious history of the world." [1]

One more illustration remains. Village pastors worked in a way worthy of remembrance. In a few instances old wealthy families might be found in the country who preserved the traditions and spirit of their ancestors, and were glad to support the rustic meeting-house, where fathers and mothers had worshipped ever since the passing of the Toleration Act. But in

---

[1] Hall's Works, vol. iv. p. 316. I have heard Mr. Hall's opinions corroborated by others, who well knew Thomas Toller.

more instances, village congregations consisted of a few peasants drawn together by spiritual sympathies, sometimes to the disadvantage of their temporal circumstances. We find placed over one of these at Killby, in Northamptonshire, a young man from Doddridge's Academy, named Thomas Strange. His parsonage was a tiny cottage of crumbling walls and thatched roof, the only parson's glebe being a rude adjoining orchard. There he managed to lay out a garden, and set up bee-hives. He had the oft-mentioned stipend of forty pounds, and, unable to keep a servant, he devolved the drudgery of the house on his wife and daughters. But they lived " in ancient simplicity, having every office performed by the hand of love," and by strict economy kept out of debt, never having recourse to the demoralizing practice of begging from wealthy friends. The minister eked out his income by taking a few pupils, on the moderate terms of twelve guineas a year. The good man was no great preacher; but he made such sermons as he could, and conducted service four times on a Sunday, walking from place to place, not less than eight miles. His influence subdued prejudice, and won reputation for his little community; it gradually increased, and it is naively remarked, such was the influence of his life and doctrine, that when one of his congregation married a member of the Established Church, the Independent pastor most likely thereby gained another proselyte.

Descriptions in reference to Dissent in the reign of George III. convey the idea that liberty, secured by the Act of Toleration, existed without disturbance. Generally, it did, but there were exceptions. Some clergymen refused to bury unbaptized children and adults. Fees for baptism were demanded when the service had been performed by a Dissenting minister, and the same kind of imposition occurred in cases where interments took place in Nonconformist cemeteries. But much more serious were riots and assaults committed during the celebration of worship. Even at Clapham, in 1760, a minister was insulted whilst preaching, and part of the building he occupied was demolished; at Midhurst, in Kent, in 1772, damage was done to a meeting-house; and at Dartmouth and at Lewes, in 1772 and 1775, peaceable assemblies were outraged by lawless mobs. In 1781 and 1782, congregations were disturbed in Staines and in Peterborough; and in 1785, a Grimsby lawyer, who from his profession ought to have set a very different example, went into a meeting-house, cursing and swearing at a moment when the people were at worship. In 1795, 1797, and 1799, similar disgraceful breaches of the peace occurred.[1] Attempts were sometimes made to excuse the persecution of Methodists, on the ground that they did not assemble in licensed places; but the instances now enu-

---

[1] "History of the Dissenting Deputies," pp. 123-130.

merated could admit of no such plea, since these acts of violence were perpetrated in buildings properly registered according to law. It does not appear in the record of these breaches of social order to what denomination exactly the insulted parties were attached; but it is probable that unusual zeal for the spiritual welfare of the population provoked the hatred of the irreligious, and that such zeal would be found mostly among those who had adopted Congregationalism under the inspiration of Methodist examples.

The old Dissent had been quiet and peaceable; the people did not think of "changing their religion:" as they were brought up, so they lived. Parish churches and meeting-houses stood face to face, and those who attended one place of worship thought not of entering another. Church and Dissent were thus, in many instances, rather distinct than opposed,—rather separate than inimical. Now a different state of things arose; not zeal for ecclesiastical principles so much as zeal for Evangelical truth prompted Congregationalists to make aggressive movements on the ignorant and careless population around them. Torpor in the parish church made the people in the meeting-house all the more wakeful; and efforts simply with a view of saving souls were pronounced sectarian and schismatic offences. However regarded at the time, a great religious movement arose in many parts of England, of which Yorkshire, Lancashire, Warwickshire, and Kent furnish typical examples.

Yorkshire Nonconformity had sunk into a low condition at the middle point of the last century. Congregations in large towns were almost wholly heterodox and apathetic, with the exception of one assembling in the Nether Chapel, Sheffield, under the care of a decidedly Evangelical minister. He, and Scott, the patriarch of Heckmondwike, were the advanced guard of a band which sprung up soon afterwards to retrieve the fortunes of Independency. Scott's congregation greatly increased, and, in 1761, it was found necessary to erect a new and more commodious building, subsequently increased as to its measure of accommodation by the erection of "lofts" or galleries. An impetus to Evangelical Dissent sprung out of this man's diligent and zealous ministry; a still more powerful inspiration flowed from his labours as tutor in the little Academy whose origin has been described. It formed a centre, whence radiated streams of light over the darkness of the neighbourhood; and the result appeared in Churches which dimly or brightly shone in the surrounding gloom. Beyond such efforts the great Methodistic revival told upon the Congregationalism of Yorkshire. Not to any surviving power in old Independency, never very strong in that district, but to the impulse of the day is the improved condition of the county to be ascribed. Methodism struck deep roots, both inside and outside the Establishment; and offshoots in Congregational forms soon appeared in different directions. The Methodism of Wesley planted itself in the parish of Haworth, under Grimshaw, and there throve with amazing vigour. Indeed, the parish and neighbourhood assumed the aspect of a Wesleyan circuit, subject to the rules of the Conference. The indefatigable clerical evangelist scoured the country, preaching thirty times a week, and thus he largely promoted the interests of the connexion founded by his illustrious friend. But some who were converted by his ministry, and encouraged by him to undertake the care and oversight of souls, forsook both the Establishment and Methodism, and became Congregational ministers.

The Methodism of Whitefield proved still more helpful. Henry Venn, in his vicarage at Huddersfield, entertained many a Calvinistic evangelist, from the great orator down to the humblest itinerant; and in his pulpit, where he was "valiant for the truth—a son of thunder," as Whitefield said, the strain of his preaching prepared many of his hearers to do, what the good man by no means desired, that is, dissent from their mother Church. Thirteen young preachers rose up out of the midst of his labours, some of whom became Congregationalists, and studied under "Father Scott," as he was called. The congregations at Huddersfield, Holmforth, Honley, and Brighouse, trace their origin to the work accomplished by Venn; and, as the Church of England would not embrace Methodistical instrumentalities within its own borders, and control them to its own advantage, dissent followed as a natural effect, however much deplored by consistent Churchmen, some of whom saw in the operations of such men as Venn only the sowing of so many dragons' teeth.

The conversion of John Thorpe at Rotherham, with its results, in the history of Dissent, is a favourite Yorkshire legend. Carousing in an ale-house, he laid a wager that he would mimic Whitefield better than any of his companions. When they had finished this exhibition, he mounted a table, exclaiming, "I shall beat you all,"—and so he did; for, opening the New Testament, where his eye fell on the words, "Except ye repent, ye shall all likewise perish," he began a discourse which strangely and irresistibly rose into a strain of the utmost religious fervour. He felt transported beyond himself, and was mysteriously carried along by the very truths which he intended to ridicule. The hearers were struck with awe, the bet was forgotten; John Thorpe became a new man, and joined the Methodists, after which his ecclesiastical opinions underwent a change, and he was chosen pastor of the first Congregational Church at Rotherham. He died in 1777, and was succeeded by Thomas Grove, one of the students expelled from Oxford.[1] Thorpe's meeting-house, built in 1764, became too

---

[1] See page 115 of this vol.

small for Grove's congregation; when another was erected at the expense of the Walker family, great patrons of Congregationalism at that time.[1]

Lancashire had been a stronghold of Presbyterianism; and, until after the middle of the last century, Independency made little way; then, in the form of new Congregationalism, animated by the revival under Wesley and Whitefield, it rose up with vigour, and laid its hand with a strong grasp upon the inhabitants of the great duchy. No professedly Congregational Church existed in Manchester, Liverpool, Bolton, Rochdale, Bury, Preston, Lancaster, Warrington, and Wigan, a century and a half ago. The great communities of this order, now so influential in the North, have mostly arisen within a much shorter period than that. The Evangelical fervour kindled in Yorkshire had much to do with the progress of Congregationalism in the adjoining county. The Heckmondwike Academy sent warm-hearted evangelists across the borders, and they gathered together little knots of people who formed a nucleus for some new congregation. A large proportion of the Lancashire ministers, during the last half of the century, went out of Yorkshire; Manchester, Liverpool, Bolton, Ashton, St. Helen's, and other places were indebted to this source for efficient pastors.[2]

---

[1] The foregoing particulars are mainly drawn from Miall's "Congregationalism in Yorkshire."

[2] Halley's "Lancashire," vol. ii. c. 9.

In some cases, Congregationalism did not so much draw off to its principles new converts from the Establishment, as gather together those who had previously dissented in practice. People were dissatisfied and uncomfortable, they did not find what they wanted in the parish church, though they had no objection either to Episcopacy or the Establishment, and greatly preferred the Book of Common Prayer to other forms; so they met together by themselves in irregular ways and formed little assemblies and read the liturgy, until, having taken certain steps, they felt necessitated to proceed further. Of this state of things Congregationalists availed themselves; and drawing around them those already in sympathy with their religious spirit, they gradually brought them over to their own usages and habits. Such is the genesis of much Independency in Lancashire. And at the same time, Methodism, as in Yorkshire so in Lancashire, contributed to Congregational progress and prosperity, but it seems to have been more the Methodism of Whitefield than that of Wesley. Calvinistic Methodism, for a time, commanded a considerable following in the county of Lancaster. Chapels of the Countess's type, ministers wearing gowns and surplices, and reading the liturgy, with the superadded attraction of organs, drew large audiences, "boasting that they had the advantages of both Church and Dissent, without the evils of either." But in the long run this movement did not succeed, and it is stated on good authority, that of several chapels more or less belonging to the Countess of Huntingdon's connexion, only one, that at Rochdale, preserves its original character and formularies.[1] The Calvinistic Methodists by degrees became Congregationalists. Their former peculiarities were dropped, and Independent modes of Church government assumed.

Wesleyanism, however, also in some measure helped on Independency. Many who were converted by the preaching of Wesley and his assistants, did not join their Society, because they wished for a form of Church polity different from that which consisted of conferences and circuits, class-meetings and change of ministers. Having received spiritual inspiration from the great home missionaries who traversed the length and breadth of the land, they settled down in communities, where they blended the new with the old, kindling sacrifices on ancient altars with fire which, they believed, was fresh from heaven. And it would also happen, that where converts had for a time been connected with Wesleyan organizations, they began to feel the want of calmer service and more instructive teaching.

Above all, the spread of Congregationalism in Lancashire is to be attributed to the labours of minis-

---

[1] Halley's "Lancashire," vol. ii. p. 438. Many of the particulars I have given are gathered from the interesting work of my honoured and lamented tutor.

ters held in honourable remembrance by the communities to which they belonged. Two Scotchmen, James McQuhae and Robert Simpson, are especially noticeable. The former settled at Blackburn in 1777, and gathered into his congregation Methodists, Presbyterians, and Independents. Even Arians came to hear him; and the story went abroad that, in an unapostolic sense, he was "all things to all men," and "had corn for all sorts of crops." The fact is, that he preached "Evangelical doctrine faithfully, but not angrily; practically, rather than controversially; and in a manner which interested intelligent hearers, whether they assented or not to his statements."[1] In short, he seems to have been a truly wise master builder, and by the blessing of God, he raised a goodly Church, built of living stones. He educated young men as preachers, and sent them into the surrounding villages. The other minister, Robert Simpson, came to Bolton in 1782. Bolton had been the Geneva of Lancashire; a thousand communicants had surrounded the Presbyterian table, but the numbers had sadly fallen off, when a congregation, gathered by itinerant Methodists, invited the Scotch preacher just named to take the oversight of them. Having caught the spirit of the Puritans, and something of the fire which burnt in the hearts of the Covenanters, he preached sermons full of Calvinistic theology, wrought

---

[1] Halley's "Lancashire," vol. ii. p. 440.

out in anything but frost; and such effusions wonderfully animated and aroused the Lancashire people. He is the same person as I have mentioned in connection with the Hoxton Academy, whither he removed when he left Blackburn. Another Independent, George Burder, who ministered in the town of Lancaster between 1777 and 1783, made his mark there during that space, not only as an efficient pastor, but as a zealous missionary.

He encouraged others to make themselves useful, sending out young men to give religious instruction in the rural districts of Amounderness and Lonsdale; and probably at that early period he provided brief discourses to read to the people, such as he afterwards published in his world-known volumes of "Village Sermons."[1]

Manchester, from the beginning of this century, proved a favourable soil for the seeds of Congregationalism, but the first sowing was by the hands of one Caleb Warhurst, who first preached at an obscure meeting-house in Cold House Lane; afterwards a better building was erected in Cannon Street. To him succeeded Timothy Priestley, who, though an able man, but without the genius of his scientific brother Joseph, made himself remarkable mainly by means of his

---

[1] These sermons became so popular as to attract the attention of clergymen, who ventured to read them in parish pulpits. There is a story told of some one who, to please the Evangelical people in church, would "tip them a Burder."

numerous eccentricities.[1] David Bradbury, the next pastor, was quite as odd and erratic, only in another way; and after quarrelling with some of his congregation, resigned his pastorate.[2] These are by no means favourable specimens; under such leaders the cause could not be expected to thrive. A new leaf was turned over, when, in 1795, William Roby, a Trevecca student, accepted the pastorate at Cannon Street, and commenced a career of prosperity which covered part of the present century.

Gloucestershire, the scene of Whitefield's earliest labours, as well as the place of his birth, came under an influence from his ministry which, after his death, effectually promoted, in that part of the country, the cause of Congregational Dissent. His name became a power scarcely less effective than himself; and in the village of Rodborough, near Stroud, there lingered long—indeed, there linger still—legends of his preaching in a beech grove, which commands a distant view of the Severn, at the end of a most charming valley, so that the tones of his voice reached the churchyard a quarter of a mile distant; and how a little boy being lifted up to see him, as he beheld tears rolling down Whitefield's cheeks, asked what the preacher cried for. People, convinced by his ministry, gathered together to promote one another's spiritual edification, and so formed the nucleus

---

[1] Halley, vol. ii. p. 448. [2] Ibid., vol. ii. p. 449.

of a Church which continues vigorous and useful to the present day. Amongst the members arose lay preachers, men uneducated, but of vigorous minds, who imitated Whitefield's example; respecting one of them, a local chronicler relates: "I remember to have heard him say that he worked half a day at haymaking, and in the afternoon of that same day took his staff and walked to Bristol, and preached at the Tabernacle in the evening; and that, likewise on a Sunday morning, he would rise early and walk to Clack, in Wiltshire, a distance of thirty miles, preach there in the forenoon, and in the afterpart of the day, travel several miles on foot to preach at other places, carrying his food in his pocket, and when he came to a spring of water, he sat down and ate of his bread and drank of the water, and on the Monday morning would resume his usual employment." A chapel was built—now much enlarged—on the edge of the beech-wood, long since turned into a burial-ground; and in an adjoining cosy parsonage have lived successive Christian teachers and men of honourable renown, preserving "the accredited chair of Whitefield in the chapel, his reputed tea-caddy and bureau in the house, and the antique fourpost bedstead, with its dingy hangings, on which slept Selina, Countess of Huntingdon."[1] Methodism settled down into Congregationalism, and

---

[1] These illustrations are gathered from "A Memorial of Centenary Services," held at Rodborough, 1866, and from several personal visits to the interesting neighbourhood.

instead of being confined to the ministrations of itinerant preachers, the people had their own pastor and deacons.

Another centre of Nonconformity was Marlborough, in Wiltshire, where the influence of Whitefield made itself felt. There lived, for some time, Cornelius Winter, his early friend and disciple, who in a series of autobiographical letters affords the best picture we have of the famous preacher's private life; and who, having been spiritually affected by his ministry and example, transferred the religious impressions thus received to the flock of which he was pastor, and to a few young men whom he educated under his roof. Amongst these was the Independent minister, William Jay. From Winter, Jay caught something of Whitefield's spirit, and he spoke of the Rodborough evangelists, of whom he had heard much from the lips of his tutor, as "rough sledge hammermen, raised up to do a great work." "They did not," he said, "secede from the work of God for fear of a flake of snow, a shower of rain, or the dread of taking cold by the inclemency of the weather. These were men who did not mistake a painted lion for a real one, nor were scarcely to be intimidated by a real one in the way."[1]

---

[1] Winter accompanied Whitefield on his last voyage to America, and after his death returned to England, where he sought ordination from the Bishop of London (Dr. Terrick), with a view to missionary work among the negroes in Georgia, under

The spirit which Jay caught at Marlborough he carried with him to Bath, where he was ordained in 1791, and became a great religious power, felt, not only throughout the west of England, but in London, where he preached every year for six weeks at Surrey Chapel. From the humblest ranks he rose to high renown, and though the popular applause he inspired was enough to turn his head; as Wilberforce said, "he seemed to shake it off as the lion shakes the dew from his mane." Amongst his admirers, first and last, were also Hannah More, William Beckford, Richard Sheridan, John Foster, James Montgomery, and Rammohun Roy; and whilst he attracted people of high rank and advanced culture, he also gathered round his pulpit multitudes of the poor who hung on his lips with unfeigned delight, and with spiritual profit.[1]

---

the sanction of the Propagation Society. The account which Winter gives of what took place between himself and the Bishop, presents the latter in an unfavourable light; and it is plain from the correspondence, published in Jay's "Life of Winter," p. 137, that a very unfriendly feeling existed between the Society and Whitefield's friends. (See Hawkins' "Missions of the Church of England" for notices of Whitefield and his opponents.) Winter devoted himself to mental improvement amidst immense discouragements. "My efforts," he says, "were frequently discovered, and as often reproached by the enemies of literature; and our connections abounded with too many, who made little discrimination between study and sin," p. 155. His Nonconformity did not forfeit the affection of his clerical friends. He died at Painswick.

[1] See sketch of William Jay, by Dr. Newth. "Pulpit Memorials."

Warwickshire, during the last quarter of the century, was the scene of a great religious revival. It emanated from three centres. The first was the old town of Warwick, where a zealous Christian, called James Moody, in 1780 became pastor of a small Independent Church,—so small, indeed, that it did not number more than twenty members. By the end of the century about 150 communicants appeared at the Lord's table, and five or six hundred hearers gathered within the walls of the meeting-house. The second centre of influence was Coventry, whither George Burder, just noticed, went in 1783, to take charge of a Church at West Orchard, in the picturesque Midland city; there, during a ministry of twenty years, he enjoyed popularity, and accomplished a mission beyond what can be expected to fall to the lot of many. A third centre of influence may be pointed out in the neighbourhood of Rugby, at a place called Little Harborough, about four miles from the great Midland Grammar School, where lived Sir Egerton Leigh, a pious and rather eccentric baronet, friend of Rowland Hill, and deeply imbued with the spirit of Calvinistic Methodism. From these triple points, and by these three men, were worked out lines of missionary operation which resulted in the establishment of numerous efficient Congregational Churches.[1] Sunday schools were established in the

---

[1] Sibree's "Independency in Warwickshire," chapters i., ii.,

county, after the example set by Raikes, of Gloucester; and, in 1793, arose "The Warwickshire Association of Ministers for the spread of the Gospel at home and abroad."

Much of the same history is found repeated in the county of Kent, old Churches, Presbyterian and Independent, came under a vivifying power, and assumed a new form, and people, gathered by ministers whom Lady Huntingdon patronized, mostly adopted Congregational forms; a County Association of Ministers and Churches appears in 1792, the second instance of the kind, it is said,—Devonshire, in 1785, presenting the first.[1]

---

and xxiii. The writer informs us that Sir Egerton Leigh, Sir Abraham Elton, and Sir Harry Trelawny, once united in conducting a religious service in the Bristol Tabernacle. "Baronets, squires, and captains, both naval and military, in their coloured clothes,—the red, the blue, as well as the black,—stood up in the pulpit, and in the open air, to preach the common salvation." p. 396.

[1] Timpson's "Church History of Kent," p. 300.

CHAPTER XXV.

1760-1800.

THE history of the General Baptists somewhat corresponds with the history of the Presbyterians; but the former resembled the latter not in intellectual power, literary culture, or social superiority, but in their spirit of investigation, and in their departure from orthodox beliefs. The West of England affords examples of their declension from earlier opinions, but, in some cases, they only pursued a course initiated at the era of their institution; since, it appears, they were never bound to particular Articles, trust deeds of their places of worship being of the most general description. An opulent and numerous congregation of this order, in the busy cloth-working town of Trowbridge, Wilts, whose meeting-house seems to have evinced some architectural pride, ran a course of the kind just indicated. Early pastors "distinguished themselves by the candour and earnestness with which they sought for truth and advocated the rights of conscience;" and no instance occurs in the history of this Church of any excommunication for erroneous sentiments. "A bad life seems to have been the only heresy of which the

Trowbridge congregation have ever taken notice. A minister, who officiated amongst them in the latter half of the century, would seem to have belonged to the Arian school; and he was succeeded by one of decidedly Unitarian views, of whom it is said, that he 'contributed to promote the knowledge of rational religion, awaken attention to free inquiry, and cherish just and liberal sentiments.'"[1] Also, in the first quarter of the century we meet with a Devon "manufacturer of serges," who was a zealous Baptist, of Arian, if not Socinian convictions, who preached every Sunday to a small sympathetic congregation in the parish of Dalwood, near Honiton.[2] Whatever might be their opinions, they retained something of a Puritan temper, and in their records express much devout feeling, of which a rather quaint and touching instance occurs in one of their documents: "Now we, the members of this little Christian Society, and those that attend among us as hearers, are in general but low in our worldly circumstances; but we that have been buried with Christ in baptism, humbly hope we have some blessed stock in faith, and a treasure in the heavens."

An instance of peculiar opinions and practice on the part of some Baptists, in the first half of the eighteenth century, is furnished by William Whiston:

"In the year 1735, that great and good friend of mine,

---

[1] Murch's "Presbyterian Churches," p. 74. [2] Ibid., p. 317.

Mr. Samuel Collet, a Baptist, who was so zealous to have primitive Christianity examined into and restored that he assured me he thinks he never once missed a meeting of our old Society for promoting that primitive Christianity, was very ill, and thought himself in danger of death at Newington Green. I went to see him, and at his desire prayed with him, and for him, as became a Christian clergyman to do. He also desired me to anoint him with oil, according to the injunction in St. James v. 14–16, upon which desire of his I hesitated, and told him I durst not venture to do that till I had examined antiquity about it." " However, he fully supposes that God took the will for the deed, and accepted of the prayers we put up to Him for his recovery; when there was nothing but involuntary ignorance on both sides, for he recovered, and he has ever since been in a better state of health than he had been long before."—"And since, it appears this practice has had great and eminent success in healing the afflicted; which the following Baptists, Mr. Killingworth, the two Mr. Stangers, Mr. Copper, and Mr. Goode, all of my own acquaintance, do fully attest. These seem to me to give a Divine approbation to it, so that any criticisms notwithstanding, I am clear that it is a certain law of the gospel, and ought to be put in practice by all Churches accordingly." In 1738, Whiston says he had been an anti-Pædobaptist twenty-six years.[1]

A great change occurred amongst the General Baptists about the middle of the century. Lady Huntingdon had a man-servant at Donnington Park, Leicestershire, named Daniel Taylor, a pious man,

---

[1] Whiston's Memoirs, pp. 354, 368.

who began to preach in the neighbourhood with her ladyship's sanction; and, at the same time, a blacksmith in Normanton, then recently converted, sat down one night on the kitchen table, talking to his neighbours about religion. He went on for two hours, and at the close was startled at the idea that he had been preaching. These persons, with others, called from the place where they tried to do good, "the Barton preachers," underwent violent persecution, being brutally assaulted by village mobs. "The Barton preachers" did not adopt Baptist principles until the year 1755, when, having made a large number of converts in the county of Leicester, they formed themselves into a distinct society. It is stated that when they became convinced of baptism by immersion, they placed a tub in the little meeting-house, and there "the ministers dipped their infants." This was the practice for several years, when they were led to believe that "the New Testament no more authorized the baptism of infants, than it authorized baptism by sprinkling."[1] The preachers therefore baptized one another by immersion, and then proceeded to administer the ordinance to their converts in the same way. In 1760, the Society divided itself into five Churches, which led to the establishment of what is called the New Connexion; and it is pleasant to find that when this community

---

[1] Taylor's "History of the General Baptists."

was insulted in villages where hand-bells were jingled in their ears, and dirt thrown in their faces, and a bucket of blood poured on one unfortunate member, the Bishop of the diocese reprimanded a curate who had stimulated the proceedings, and recommended the preacher to his own Registrar for a certificate, according to the Act of Toleration. If the circumstance reflected credit on the Bishop, it must be added to the discredit of this subordinate officer, that he, somehow or other, evaded his lordship's injunctions. County magistrates did all they could to crush the new party, but failed; and the latter succeeded in placing themselves under legal protection.

It appears that the New Connexion of the General Baptists sprung from an impulse created outside the circle of the elder denomination which bore the same name, but in the midst of the latter were those who retained Evangelical sentiments in an anti-Calvinistic form; such Churches were found in London, Kent, Essex, and Lincolnshire,—these, in time, were absorbed into the new body, which had come to be pervaded by a similar belief and by a similar spirit.

In 1770, a meeting was held in London, "with a design to revive experimental religion, or primitive Christianity in faith and practice," when six Articles were adopted and signed, setting forth the Fall of Man, the Obligation of the Moral Law, the Divinity and Atonement of Christ, Salvation by Faith, Regeneration by the Holy Spirit, and Adult Baptism.

No allusion appears in these Articles to the Calvinistic controversy. Besides subscriptions to Articles, there was instituted another term of communion; every minister was to give an account of his religious experience, that his brethren might be satisfied concerning the reality of each other's conversion.[1]

The history of the body, after these initiatory transactions, resolves itself into a history of each Church, and of the meetings of representatives held at particular times. Churches were formed in the midland counties, also in Yorkshire, in Lincolnshire, and in London; though neither large nor numerous, they were devoted and zealous.

Amongst the ministers, Daniel Taylor appears most prominent. He is described as a man of distinguished ability, and was successively pastor of a Church at Birchcliffe, and another at Whitechapel, London, whither, in 1785, he came for the remainder of his life. We find him at the annual meetings giving counsel to his brethren, writing circular letters, and otherwise promoting the knowledge of his principles; in 1798, he appears presiding over an Academy at Mile End, for the education of young ministers.[2]

The Particular Baptist body retained their primitive organization, with, perhaps, a stronger demo-

---

[1] These particulars are drawn from Taylor's "History of the General Baptists," vol. i. p. 143.

[2] Ibid., vol. i. pp. 192, 331.

cratic element in it than existed amongst the General Baptists, who seem in some cases to have verged towards Presbyterian habits of government and discipline,—Church meetings for the admission of members, and the discussion of affairs; a demand for detailed experience from candidates seeking fellowship; worship of the most inartistic kind, often conducted by poor laymen; jealousy with regard to Independency; decided alienation from the Establishment, and a strong bond of mutual attachment, drawing together not only member with member but also Church with Church;—these were characteristics of the Particular Baptist body during the two last generations of the eighteenth century. Many pursued the practice of strict communion, while they tenaciously held the doctrine of Particular Redemption, from which they derived their distinctive name.

There were not wanting in the first half of the century, amongst either General or Particular Baptists, men of considerable learning, some of whom had been educated either at foreign universities, or at English Dissenting Academies. In general culture one Baptist minister stands out prominently in the middle decades of the century—the well known Dr. Gifford, of the British Museum; not to mention for the present a few others eminent for theological acquirements. But no Academy expressly instituted for the education of Baptist ministers existed before the reign of George II. One appears under the charge of "a man of fine talents matured by constant and severe studies," named Foskett, who died in 1759, and was succeeded by Hugh Evans, "an able an eloquent preacher," whose son, Dr. Caleb Evans, assisted him, and then, at his father's death, took his place, as Principal of the Institution. By him, the Bristol Education Society was formed, and the Academy being then based on a deeper and stronger foundation, another Bristol Baptist, named James Newton, qualified by classical and Hebrew studies, was associated with Evans. Both dying before the end of the century, the Institution was transferred to the hands of the celebrated Dr. Ryland, and the not less celebrated Joseph Hughes. But the majority of the Baptist ministers during the period included within this chapter were men who had received but little education, though some of them, by dint of study, rose to eminence in theological acquisitions. They were strict Calvinists, some of them very high in doctrine, deprecating with vehemence the latitudinarian sentiments of the sister denomination, and confining the idea of Christian piety almost wholly to those who theologically sympathised with themselves.

Lapses of the description so common amongst General Baptists are not to be found, except in rare instances, amongst Particular Baptists; but one signal instance, showing that Calvinistic opinions at the outset provided no sufficient safeguard against heresy, requires attention, not only on that account, but because of the remarkable character of the man in whose life the instance occurs. Robert Robinson, a native of the county of Norfolk, born in 1735, when an apprentice to a London hair-dresser, heard Gill, Guyse, and Romaine, but preferred George Whitefield to any other preacher. Imbued with a Calvinistic spirit, he soon began himself to preach, and joined the Calvinistic Methodists at Norwich. Leaving them, and becoming an Independent, he settled down at length into Particular Baptist views; and, just on the edge of George III.'s reign, accepted the charge of a Baptist Church at Cambridge. It was then in a miserably low condition: strict in communion, high in doctrine, narrow in sympathy, the people had just lost a minister who is described as a "lord in his Church, a tyrant in his family, and a libertine in his life."[1] It may be hoped that this uncomely portrait is overcoloured; but the little flock he left, there can be no doubt, quarrelled and separated immediately after his death, so that Robinson, when he arrived, found empty walls, and a few devout souls who, amidst prevalent darkness and confusion, waited and prayed for brighter days. Thirty-four members assembled together, and all they could raise their new pastor, the first quarter, was sixty-six shillings. But the tide soon turned. Rarely has any man appeared in a pulpit with such extraordinary gifts

---

[1] Robinson's Works, vol. v. p. 283.

for popular impression as Robert Robinson; with a commanding presence, a beautiful voice, a graceful delivery, a slow measured dignified tone of utterance, perfect self-command, wonderful skill in the use of language, a most felicitous method of quoting Scripture, directness of address, and pungency of appeal, he riveted the attention of his hearers. They gradually increased. The little one became literally a thousand. All Cambridge went to hear him: the gownsmen, at first to mock, afterwards to listen—if not to pray.[1] The University Professor of Music attended the meeting-house, except when official duties obliged him to be absent, and by his influence the psalmody was greatly improved, a very notable circumstance in those days. Throughout life Robinson was the uncompromising advocate of civil and religious liberty, and by that means secured friends and created enemies.

"His name," said Dr. Rees, "has been often mentioned in the senate of the nation, sometimes with respect, but generally with a view of criminating and reproaching him."[2]

Robinson was very eccentric,—eccentric in his dress, for he would appear in the pulpit with coloured

---

[1] See his remarkable sermons upon "A becoming behaviour in religious assemblies." He set up a Sunday night lecture, and "it is supposed that not less than 150 or 200 gownsmen generally attended."—Funeral Sermon by Toulmin, p. 28.

[2] Funeral Sermon by Dr. Rees, p. 60.

clothes; eccentric in his studies, for he would borrow books in enormous numbers, availing himself of the college and university libraries until he had emptied many shelves to fill his own, and had to send them back a cartload at a time; eccentric in his employments, for he combined trade and farming with ministerial duties, and has left behind him a diary for one day, in a letter as strange as was ever read.[1]

But the point to be particularly noticed is the change which took place in his opinions. He began with orthodoxy, and wrote a powerful essay on the Divinity of Christ. He believed the doctrine of election in a moderate form, and ably expounded it in a characteristic treatise. He preached Evangelically, and wrote charming hymns, full of tender devotion;[2] and for some time associated with his brethren of the Particular Baptist denomination on terms of affection and confidence. But from the beginning he manifested a spirit of bold inquiry, coupled with great self-reliance, and with contempt

---

[1] Robinson, Works, vol. iv. p. 231. A curious instance of eccentric opinion appears in the following passage: "We never pray at a grave, lest we should mislead our little children, who know not yet their right hand from their left, in the way to heaven. We would not ensnare their unwary steps, or tempt them to form one idea favourable to that exploded popish practice, praying for the dead."—Address at the interment of Mrs. Susanna Borley, 1782; with sermon by D. Taylor.

[2] The well-known hymn, "Come, thou fount of every blessing," etc., was written by Robinson.

for other people's opinions. This, of course, provoked criticism, and at length produced alienation. Whether if he had been differently treated he would have pursued the course he did, it is impossible to say; but it is pretty clear that his speed in the race of what he regarded as free inquiry was accelerated by the conduct of his brethren.[1] This is certain, that at the end of life he had given up that which he held most dear at the beginning. It is difficult to determine what were his positive opinions at last. His works do not express his final views, but it is said that he passed by a rather rapid transition, not to Socinianism, but far beyond,—to the very border of infidelity. Such at least was the substance of his declaration to Dr. Priestley, whom he thanked for preserving him from that awful gulf.[2]

In not a few cases where a minister was the opposite of Robinson—where Calvinism was advocated with zeal—Baptist Churches were in a feeble condition for some time before the end of the century. Indeed, Calvinism rose to such a pitch as to produce a state of things resembling that of advanced Rationalistic

---

[1] Jerome said that Tertullian was driven into schism by the Roman clergy.

[2] Dr. Olinthus Gregory's "Life of Hall." Hall's Works, vi. p. 28. Mr. Robinson died suddenly at Birmingham, when on a visit to Dr. Priestley.

"I have been informed that it was always the wish of Mr. Robinson that his death might be sudden."—Funeral Sermon by Dr. Priestley.

congregations. Spiritual torpor prevailed. The religious faculties were benumbed. If some Churches folded their hands in slumber, because they had little truth they cared to promulgate, others were just as listless and idle, because preaching the Gospel to the world was no business of theirs,—God would take care of His own elect. It is to be feared that where there might be no downright Antinomianism,—a thing much more unfrequent than some people suppose,— there was thoroughgoing Antinomianism in practice. The state of things at Trowbridge was reversed in Northamptonshire and other places. A bad life was treated as no heresy whatever, provided people were not Arminians, or "free willers." When a member fell into immorality, excuses were alleged on his behalf, arising from an idea of human inability to obey God's commandments.[1] The low tone of religion in the midland counties became a subject of lamentation amongst exemplary Baptists of the neighbourhood; and they set apart seasons for prayer to the Father of spirits to recover from devious ways His backsliding children. It is very remarkable that at this very time the denomination, whether cognisant of it or not, really caught the bracing breeze which had come sweeping down from the hills of Methodism over Baptist meadows, as well as Independent fields.

---

[1] Morris's "Life of Andrew Fuller," p. 27.

There was Benjamin Beddome, in the middle of the century, at Bourton-on-the-Water, in the county of Gloucester, a man whose life and ministry resembled the streams which refresh the broad street of that pleasant little village. "Favoured with the advantage of a learned education, he continued to the last to cultivate an acquaintance with the best writers of antiquity, to which he was much indebted for the chaste, terse, and nervous diction which distinguished his compositions both in prose and verse." "As a preacher he was universally admired for the piety and unction of his sentiments, the felicity of his arrangement, and the purity, force, and simplicity of his language, all of which were recommended by a delivery perfectly natural and graceful." "As a religious poet his excellence has long been known and acknowledged in Dissenting congregations, in consequence of several admirable compositions inserted in some popular compilations."[1]

Dr. Samuel Stennet, a native of Exeter, laboured with his honoured father in that beautiful city, and then succeeded him in the pastorate of the Baptist Church within its walls. To zeal for the progress of civil and religious liberty, and attachment to his own denomination, he added a catholic spirit, and also much tender and persuasive eloquence. "He was, perhaps, the last of the Dissenting ministers who cul-

---

[1] Robert Hall's Works, vol. iv. p. 438.

tivated social intercourse with the great,—a practice common in the former generation, and conceived to be beneficial to the body."[1]

The religion of Samuel Pearce, of Birmingham, had in it a seraphic ardour which passed beyond the bounds of ordinary experience. Dying at the end of the century, when only in his thirty-fourth year, he left behind him a memory which has since inspired with zeal many of his successors in the ministry. In labours more abundant, he also animated contemporaries by his example, and by his singular fervour in worship led many to exclaim, as they heard him, "We scarcely ever seemed to pray before."[2]

John Sutcliff, another Baptist minister, is described as possessing ample stores of knowledge far beyond what most of his hearers imagined, "for he seemed almost as anxious to conceal as some are to display." "Humility diffused itself over the whole of his character and deportment, and gave it a certain beauty which no artifice could successfully imitate." "As his disposition little inclined him to ecstasy and rapture, so his piety shone with a mild and steady lustre, perfectly free from the false fire of enthusiasm, and equally from a lukewarm formality."[3] Such unobtrusive excellence in a Christian pastor, little

---

[1] Bogue and Bennett's Hist., vol. ii. p. 651.
[2] Ibid., p. 653.
[3] Robert Hall's Works, vol. iv. p. 302.

known beyond his own circle, deserves to be recorded, and in this instance it is brought the more distinctly under our notice by the important services rendered by the subject of it to the Church at large. For he superintended an Academy at Olney for the education of ministers, and took a prominent part in the establishment of the Baptist mission.

The two Rylands, father and son, were men of strong mental calibre, and renowned for their spiritual prowess. The father, John Collett Ryland, of Northampton, was eccentric in the extreme, as appears from a strange vow, written by him at the age of twenty: "If there is ever a God in heaven or earth, I vow and protest in His strength, or, that God permitting me, I will find Him out, and I'll know whether He loves or hates me, or I'll die and perish, soul and body, in the pursuit and search." Such a man was not likely to do or say things like other people; and, accordingly, his preaching and conduct were often of an *outré* description,—but rich and racy sayings dropped from his lips; his sermons were bold and original in the extreme, sublime thoughts bursting forth from amidst baser matter. The character of the son, Dr. John Ryland, the Principal of the Baptist College, at Bristol, may be best delineated in words borrowed from Robert Hall. As to erudition, he was a scholar from his infancy; his attainments in the Hebrew language were profound; he had a general acquaintance with the principles of science, and his reading was various and extensive. "He had a passion for natural history, in the pursuit of which he was much assisted by the peculiar structure of his eyes, which were a kind of natural microscopes." "His religion appeared in its fruits, in gentleness, humility, and benevolence; in a steady, conscientious performance of every duty, and a careful abstinence from every appearance of evil." "His love to the Great Supreme was equally exempt from slavish timidity and presumptuous familiarity; it was an awful love, such as the beatific vision may be supposed to inspire when the worshippers veil their faces in that presence in which they rejoice with ecstatic joy." "The two extremes against which he was most solicitous to guard the religious public, were Pelagian pride, and Antinomian licentiousness: the first of which he detested as an insult on the grace of the gospel; the last on the majesty and authority of the law."[1]

Two of the men now mentioned, John Sutcliff and John Ryland, were intimately connected with an enterprise which commenced within the last decade of the century, and this, with a kindred undertaking described in another part of this volume, constitutes a memorable epoch in the history of Christianity and the world. But the enterprise did not originate with

---

[1] Detached Sentences, from Hall's Funeral Sermon for Ryland Works, vol. i. pp. 392-405.

them; though but for them and another eminent individual to be presently mentioned, probably it would not have been carried out.

The originator of the movement was William Carey. Up to the age of twenty-six he was a man in humble circumstances, first employed as a shoemaker, and then as a village schoolmaster. But the force of his genius rose above the difficulties of his position, and even when cutting leather and working on the last, his mind was occupied in the study of languages, the problems of geography, and the construction of maps. He acquired a knowledge of Dutch in an incredibly short time, in addition to that of Latin and Greek, with which he soon made himself so acquainted as to lay the foundation for acquirements which ultimately rendered him a wonder to his age. He had a rare faculty for the acquisition of foreign tongues, and a facility—it would seem quite as rare—in all kinds of geographical investigation. Here, then, were the scientific elements out of which to form an eminent missionary; and in this case the moral power to mould and apply them was not wanting. Animated by fervent piety, and conscious of a call from Heaven, Carey left the village school, for which he had exchanged his ignoble trade, and became a minister of the Gospel, receiving ordination at Moulton, in Northamptonshire, in 1787, where he had been chosen pastor of a Baptist Church. There the duty of Christians to propagate the Gospel in heathen lands so impressed his mind that it wrought in him a passion for missionary work. He pondered the subject in silence. It produced in him fits of absence at which observers marvelled. He would pause as he walked in his little garden, and stand motionless for an hour and more, wrapt in the contemplation of this absorbing theme. He removed to Leicester in 1788, and took with him that one idea of his life, which kept burning in his breast—a coal from off no earthly altar. At a Ministerial Meeting held in the town of Clipston, he renewed the question, to him full of spiritual fascination, "Whether it were not practicable, and our bounden duty, to attempt somewhat towards spreading the Gospel in the heathen world." For some time afterwards, in London and elsewhere, numbers doubted and hesitated and objected, urging that the season had not come for such attempts. As the thought became more familiar, however, it acquired increasing strength, and began to wear a look of likelihood. In May, 1792, Carey preached a famous sermon at Nottingham, in which he sharply brought out two simple exhortations, which have since been placed and trimmed as lamps of Heaven-kindled fire, on Baptist altars : "*Expect great things from God; attempt great things for God.*" "If all the people had lifted up their voice and wept, as the children of Israel did at Bochim, I should not have wondered," are the words in which Ryland records the impression made that memorable day. He, Fuller, and Sutcliff, were now satisfied that the time had come for attempting a great work in the strength of God. So, on the second of October, 1792, they met in "the back parlour" of a good woman's house at Kettering, and resolved: "As in the divided state of Christendom, it seems that each denomination by exerting itself separately is most likely to accomplish the great ends of a mission, it is agreed that this Society be called, 'The Particular Baptist Society for Propagating the Gospel amongst the Heathen.'" Thus the Society was established, not in a church, a chapel, or a hall, but in a little "back parlour," when twelve men—probably the whole number present—signed the minutes, and the subscriptions altogether amounted to £13 2s. 6d. Ryland, Carey, Sutcliff, Fuller, are among the subscribers.[1] When once these men had started on their path, they did not let the grass grow under their feet. Meeting after meeting followed in the now famous Northamptonshire town, and the first subscriptions received additions,—seventy pounds being contributed by the hands of Samuel Pierce, of Birmingham, who threw himself into this missionary enterprise with intense ardour, and would have gone to Bengal had his health permitted; but God cut

---

[1] These particulars are drawn from "Memoirs of Fuller," by Ryland, chap. vii.; Morris' "Memoirs of Fuller," chap. iv.; Cox's "History of the Baptist Mission," chap. i.; and "Periodical Accounts relative to the Society," vol. i. pp. 1-45.

short his days and took him to another sphere of service. Of course, everybody who joined the Society saw at once that the heaven-sent man, who had stirred them up to work, was the messenger whom they should despatch to the heathen. He was willing to go. "We had no one to guide us," Fuller used to say, talking the matter over with friends, and comparing the work to the opening of a mine ; "we had no one to guide us ; and while we were thus deliberating, Carey, as it were, said, 'Well, I will go down if you will hold the rope.' But before he went down, he, as it seemed to me, took an oath from each of us, at the mouth of the pit, to this effect, 'that while he lived, we should never let go the rope.'" That, and the other legends which gather round the origin of the Baptist Missionary Society, will never die.

Another mission was attempted soon afterwards, not so well known. The cuckoo-note objection, that there is enough work to do at home without going far abroad, was then often heard ; and practically to answer it by doing the one, and not leaving the other undone, was the course adopted by the Fathers and Founders of the Baptist Society. They organized efforts for the propagation of the Gospel at home. Two brethren were sent down to preach in Cornwall, their names were Saffery and Steadman, both well known in their own denomination ; and a list is preserved of the places where they preached, with notes of circumstances which occurred. Sometimes they occupied the pulpits of meeting-houses, sometimes they stood on platforms in town-halls, sometimes they addressed people in private houses, sometimes we find them "out of doors," in a back yard, in the street, amidst the romantic scenery of the Land's End and at Tintagel, rich in British legends. Also in the natural amphitheatre near Redruth, where Wesley gathered thousands together—the brethren delivered their message. Once, at Merthyr, the service was carried on in a meadow, partly by moonlight; and once, at Kellington, it being harvest-time, the stars began to appear before the preacher commenced, and a "large lime-tree spread itself over nearly all the assembly; these circumstances, added to the seriousness of the auditory, rendered the opportunity highly solemn and delightful."

Of "the lovely triumvirate," celebrated by Robert Hall—Fuller, Ryland, and Sutcliff, co-founders of the Baptist Missionary Society—the first requires separate attention from his eminence as a preacher and a theologian. Without the grace of delivery and the brightness of imagination conspicuous in Robinson, and without the sublimity of thought and the felicity of diction which marked the discourses of Robert Hall, Fuller, in concentrated power of reflection, and in originality of theological speculation, surpassed them both. The momentum of his arguments and the incisiveness of his appeals have been again and again attested by those who were personally acquainted with his ministry;[1] and specimens of them, perhaps after all not the best, may be found in his published discourses. Sometimes familiar and homely, he would turn to account passing circumstances: as, for example, once going to Nottingham, to preach before an association of ministers, he had to cross a swollen river, in the midst of which he became alarmed, and was about to turn back to his peril, when the voice of a friend well acquainted with the spot, cried "Forward, forward," and encouraged him to advance. On reaching his destination, he alluded in the pulpit to this familiar incident, as suggesting the privilege and security of walking by faith and not by sight, and the blessedness of His guidance who is ever present to direct our way.

Andrew Fuller once preached in a parish church.[2]

"In the spring of 1796, a reputable grazier at Braybrook, in Northamptonshire, who has since emigrated to America, lost his eldest son, and requested Mr. Fuller to preach a funeral sermon at his interment. When the sermon was about to commence, the little meeting-house in the village was found by far too small to contain the congregation; the weather also was too cold to admit of preaching in the open air, and no convenient place was at hand. An urgent request was presented to the aged vicar for the use of the parish church." "The parent of the deceased youth was

---

[1] Some of them were my early friends.
[2] "Life," by Morris, p. 49.

willing to engage for any pecuniary consequences that might ensue; while the preacher promised to make his best apologies to the bishop, if they should be demanded. The interment took place in the churchyard; and the aged and infirm vicar, having performed the burial service at the grave, actually introduced the Nonconformist to his pulpit, and became himself a hearer, while Mr. Fuller delivered a most impressive discourse from Jer. xxxi. 18-20, to a numerous and deeply affected audience." "When the service was over, the clergyman, whose name was Chapman, shook hands with the preacher before all the people, and thanked him for his serious and pathetic discourse, saying, 'I hope that no ill consequences will befal either thee or me.'" "At a following visitation, however, the bishop inquired into the fact, which was freely admitted by the clergyman; and particularly asked whether the preacher prayed for the king; for possibly his lordship imagined that none but bishops pray for royalty. The answer was 'Yes, very fervently.' 'And what did he preach about,' said the diocesan. 'Why, about the common salvation,' was the reply. The bishop only added that he must not do so again."

But Fuller's fame as an author, even while living, exceeded his fame as a preacher. He was not a scholar, he could not be called a learned divine, but as an original thinker few equalled him. Of his numerous works many are controversial; one on Socinianism, another on Universalism, a third on Deism; some of his writings, unfortunately, are in reply to obscure persons, or they relate to subordinate points which retain now but little interest. Passing over the former, I would venture a brief remark in reference to one of the latter, namely, a controversy with a Scotch divine named Maclean, who advocated Sandemanianism.[1] The Sandemanian view, is that faith, as an intellectual exercise, precedes, in the order of nature, the production of moral obedience. Fuller contended that faith itself is a moral act, that it is the root of all Christian virtue, and that the turning-point of individual salvation is found in the heart. But both these good men ascribed Regeneration to the work of the Holy Spirit, to the communication of Divine grace, and therefore, though their debate was not strictly speaking a piece of logomachy, it possessed no practical importance. Each writer believed that intellectual perceptions, and moral dispositions entered into the character of personal religion; they merely differed as to which is to be placed first. No doubt there underlie the question some important interests visible to metaphysical eyes, and these were detected by Fuller. With terrier-like tenacity in this, as in all his other debates, he kept hold on what he deemed the error of his opponent, and shook it to death; but the form in which the subject was discussed by these two writers has now entirely lost its edge and interest.

Much more was involved in another controversy. Against High Calvinists Fuller waged incessant warfare, contending not only that the Gospel is worthy

---

[1] "Strictures on Sandemanianism, in Twelve Letters."

of all acceptation, but that men are, on moral grounds, bound to believe and obey it; that a sufficient provision has been made for their salvation, and that the invitations of peace are to be universally offered; at the same time he believed that a Divine power wrought on men, constraining them to yield up their souls to God in a life of holy love.[1] Fuller was one of that class of theologians who are equally impressed by the facts of God's gracious sovereignty, and of man's moral obligation. In contemplating the one he could not lose sight of the other. He saw that on neither of these two principles, taken *alone*, can a system of divinity be securely based; it must cover both. He did not think that he was shut up to the alternative, on the one hand, of receiving the doctrine of Predestination, and of renouncing the doctrine of Universal Atonement; or, on the other, of rejecting the first, whilst embracing the second. In fact, he did not feel himself bound to become a thorough follower of John Calvin, or a thorough follower of James Arminius; a tendency wrought in Fuller, similar to that which had appeared in John Howe and Richard Baxter. Without the Platonic culture of the one, or the dialectic skill of the other, he had much of the theological catholicity and comprehensiveness of both; but he wrought out his

---

[1] See Fuller's "Essays," and his "Gospel of Christ Worthy of all Acceptation."

results, not as the copyist of any one, but after a fashion of his own. He belonged to the same school of Evangelical divines as John Newton and Thomas Scott, but was far more inventive in method and distinct in conclusion than either of those good men. For native force he stands first in the Evangelical school of his day; and perhaps no one had so much influence as he upon Nonconformist theological opinions during more than the first quarter of the present century.

If Andrew Fuller bears away the palm as a theologian, to Robert Hall, as a preacher, it must certainly be assigned. Traditionary descriptions of his eloquence, and recollections of it lingering amongst a few who, when young, had the privilege of hearing him, are quite sufficient to place him amongst the first pulpit orators of the last, or any other age. The rapidity of his utterance had the effect of giving additional momentum to his exhortations and appeals; and these were sometimes so impassioned that, as if by an electric shock, he moved his hearers till they started to their feet, and bent forward in trembling expectancy of what would follow. The perfect stillness of the entire audience rendered the modulations of his voice, not naturally powerful, all the more impressive, whether his tones were pathetic or argumentative, denunciatory or persuasive. It is said, however, that like many other distinguished speakers, he was very far from being always himself, that he could sink as well as rise, and that there were occasions when listeners, though favourably disposed, would be unable to form any conception of the grandeur of his discourses at other times. In the case of George Whitefield, as we read his published sermons, we wonder at the impression he produced. His thunder and lightning could not be represented in print. But Robert Hall's eloquence was of a different description; and as we read his luminous pages, we are not surprised to learn that his hearers were carried away by the charm of his utterances. Of his style it may be truly said, " that it is one of the clearest and simplest; the least encumbered with its own beauty of any which ever has been written. It is light and lucid as a mirror, and its mood highly wrought; and sparkling embellishments are like ornaments of crystal, which, even in their brilliant inequalities of surface, give back to the eye little pieces of the true imagery set before them."[1] Language was with Robert Hall a magician's wand, with which he could accomplish surprising transformations in the minds of attentive and sympathetic hearers. Their thoughts, obedient to his touch, glowed for the moment with an imagination like his own. When the essence of his meditations or the substance of his reasonings was not original, the words in which he clothed them were such as to lend a fasci-

---

[1] Hall's Works, vol. vi. " Memoirs," p. 132.

nation which the same thoughts did not exercise at other times. In many of his reported discourses there is little originality as to the line of reasoning pursued ; but his sermon on Infidelity, to mention no other, is surprising throughout for the majesty of its ideas, as well as the felicity of its diction. The publication of it produced an unusual excitement in the most refined literary circles, and Parr and Macintosh vied with each other in expressing their admiration.

Perhaps the force of Hall's intellect was nowhere so manifest as in conversation with his friends. In Cambridge, at Alderman Ind's Club, as it was called, where the Baptist minister mingled with men of different denominations, the flashes of his wit, the dexterity of his arguments, and the incisiveness of his axiomatic remarks, were such as to leave on the memory an indelible impression of the versatility of his genius. But what concerns us most is his eminent piety of heart, humility of mind, and devotedness of purpose. He did not live to build up fame, any more than to amass wealth. The end of his existence, the one object of his will, was to preach the Gospel, and to gather souls into the Church of Christ. And I have alluded to his power and his culture as means which he employed to promote the supreme design of his great endeavours.

Mr. Hall was an advocate for the practice of open communion, thus walking in the steps of John Bunyan, and other members of the same body. Some years after the close of the last century he published a book on the subject,[1] going into it very thoroughly, both on grounds of Scripture, and on principles of Christian reason and equity. This elicited a reply on the part of another eminent Baptist minister, the Rev. Joseph Kinghorn, of Norwich, who permanently adhered to the practice of strict communion. The controversy lies beyond the chronological events of this history, and is only noticed to indicate that the long-continued difference on this question amongst the Baptists continued down to the close of the century; and that an advocate on the side of free communion was then rising up to defend and encourage the broader view, so effectively as to prepare for a widespread change in that particular throughout the Baptist denomination of this country.[2]

---

[1] "On Terms of Communion, with a Particular View to the Case of the Baptists and Pædobaptists," published in 1815. Hall's Works, vol. ii. pp. 1–232.

[2] "Baptism a Term of Communion," by Joseph Kinghorn, 1816.

Hall's "Reply to the Rev. J. Kinghorn," 1818. Works, vol. ii. p. 233.

"A Defence of 'Baptism a Term of Communion,'" 1820. By J. Kinghorn.

CHAPTER XXVI.

1702–1800.

QUAKERS, in the middle of the eighteenth century, described their "convictions" much after the same manner as did their predecessors in the seventeenth.

The words of Christ, "*I am the Truth*" constituted the sheet anchor of their distinctive faith—"*This I am*" to use their own characteristic phraseology, "the essential, everlasting, saving truth, is that of which they were convinced, and in which they believed. Convinced of Him by His own immediate, self-evident operation upon their minds; convinced that this was the Spirit of Truth of whom it was said, when He came, He should convince the world of sin, of righteousness, and of judgment. And being brought to this Rock and sure Foundation of living Faith, they became convinced that as the Holy God is an omnipresent Spirit, so in Spirit and in Truth must He be acceptably worshipped; that as He is in Himself infinite and incomprehensible, dwelling in the Light which no man can approach unto, whom no man hath seen or can see; so through this Spirit of Truth, this Holy Mediator, access only could be had, and true worship performed, to the Father of spirits. They were convinced that as He is perfectly holy, so, except they were made in degree holy, their prayers could never ascend with acceptance as the incense of saints, before the throne of glory. And although the command and declaration to Abram is plainly exhibited in Scripture, viz., I am the Almighty God ; walk before Me, and be thou perfect ; it seemed to them an impossible attainment, till opened by Him who hath the key of David. They then saw, that perfection arose from the relation Abram stood in to an Almighty Creator ; and were convinced that this call extended to the seed of Abram through all generations. And being convinced of the purity, so they were of the peaceableness of this gospel dispensation. They not only read but felt it breathe peace on earth and good-will to men ; that there was to be no hurting nor destroying in all God's holy mountains."[1]

This was a kind of spiritual manifesto, issued in the year 1760, "by the people called Quakers."[1] Every denomination has its own type of excellence. Such was the standard set forth by Friends ; but it is not to be supposed, that in this, any more than in other instances of ecclesiastical history, the actual always corresponded with the ideal.

Yet there can be no doubt that in a good deal of Quaker life the principles inculcated by George Fox received a fair practical expression. Reticent as were his followers in some respects upon what is mysterious in spiritual experience, they carefully preserved brief biographical records of deceased members who had been preachers amongst them,—

---

[1] Preface to "A Collection of Testimonies concerning several Ministers of the Gospel." London, 1760.

"testimonies," as they were termed, "concerning, ministers of the Gospel, with some of their last expressions and exhortations." The quarterly meetings in the provinces sent up to the yearly meetings in the metropolis written accounts of this nature, "to promote and encourage the practice of virtue, and of that obedience and self-denial which the Gospel of Christ requires of His servants." Some of these documents were published, and examples of them, in their original form, supply interesting illustrations of that cast of sentiment and conduct which, from the beginning, marked off this peculiar people from other sections of the Christian world.

One of these worthies being by trade a tailor, "soon after his convincement could not comply with the making of such needless and superfluous fashions in apparel as were then used by his customers, and thereupon gave over the chiefest part of his trade, and betook himself to other business in order to get a livelihood; wherein Providence was favourably pleased to bless his labours with success, so that although he never had a great deal as to the things of this world, yet he had a competency sufficient to support him, and to carry him through the same with satisfaction and comfort."

A Yorkshire female member, in the twenty-second year of her age, had "a part in the ministry committed to her which became a very close concern upon her, being such a cross that she said she had rather have parted with her natural life, but could find no peace without answering the Lord's requirings; and therefore she resolved, through His Divine assistance, to be obedient unto Him, though all sorts of people might hiss at her."[1] The testimony respecting John Gurney—a famous Norwich Quaker, whose father had suffered much for conscience' sake—brings him before us in the middle of the century as a pillar of strength, and an ornament of beauty, to the large and prosperous community of friends in the old East Anglian city.

"About the twenty-second year of his age, his mouth was opened in the assemblies of his friends as a minister, much to their edification and comfort; and, as he advanced in years, that excellent gift was more plentifully bestowed upon him, being an eloquent man, and mighty in the Scriptures; his ministry having often the demonstration of the Spirit and power of life attending it, being delivered with much plainness, and so suitably adapted as generally reached the meanest capacities, and answered to the witness of God in the auditors; which made him very acceptable to many, who for the most part delighted to sit under the same, and sought for opportunities so to do: Though it may be said, he endeavoured rather to be hid, than to appear to gratify the curious, or only to satisfy their itching ears, being careful in attending to the immediate pressures on his own mind before he entered thereupon; and often gave way to others, though perhaps inferior to himself in many respects, which made service more available, and better accepted."
"The first day, two weeks before his last illness, he was at our

---

[1] " Collection of Testimonies," pp. 7, 21.

meeting in the forenoon, when he appeared in a lively Testimony amongst us: He pressed us to consider, How our time passed away! and to examine How far our minds had been religiously disposed since our meeting together. Some of us, he said, seemed to be at the top of the mountain, where it pleased God sometimes to remove the clouds, and give us a clear prospect into the promised land, though we were not yet quite arrived so as to take possession thereof. It was a melting time, and an opportunity that will leave a lasting remembrance on the minds of many. He drank large draughts of affliction in this life; yet he bore them with great patience and resignation to the Divine hand which permitted them. He saw clearly they must soon finish him, as to this world; and as they did greatly wean him from it, so they did abundantly increase his faith in the dealings and goodness of God, by which, we doubt not, they were sanctified unto him; and though they were permitted to end his days in this world, yet, we doubt not, they did work for him, through Divine assistance, a more exceeding and joyful inheritance in the world to come."[1]

It is a curious fact, that in connection with their extreme spirituality and contempt for worldly things, the Society of Friends maintained two principles of a counter description : the one was what is called *birthright membership;* the other, that of *the minutest legislation touching the common affairs of life.* George Fox, the founder, had insisted upon the idea that the Church is made up of "living members," that is, of " a spiritual household, of which Christ is the head ;"

---

[1] "Collection of Testimonies," pp. 134 138

and Robert Barclay, the apologist, in a tone of disapproval had remarked, that when Christianity ceased to be a ground of reproach, men became Christians "by birth and education, and not by conversion and renovation of spirit."[1] From this principle there was a departure in 1737, when a sort of Quaker poor-law was passed, and the community resolved to save its indigent members from pauperism. A spirit of comprehensive sympathy appeared, when Friends decided that wives and children should be deemed members of the monthly meeting to which their husbands and fathers belonged, not only whilst those husbands lived, but after they were dead.[2] Then the desolate widow and her offspring were bequeathed as a legacy of love to the Society with which the supporter and guardian of her life had been identified. Very beautiful! But they seem not to have discerned that this implied adoption of the rule, that membership was a natural inheritance—that it descended from parents by birthright—could not fail, in the end, to incorporate within their select community a number of persons destitute of those religious convictions which formed the very strength and life of Quaker fellowship. Friends *had* been Friends by virtue of professed "convincement," as it was quaintly termed;

---

[1] See quotations in Barclay's "Inner Life of the Religious Societies of the Commonwealth," 1876, p. 361.
[2] Barclay, p. 520. This writer died recently.

now they could be regarded as such, by virtue of the law of descent. They have been blamed for what they did on this occasion ; no doubt they departed from the original basis of their communion, but if they were blind, it may be pleaded that charity, that tender kindness towards widows and orphans, bandaged their eyes.

The minute legislation of the Quakers respecting the commonest affairs can hardly be called a departure from early principles, because from the beginning they had been extremely punctilious in reference to trifling matters, regarding minor peculiarities as so many outworks against invasions of worldliness, so many advanced defences around the citadel of their spiritual life. Nothing seems to have been beneath their notice. From the cradle to the grave they provided for the conduct of their members. The time children were to be kept at school, the books they were to read, how they were to be apprenticed, and rules for marriage, were specified with much minuteness. No feasting or gaiety was allowed at weddings; bridesmaids were not to be led out of meeting by groomsmen ; and the use of a coach on one marriage occasion led to grave remark. "Great superfluity and too great nicety in gardens" came in for serious censure, so that floral decorations, and pretty bouquets such as now-a-days grace with tender beauty our nuptial gatherings, would have filled the old Friends with sore dismay and sorrowful concern.[1] Nor did funerals, any more than weddings, escape legislative control. The last, as well as the first wants of life were comprehended within orders issued at important meetings. As ornaments on cradles were to be dispensed with, and mothers were to suckle their children; so burials were to be conducted with the utmost simplicity; coffins were "to be made plain, without covering of cloth, or needless plates."[2] Even floor-cloth in houses was forbidden; also "the fashionable using of tea," the taking of snuff, and the smoking of tobacco. Curiously enough, they anticipated modern legislation in reference to killing salmon or trout in the breeding season; for at a monthly meeting they said, this violates "the decree, or command of God, in the beginning, when He blessed them, and commanded them to increase and multiply."

Dress attracted great attention. The attempt to repress its extravagances occasioned an amount of time and thought and trouble which defeated one of the ends which those well-meaning people had in view. George Fox had launched his thunderbolts against the costume prevalent in his day: "Away with your long slit peaks behind, in the skirts of your waistcoats," your "skimming-dish hats," your "unnecessary buttons," "your short sleeves and short black aprons," "your vizzards," and great needless

---

[1] Barclay, pp. 494-8.   [2] Ibid., p. 495.

flying scarfs like colours on your backs."[1] This, after all, however we may smile at it, was but a revival of those sumptuary antipathies which had burst forth again and again in the discourses of mediæval monks; and the spirit which it evinced reappears in orders issued at monthly meetings after Fox had gone to a world where such things no longer give trouble. Young women were to come to meeting in long cloaks and bonnets, and to take the advice of their elders as to what they should wear. In smaller gatherings they were to show themselves in just such apparel as that in which they meant to appear at larger ones, so that the costume might be criticised and endorsed at these strange rehearsals. In monthly meetings of the West Riding, the fair Rachels were to present themselves, "in those clothes that they intend to have on at York." "Let no coloured plaids be worn any more, but either mantles or low hoods." "Let none want aprons at all, and that either of green or blue or other grave colours, and not white, upon the street, or in public at all, nor any spangled or speckled silk or cloth, or any silk aprons at all."[2] These were rules solemnly issued for the government of that most refractory of all subjects—fashion in dress. And refractory it continued amongst Quakers as among

---

[1] Crisp's "Testimony concerning Isaac Pennington," 1681, p. 23. Barclay, p. 440.
[2] Aberdeen Minutes. Barclay, p. 491.

other people, notwithstanding all the trouble taken about it. In 1720, came lamentations over "quilted petticoats, set out in imitation of hoops, cloth shoes of a light colour, with heels; white and red, scarlet or purple stockings, and petticoats made short to expose them." Scrupulosity sometimes went great lengths. As to bonnets, the question was raised, "whether any should be worn, yea or nay"; and this is the conclusion reached, "though they might be lawful, it was not expedient to wear them."[1] All this concern respecting outward adornments—the plaiting of hair, and the putting on of apparel—was not confined to the young of one sex; young men were justly censured for "cutting off good heads of hair," and putting on "long extravagant gay wigs."[2]

Quakers sought some important ends. They wished to promote honesty in trade, to secure, that articles in commerce should be perfectly genuine, that goods should be made for use, and not simply for sale; in short, they fixed on the object aimed at by one sumptuary law in the middle ages. Linen and woollen articles were to be honest and substantial; and people guilty of manufacturing things slightly and of little service to the wearer, were, in case of unrefractory non-compliance with good Quaker law, to be excommunicated from all Quaker society. To prevent members from falling into debt, power was

---

[1] Barclay, p. 491.   [2] Ibid., p. 493.

given to examine into their condition. Every one was to give to properly deputed persons an account of his circumstances and his way of living. No more business was to be undertaken than could be reasonably managed. Families were to be provided for, and reputable and solid credit maintained; the bread of idleness was not to be eaten; people were to live by the labour of their hands. Admirable advice! and, though it sometimes failed, yet on the whole perhaps, the Quakers were much more exemplary than other people in their diligence, their honesty, and their abstinence from extravagantly expensive habits.

Registration of births and marriages and deaths, the making of wills, the disposal of property, domestic disputes, the prevention of fire, and the use of fire-engines—these and other matters are comprised within the scope of Quaker rules and regulations adopted in solemn assemblies.[1] The tendency was to form a sort of secular *imperium* in a spiritual *imperio*, and so to depart from the spirituality of ecclesiastical government; also, there might be a forgetfulness of the importance and efficacy of a few general principles in the conduct of life, beyond a multitude of preceptive details; yet it would appear from the history of the Society, that what they did in the way of law making, though it may, in some

---

[1] Ibid., p. 487.

particulars, draw forth a smile, effected some valuable social results. The morality and good behaviour of Quakers in their mutual relations, and in their intercourse with the world, during the last century, redound immensely to their credit; the more so when we remember the vice, the falsehood, and the manifold wickedness of the age in general.

Quakers, like other religionists, came in contact with Methodism; and it is interesting to notice some particulars illustrative of this point. Wesley mentions the Friends in his journal, and says, in July, 1765, he saw that, when preaching, many of them were present, and that he read the life of one of their preachers with admiration. "If," he says, "the original equalled the picture, which I see no reason to doubt, what an amiable man was this. His opinions, I leave; but what a spirit was here! What faith, love, gentleness, long-suffering! Could mistake send such a man to hell? Not so. I am so far from believing this, that I scruple not to say, Let my soul be with the soul of William Edmundson." The Great Methodist Revival undoubtedly influenced the Society, but not to any very large extent. Wesley seems hardly to have moved them as much as Whitefield. Whitefield had more sympathy with them; for he dwelt on the hidden life of the soul,—"a light which never was on sea or shore:" "Christ in the heart, the secret of spiritual mindedness." Quakers gathered round the great preacher. He preached to them, talked with them, and received from them assistance. A Quaker acted as a kind of curate to him, when on shipboard. Quakers went to hear him in Scotland and America, and "cheered him not a little ;" and a Quaker prepared a pulpit for him in Marylebone Fields.[1] "And," said he, "the Quakers, though wrong in their principles, yet I think have left us an example of patient suffering, and did more by their bold, unanimous, and persevering testimonies, than if they had taken up all the arms in the kingdom." [2]

Once we find Lady Huntingdon crossing a Quaker's path; and as the anecdote is interesting, I give it in the words of Mrs. Schimmelpenninck, who relates it in her memoirs.

"When at Bath, as my mother grew better, she frequently took me with her to the Pump Room, and she sometimes told me anecdotes of those she had seen there when a child. On one occasion, when the room was thronged with company,— and at that time the visitors of Bath were equally distinguished for rank and fashion,—a simple, humble woman, dressed in the severest garb of the Society of Friends, walked into the midst of the assembly, and began an address to them on the vanity and follies of the world, and the insufficiency of

---

[1] Gladstone's "Life and Travels of Whitefield," pp. 126, 170, 177, 275.
[2] Letter dated Nov. 10th, 1739. "Whitefield's Letters," vol. i. p. 79. There are no less than thirty-eight letters bearing that date. Some were written on board ship, and dated after Whitefield's arrival in America.

dogmatic without spiritual religion. The company seemed taken by surprise, and their attention was arrested for a few moments : as the speaker proceeded, and spoke more and more against the customs of the world, signs of disapprobation appeared. Amongst those present was one lady with a stern yet high-toned expression of countenance; her air was distinguished, she sat erect and listened intently to the speaker. The impatience of the hearers soon became unrestrained; as the Quaker spoke of giving up the world and its pleasures, hisses, groans, beating of sticks, and cries of ' Down, down,' burst from every quarter. Then the lady I have described arose with dignity, and slowly passing through the crowd, where a passage was involuntarily opened to her, she went up to the speaker, and thanked her in her own name and in that of all present for the faithfulness with which she had borne testimony to the truth. The lady added, ' I am not of your persuasion, nor has it been my belief that our sex are generally deputed to be public teachers; but God who gives the rule can make the exception, and He has indeed put it into the hearts of all His children to honour and venerate fidelity to His commission. Again I gratefully thank you.' Side by side with the Quaker she walked to the door of the Pump Room, and then resumed her seat. This lady was the celebrated Countess of Huntingdon."

We turn for a moment to look at the inner life of Quakerism during the latter half of the eighteenth century.

They taught their children to believe in the constant presence of God, and in that interior voice, Conscience, or the Holy Spirit, by which He speaks to human hearts, but they did not inculcate any distinct, or rather, any doctrinal views of Christian truth.[1] It is curious to find how they daily endeavoured to impress their own peculiar taste on the young, claiming sanction and precedent in the works of creation. "See how beautiful are the sober and unobtrusive colours of the linnet, the dove, and the redbreast. I hope thou wilt imitate them in thy attire," said a sedate friend to a thoughtful girl, who naturally replied, "But art thou not glad, though, that it pleased God not to create grandpapa's peacocks and golden pheasants, on Friend's principles?" It must have been wearisome for young folks unendowed with reflective instincts to sit for an hour or two in a silent meeting-house; but a thoughtful young Quakeress[2] could say, "I felt the influence of that holy presence of God, visibly recognised by so many persons, whose garb marked them as withdrawn from the world, and whose countenances, for the most part, bore the impress of love and peace. I felt as one entering an overshadowing summer cloud, where the presence of light is felt, though no distinct object is seen." If Friends did not bring

---

[1] "The religious Society to which we nominally belonged—Friends—was at that period at the lowest ebb; and we never had the opportunity which all may now enjoy of hearing the truth in Christ commonly set forth."—Autobiography of Mrs. Schimmelpenninck, p. 11.

[2] Mrs. Schimmelpenninck.

forward dogmatic truths, neither had they the irreverent habit of bandying about the most sacred subjects in colloquial discussion. But they spoke with a religious voice more eloquent than verbal utterance in their untiring activity for the improvement of the temporal and spiritual condition of their fellow-creatures. When the emancipation of the slave, and the education of the lower classes, came to be objects of public interest, the Friends led the van of the host, in the warfare against oppression and ignorance. Spiritual conflicts and changes occurred in their experience of a singular kind; we hear of a young lady abandoning Quakerism, submitting to baptism, entering the Church of England, and then leaving a fashionable party of her acquaintances, to prostrate herself before God in her silent chamber, whence, she at length returned, in the attire of a plain Friend, determined to abide ever afterwards in fellowship with the people among whom she was born.

Quakers with all their strictness sought help at times from other Societies, and in forms of fellowship unlike their own. Whiston tells us, in reference to his own peculiar services in Hatton Garden,—

"Mr. Joshua Martin, the most learned of all the people called Quakers that I ever knew, offered himself to be a member, and was readily received as such. I then proposed that we should use some short collects taken out of our common Prayer-book, before we began and after we ended every meeting, to implore the blessing of God upon our inquiries. To which proposal all readily agreed but Mr. Martin, who entirely scrupled joining with us in such prayer, unless when the spirit moved him, which occasioned a good deal of difficulty to the Society. Yet at last we agreed to leave him to himself, to stay either with his hat on or off, as he pleased, and he gave us leave to say our prayers ourselves; nor did he ever disturb us, nor was he afterwards an unuseful member when he came to the Society." [1]

Towards the close of the last century there seems to have been some relaxation in that strictness of limited intercourse which marked the early Friends. Not only did a distinguished Quaker family in Coalbrook Dale mingle with the Madeley Methodists, but another distinguished family, living not far from Birmingham, and entering with zest into scientific pursuits, had large and miscellaneous reunions; amongst their guests might be seen Dr. Parr, Dr. Darwin, Sir William Herschell, Sir Joseph Banks, Dr. Priestley, and the Rev. Joseph Berrington, the literary Roman Catholic priest at Oscott.[2] This family was so considerate with regard to their Roman Catholic neighbours, that in case any of them should

---

[1] Whiston's "Memoirs," p. 237.
[2] All these particulars are gleaned from Mrs. Schimmelpenninck's Autobiography, particularly pages 4, 18, 37–45, 192. She says of Mrs. Berrington, "How I delighted in his anecdotes of Cowper the poet, of Mr. Unwin, Lady Austin, and Lady Hesketh, all of whom he continually met at Sir John Throckmorton's." P. 123.

drop in during seasons of abstinence, fish was regularly provided on Wednesdays, Fridays, and Saturdays.

Of this extended intercourse with the outside world, another example occurs in the history of the Gurney family, at Earlham, near Norwich. In that hospitable mansion, at the latter part of the last and the beginning of the present century, the young people with an indulgent father, cultivated friendships with those in the same rank of life as themselves, without regard to sectarian distinctions or political differences. They also entertained members of the nobility and even one of the royal family—at the same time deviating from Quaker modes of dress and conversation. But, after a time, some of the family returned to their former strictness—and not "a more beautiful, consistent, and exemplary Friend's home than that at Earlham could be found in the three kingdoms."

Such was the inner life of Quakerism. What was its outward appearance? Something different from what it had presented in the seventeenth century. No stories were now circulated respecting it, similar to those about James Naylor, in Oliver Cromwell's time. Even good George Fox's eccentricities, seen through the haze of antiquity, did not appear as they did a hundred years before. Robert Barclay by his masterly exposition had given the peculiar doctrine of the Friends a place amongst well-digested systems of divinity; and William Penn, by his social position in England and his political achievements in America, had elevated his denomination to worldly respectability. Moreover, the temperate habits, the economical conduct, and the industrial activity of the members, had secured for them great wealth in the manufacturing districts ; also their mental culture, refined tastes, and literary intercourse, had, in several cases, secured for Quaker families the highest consideration and respect.

Quakerism flourished in the city of Norwich. Some of the members who had been poor at an early part of the century, became rich before the end, and with increasing wealth came corresponding external manifestations. A large commodious edifice was built in what is called the Gildencroft; and everything about the building, if not elegant, was made appropriate for the meeting of Friends.[1] The floor was covered with benches in rows, broken up into three divisions by two spacious aisles. A long low gallery ran along one side of the structure, opposite the doors ; and there sat public Friends, as those who preached were often called. Goodly congregations often assembled, especially on the afternoon of first day, during the summer months, when the retirement

---

[1] The roof is supported by two oak pillars cut out of single trees, and it is reported that after one of them had been provided, a person rode about the county for a fortnight, before he could find another sufficiently large and long to match the other - "History of the County of Norfolk," vol. ii. p. 1262.

of the situation, and the airiness of the building added attractiveness to the simplicity of the service. The men sat on one side, and the women on the other, all attired in a fashion familiar to us half a century ago, but now vanishing away. Here, drab coats and broad brimmed hats were numerous,— there, dark bonnets, pearly white shawls, and leaden coloured dresses were equally so. Among Quaker merchants of the East Anglian city were two or three persons of considerable eloquence, accustomed to lead the devotion, or to stir up the faith of the assembly; not only on the Lord's-day, but on Thursday mornings, when business being laid aside for an hour or so, the good people found spiritual rest and refreshment amidst the secular toils of life. When public Friends came from a distance, conducted from some neighbouring town by a guide on horseback, as was the custom in those days, larger numbers than usual met to hear the strangers; and, on first day evenings, sometimes the place would be crowded to the doors. There sat the preachers in the low gallery, side by side, men and women, each of the former leaning on his staff, each of the latter with head bowed down; all in reverential silence awaiting an impulse from the Teacher of all truth, the inspirer of all pure thought. One of the speakers, removing his hat, would rise and address the meeting in solemn tones, or bow down in lowly worship before the Invisible One. At length, when time came for concluding the service, some one of the public Friends would rise and shake hands with a neighbour, as a signal for the people to disperse.

Marriages were celebrated in the meeting, the pair to be wedded standing up and solemnly acknowledging one another as man and wife. Hard by was a large burial ground, with no tombs or gravestones, but with a large number of grassy hillocks, beneath which slept the early fathers of the Quaker faith in the old city. When funerals took place, the dead were committed to their last resting-place in perfect silence, unless some one present would offer prayer, or administer words of consolation. A solemn air hung about the place which touched the heart—a real *campo santo*, where those who had engaged in no warfare but the spiritual, rested in peace.

Yearly meetings were Quaker festivals well known by all the citizens. So great was the access of strangers on those occasions, that the price of provisions used to rise; and quiet but busy housewives were accustomed to lay in large stores of simple cheer for the entertainment of their guests. In the streets might be seen, when the great meeting was to be held, "troops of the shining ones," on their way to the Gildencroft; accompanied by parents and husbands and brothers, all attired in a costume which made the distinction between them and the ordinary wayfarers visible enough. No gay ribbons were to be seen on any damsel's head; and the sight of a jauntily-tied neckerchief on the bosom of a young Quakeress has been known to disturb the spirit and spoil the meeting of one of the rigid elders.

Anecdotes of Divine guidance and protection vouchsafed to Friends in journeys of religious service were circulated in these pleasant gatherings; and faith in the inner light, and a sense of the all-comprehensive providence of God, were strengthened by related facts, often full of romantic dangers and deliverances. Amongst the visitors to these yearly meetings were sometimes seen American Friends, then numerous and influential. Attired in still stricter uniform than their co-religionists on this side the Atlantic, they attracted much attention, especially the female Friends, who used to wear over their drab gowns small dark green aprons.[1]

The Friends constituted a Society pre-eminently spiritual. There was another Society appearing in England towards the close of the century, which also claimed to rest on an exclusively spiritual basis; but in other respects, when compared with the Quaker denomination, it is seen to be wide as the poles asunder. One Robert Hindmarsh in 1788 organized a sect based on the strange theology of Emanuel Swedenborg, who began to publish his *Arcana Celestia* in 1749. The spirituality of the system taught by

---

[1] For these particulars I am indebted to the traditions of my childhood, some of my ancestors having been Quakers.

George Fox took a form which was no less moral and practical than religious : the spirituality of the system broached by Emanuel Swedenborg was mainly, if not entirely, intellectual and speculative. He was possessed of a brilliant genius, steeped in Mysticism. He imagined himself transported into the invisible world, where he saw visions of heaven and hell ; and the Church of the New Jerusalem, revealed to him in his dream, he regarded as the oracle and ideal of truth and life. He employed himself in developing Scripture, and, as he supposed, in adding to its contents, under the illumination of the Spirit, after the manner of a second Montanus. He sought to break through veils of sense, and to plant his foot upon the invisible threshold of a world which he beheld opening its gates amidst his apocalyptic reveries. There is scarcely any orthodox doctrine which he did not either reject or rationalize. His explanation of the Trinity reduced it to a mere philosophical myth. In his hands, the Incarnation became a simple union of things Divine with things human. Redemption was but the vanquishment of infernal foes. Angels and devils were departed spirits in a state of triumph or despair. There was to be no resurrection of the body ; and the Second Advent was simply the institution of the Church of the New Jerusalem, as revealed to himself in the year 1757.[1] The new denomination thus

---

[1] See his " Apocalypse Revealed."

formed made but little progress; very few distinct Societies were instituted; but it is said that several clergymen of the Established Church adopted Swedenborgian views. The British and Foreign Swedenborg Society was not commenced until 1810.

CHAPTER XXVII.

1790-1800.

METHODISM, both in Arminian and Calvinistic forms, served to give personal religion ascendency over ecclesiastical government. Not that the latter was overlooked. Both representatives of the new movement—Wesley and Whitefield—set out on their career with decided convictions in favour of Episcopacy; and neither of them ever formally renounced their early views. When forced by circumstances into a position separate from the Church, Wesley saw that organization was essential to the permanence of his work; his attention was occupied by principles of Church government, and the religious body he brought into existence found itself constrained, by the necessities of its condition, to imitate his example in this respect. Still, Methodism grew out of the feeling that religious experience and the truth which produces it take precedence of everything else, and that to these primary objects all which is merely ecclesiastical must be kept in strict and lasting subordination.

Out of such an idea there arose another, namely, that in Evangelical piety we are to look for a centre and ground of union, that men may differ in Church views and yet be one in spiritual sentiment. This proceeded upon the principle that the Church is not to be identified with any visible association, however numerous; that it includes many more than are ever embraced within any single fellowship, however vast; and that a clear distinction is to be drawn between local and limited Societies on the one hand, and, on the other, the aggregate of souls renewed by truth and affiliated to the Divine Father—who leads His children home through one living Way, yet by varieties of discipline. From this manner of looking at the subject, there emanated a conviction that it is possible for persons of different denominations to co-operate in acts of charity—not only for temporal but for spiritual objects. It was believed that the disciples of Christ might combine in making their common faith known to their fellow-creatures, through the medium of the press and through the instrumentality of the pulpit. Whether these views are correct is not the present question; the fact is simply stated, that such was the form of opinion, and such the consequences flowing from it, in the midst of the memorable Methodist Revival.

This is a different order of thinking from that which belongs to Anglo-Catholicism. Anglo-Catholicism identifies the visible with the invisible Church, orthodoxy with Orders, faith with early Creeds, spiritual life with the administration of Sacraments, and devotion, at least in public, with liturgical worship. It may not deny that salvation is possible outside its own enclosure; it may recognise the largeness of Divine mercy, and cherish what it considers a charitable hope, on behalf of those separate from its communion; but the worship offered by such persons is maimed, their privileges are limited, and their faith is imperfect. They do not belong, in any proper sense, to the unity of the Church; they are but outer-court worshippers, proselytes of the gate, to be treated kindly, but not to be recognised as belonging to the chartered commonwealth of the true Israel. This conception is irreconcilable with the ideas which we discover in the folds of Methodism. Christian union, in the one case, is quite of a different type from Christian union in the other. The possibilities of co-operation are therefore in the two cases entirely different. Co-operation in ministering to the physical wants and even to the mental culture of mankind, within certain limits, there may be on the Anglo-Catholic theory, and perhaps even a little further, impulses of love and zeal may carry the Anglo-Catholic; but with his theory, united action in propagating the Gospel is inconsistent. Common efforts for the circulation and advancement of Christian literature, combined endeavours for preaching the truth of the Bible and for promoting and guiding Christian worship, are out of the question.

The distinction now pointed out is necessary to be

kept in view, if we would duly estimate the character of certain associations about to be described. Their originality, as compared with the current High-Church notions of the day, their boldness, almost amounting to audacity in the estimation of many clergymen, and their tendency to undermine the exclusive claims of sacerdotalism, cannot be comprehended unless by a reference to the different theories of union and co-operation thus brought face to face with each other. Nor is it sufficient to refer to the Anglo-Catholic theory alone. To some other theories this idea of union stood opposed. There may be exclusiveness in Presbyterianism and in Independency as well as in Episcopalianism. Extreme ideas of the Divine right of any particular system may stand in the way of co-operation between members of different denominations. The charge of bigotry may be sincerely repelled, Christian charity may be honestly professed; yet union of the kind which sprang up at the end of the last century may be regarded with suspicion, and connection with it may be consistently declined. Generous sympathies had been expressed by Puritans and Nonconformists long before. Baxter and Howe, Watts and Doddridge had panted for union with intense desire. Methods of co-operation, such as were started eighty years since, would have rejoiced their hearts; but many Presbyterians, Independents, and Baptists were so attached to their own Church ideas, that they could not see their way at once to step out of enclosed vineyards, to work on a broad, open common. Nonconformists might think, and some did think, that their own ecclesiastical organizations were the best instruments with which to labour for saving souls and blessing the world. It is not wonderful that some of them should regard missionary work of all sorts as Church work, Gospel preaching as subject to the control of ministers and people in their corporate capacity, and religious teaching as necessarily involving a denominational element.

Sentiments of brotherly love, and a sympathetic desire to promote the common salvation, however, overcame in a great many ministers and laymen the objections they felt at first. Judgment, prudence, expediency, and the like, were the grounds on which their difficulties rested; not any sacerdotal claims, not any confusion of spiritual unity with visible organization. Gradually they came to see that some of the proposed methods of united activity involved no compromise of ecclesiastical principle, required no surrender of distinctive practices, and endangered no denominational interests.

The publication of a periodical for the exposition and enforcement of Evangelical views, and for the conveyance of information respecting the progress of religion, was one of the first objects which attracted attention. "A New Spiritual Magazine, or Evangelical Treasury," appeared in 1783, conducted, according to the title page, on "moderate Calvinistic principles, the only doctrines which are agreeable to the Holy Scriptures and the Reformation." It is further strangely described as presenting "the valuable labours of a *Real Society* of Gospel ministers and others." Another company projected another periodical at a rather later period. They looked, to use their own language, with unaffected concern, upon the infidelity of the age, and watched with painful apprehension what they considered the abuse of free inquiry. They deplored the progress of opinions militating against their own cherished convictions, and they sought, by means of the *Evangelical Magazine*—as their new work was entitled—not only to maintain the Divine authority of the Christian religion, and to answer objections to it current in the days of the French Revolution, but also to prove from Scripture the doctrines taught by the Puritans in general, and by most of the Reformers. Within those lines they were agreed amongst themselves, and in this respect they believed they were in possession of what is more precious than any peculiarities dividing one communion from another. Churchmen, Presbyterians, Independents, Baptists, and Calvinistic Methodists, joined in the undertaking. The idea is said to have originated with a literary gentleman belonging to the *Globe* newspaper; but, however that might be, the first editor was an Episcopalian clergyman, John Eyre, at that time incumbent of Ram Chapel, Homerton. Impressed by reading the works of James Hervey, he had united with the Evangelical party in the Establishment, and after having studied at Trevecca and preached in Lady Huntingdon's chapels, he entered Emanuel College, Oxford, and was ordained by Dr. Lowth, Bishop of London. First, curate to Richard Cecil, next curate to the Honourable Mr. Cadogan, his Churchmanship assumed no rigid form; he engaged in what his brethren pronounced irregular services, his friendships embraced many Nonconformists, and thus he had fitted himself for this new service, and for others of a like kind, which speedily followed. Amiable and gentle, he found a coadjutor in a man much more robust and vigorous than himself. This was Dr. Bogue, a minister educated for the Scotch Establishment, but who, from his objections to the law of patronage, then under discussion, left the land of his fathers to preach on this side the Tweed. He accepted the pastorate of a congregation at Gosport, where he manifested more decided opposition to the English Establishment than did many of his brethren; nor did he scruple to express sympathy with the French Revolution in the early stages of its history. He, in consequence, fell under the suspicion of Government, and had his name taken down as a person to be watched in political proceedings. Those who knew him best were aware that treason or sedition was foreign to his thoughts; notwithstanding hurtful rumours, he enjoyed the friendship of distinguished naval officers, and numbered amongst his hearers the wife of Lord Duncan.[1] With the discharge of pastoral duties, he united the employment of preceptor, and received as a pupil Robert Haldane, destined in his day to exert a wide religious influence. Still more important it is to notice Bogue's work in educating young men for the Congregational ministry. The Gosport Academy, conducted by him, originated in 1789, and during his long term of office, he enjoyed the satisfaction of sending forth eminent ministers and missionaries. Bogue helped Eyre in conducting his magazine; and, in the September number for 1794, addressed an appeal to "Pædobaptist Christians" to imitate the example of their Baptist brethren, who had just commenced their Society at Kettering. In this address he proceeded upon a denominational principle, and after referring to Roman Catholic, Church of England, Kirk of Scotland, Moravian, Methodist, and Baptist Missions, he says respecting Churches of his own order: "We alone are idle. There is not a body of Christians in the country, except ourselves, but have put their hand to the plough. We alone, and it must be spoken to our shame, have not sent messengers to the heathen to proclaim the riches of redeeming love. It is surely full time that

---

[1] See Bennett's "Life of Bogue," Morison's "Fathers and Founders" of the London Missionary Society, and the history of the Society by the Rev. William Ellis.

we had begun." In consequence of this appeal a meeting was held the very next month, October, 1794, at the old Castle and Falcon, Aldersgate Street; and the ministers and other brethren who assembled in a room of the well-known hostelry afterwards used to talk of their gathering with all that enthusiasm which lends enchantment to the origin of great undertakings, as "a hallowed circle, like a type of heaven." In arranging for their conference, a step had been taken beyond the range of Bogue's proposal, for members of *different communions* were present; and in a second Address on Missions, published in the *Evangelical Magazine* for January, 1795, the ground taken by the writer, Dr. Love, an active Scotch minister presiding over a congregation in Artillery Street, Bishopsgate, was that of a comprehensive union.

"That something may be done with effect," he writes, "it is hoped that not only Evangelical Dissenters and Methodists will be found generally disposed to unite in instituting a Society for this express purpose, but that many members of the Established Church, of Evangelical sentiments and of lively zeal for the cause of Christ, will also favour us with their kind co-operation. Indeed, the increase of union and friendly intercourse among Christians of different denominations at home, is one of the happy effects which will immediately flow from an Institution of this nature."

The Address was circulated with an accompanying letter, which invited attendance at a second meeting, to be held at the same place in the same month, when a document was signed by Episcopalians, Presbyterians, Methodists, and Independents to the effect, that they would exert themselves to form "an extensive and regularly organized Society, to consist of Evangelical ministers and lay brethren of all denominations." The appointment of a Committee followed, consisting of two Episcopal clergymen, two ministers of the Church of Scotland, two Methodists, three Independents, and one English Presbyterian.

The Society was launched in the September of the same year, 1795, and a clergyman of the Church of England, Dr. Haweis, already noticed in connection with the Countess of Huntingdon, preached the first sermon in Spa Fields, when the Liturgy of the Episcopal Church was read and extemporary prayers were offered. A public meeting immediately followed, when Mr. Eyre explained the plan of the new Institution. Burder, Greathead—Cowper's friend—Dr. Hunter, Rowland Hill, and David Bogue, were also preachers on the occasion; the last, though not present at the Castle and Falcon meeting, thus showing his accord with the friends of the comprehensive system substituted for the denominational movement proposed by himself.

Besides these men, others, already mentioned in these pages in different communions, are to be ranked amongst the Fathers and Founders of *The Missionary Society*, as it was originally designated. Matthew

Wilks, Edward Williams, William Roby, Alexander Waugh, Robert Simpson, and Edward Parsons. To these may be added, the two Townsends, John and George, the first educated at Christ's Hospital, the second at St. Paul's School—both Independent ministers. The first of these founded the Deaf and Dumb Asylum; and there stands now in the Hall a marble bust of the good man, presented by the late Duke of Gloucester, who zealously co-operated with him in the foundation. The Congregational School, Lewisham, also originated in his philanthropic efforts. George was for many years a respected minister in Ramsgate, and his son, named after him, became well known as prebendary of Durham, and a laborious author in criticism and history. Others, less known, were George Lambert, a Congregational minister at Hull, of whom his tutor said, "I have a student who is sufficiently dignified to be chaplain in the palace, and sufficiently simple to preach to poor travellers under a hedge;"[1] and John Mead Ray, for sixty-three years Congregational minister at Sudbury, a perfect type of the country gentleman, whose dignified appearance excited the admiration of George IV.,[2] and whose character and preaching greatly con-

---

[1] Morison's "Fathers and Founders," etc., p. 381.
[2] This occurred at Windsor, a short time before I became minister there. He was a very old man at that time, having been born in 1753. I have heard his son speak of him as having been a good shot.

tributed to the high position of Nonconformity in the county of Suffolk. The number of Scotch ministers who took a leading part in this movement is very noticeable. Not less than nine of this class appear in a list of about thirty; and we further discover that of the rest about one-half owed their Evangelical convictions, in some way or other, to the influence of Calvinistic Methodism.[1] Not more than a third of the whole number belonged to the Independent denomination.

Laymen were actively engaged from the beginning, and the names of a few are conspicuous. Sir Egerton Leigh presided at one of the preparatory meetings. John Wilson, one of George Whitefield's converts—for thirty years manager of the Tabernacle, Moorfields, uncle to the Bishop of Calcutta, and the confidential friend of Matthew Wilks—was a much more efficient helper. His Calvinism is prominently noticed in the funeral sermon preached for him by Matthew Wilks, who remarked, in relation to his domestic life—and it was characteristic of most wealthy London merchants of the Methodist type—"He had his abode large and commodious for his family, and large enough for his Christian friends; but not for worldly company."[2] William Shrubsole, son of the well known

---

[1] I trace such influence in the lives of Rowland Hill, Matthew Wilks, George Burder, Edward Parsons, William Roby, the two Townsends, and the two clergymen, Haweis and Eyre.

[2] Morison, p. 566.

mast-maker at Sheerness, hereafter described,[1] acted as one of the first Secretaries of the Society; and it may be mentioned as indicative of the kind of men who took part in its early management, that at first he communed at Blackfriars Church, where an Evangelical clergyman officiated, and did. not identify himself with Dissent till long afterwards, when he became a regular attendant and communicant at Hoxton Academy Chapel. The first Treasurer was Joseph Hardcastle, the friend of Zachary Macaulay, Thomas Clarkson, and Granville Sharp,—a well-known city merchant, a man of considerable ability, not only fitted to preside at meetings, but ready with his pen in sketching reports and appeals; and, at the same time, possessed of a calm temperament, which led him to say, when charged with finesse, "On entering the Missionary Society, I made this resolution, in the strength of the Lord, never to be offended." He had a counting-house near London Bridge, a quaint building, long since swept away, called "Old Swan Stairs," and there the early Committees were wont to be held. The Religious Tract Society, the Hibernian Society, and the British and Foreign Bible Society also found a nursery during their infant years within the same walls, throwing round the spot a charm which lingered in the memory of many who talked about such things in later days. Mr. Hardcastle occupied a house at

---

[1] See p. 387 of this volume.

Hatcham, a pleasant retreat from the bustle of the metropolis; and there were wont to gather round his table many of the Evangelicals of that day. "I am not sure," said one of the number, "that the missionary flame, which now burns so bright and strong among the Evangelical clergy, if it had not its first spark from the circle at Hatcham House, was not fanned and strengthened there."[1]

An expedition to the South Seas formed the first undertaking of the Society; and for the purpose the ship *Duff*—a famous name in the Society's annals—having been purchased and fitted up, was placed under the command of Captain James Wilson, who had offered to go, without fee or reward, wherever the Directors chose to send him. He was present at the battle of Bunker's Hill, in the great American war, and his early history teems with romantic adventures; on his return, we find him brought into fellowship with the Congregational Church at Portsea, under the pastoral care of the excellent John Griffin, who first convinced him of the truth of Christianity, and then led him to feel its power. The *Duff* set sail in August, 1796, and the history of the voyage is marked by striking adventures, which, when they came to the knowledge of the friends of the Society in England, must have produced an immense degree of excitement. A hurricane, blowing for four days off the Cape of Good Hope,

---

[1] Morison, p. 77.

imperilled the safety of the vessel, but when it reached Tahiti—one of the Georgian or Society Islands, discovered by Captain Cook—the natives rowed out in seventy-four canoes to welcome the visitors with a frantic joy. There had been much talk in England about Otaheite, as the island was called by its great discoverer; enchanting tales had been told of the simplicity of the natives, and now the friends of missions were delighted beyond measure to learn how the king had presented the missionaries with a large house; how they were assailing the idolatries and vices of the inhabitants; how they were building forges, and working at the anvil, while the natives looked upon the bellows as a sort of supernatural contrivance, and fled with alarm when the hot iron hissed in the water; how his majesty embraced the blacksmith; and how, better than all, the people were listening with interest to their new instructors and were beginning to embrace the truths of Christianity. The *Duff* came back. Hopes ran high amongst the Fathers and Founders. Meetings of congratulation and thanksgiving were held in London chapels.

Dr. Haweis preached, and gave "a glowing picture of God's goodness to the Society in the safety of the ship, the speed of the voyage, the health of the missionaries, and their cordial reception and kindly treatment by the natives. Such was the prevailing enthusiasm, that the Society resolved, on the following day, upon a second and similar voyage to the South Seas, with the view of reinforcing their staff, encouraging the missionaries in their labours, and more thoroughly exploring the country. The feeling was not confined to the Society but pervaded Britain. Periodicals were enriched with the intelligence, platforms echoed the gladdening notes, and the pulpit poured forth its best eloquence upon the result of England's great missionary enterprise."[1]

In February, 1799, the *Duff* was despatched again. Now came trouble. The ship was captured off Cape Trio by a French privateer. The missionaries were separated from their families and transported to Monte Video, and though the rigour of their captivity was relaxed, and the wives and children were treated with consideration and delicacy, the separation was most distressing, the seizure of the vessel was a great calamity, and the event altogether grievously impeded their missionary efforts. To add to these troubles, intelligence reached this country that the natives were pilfering the missionaries and persevering in their accustomed vices, whilst, at the same time, they were entertaining unreasonable expectations of the temporal benefits to accrue from the efforts of their new benefactors. A stormy passage in the ship *Nautilus* in 1798, with certain adverse adventures of the missionaries on board, contributed to check, but not destroy the hopes of the friends at home. In the year 1800, there came the good news

---

[1] Aikman's "Cyclopedia of Christian Missions," p. 49.

that the first missionary chapel had been erected in Tahiti, the chiefs having furnished materials, and the king having sanctioned the proceeding; but within two years there arrived tidings of a sad reverse, a native war broke out, and the structure was demolished, that it might not fall into the hands of the enemy. Again it was joyfully reported that the missionaries were making a tour of the island, and preaching with acceptance and interest, though not without some opposition; next it appeared that the Christian assemblies were disturbed by heathen boys, who brought amongst their elders cocks and dogs, and made them fight at the time of worship. Such incidents, related in England, kept that part of the religious world which was most interested in the enterprise in a state of constant but variable excitement; yet with steadiness of purpose, as well as with alternations of feeling, the design was carried forward, so that results have been achieved in the South Seas during the present century equal to the most glowing expectations of the original promoters of the mission.

The Friendly and the Marquesas groups were, before the year 1800, added to these scenes of hallowed toil: and at the same era, new ground was broken up in the wilds of Africa, and Dr. Vanderkemp, with three companions, commenced the conversion and civilization of the bushmen of Kaffraria. Vanderkemp was pioneer in the path so successfully pursued by the later agents of the same Society,

Moffat and Livingstone, and the civilizing career alike of the brethren in the South Seas and in Africa gave an interest to their history in the estimation of numbers, who lived quite outside the religious circles of Church or Dissent. Novelty, romance, and amusement lent charms to the story of Christian enterprise, as Englishmen were told how savages were taught to weave and build, to forge and hammer, to read and write. Useful arts were imported from Birmingham, from Sheffield, and from Bradford to the latitude and longitude of the Cape. Articles manufactured by our artisans threw the natives into rapture; they shouted with delight at the sound of a cuckoo clock; and in their restless curiosity pulled it to pieces to discover the secret of its wonderful voice: all this, when related to our countrymen, especially the young, kindled an unprecedented enthusiasm in these missionary efforts. The men who established the London Missionary Society were remarkable for their childlike piety and strong faith. They did not participate in the inquisitive spirit of the age, and they viewed with extreme jealousy the freedom of thought advocated by many of the old Presbyterians, and by some clergymen in the Church of England. They had not attained to the breadth of view, the variety of culture, and the tolerant consideration of diverse theological opinions, reached by their successors; but they exceeded most men in an Abrahamic faith in God, a firm trust in the Eternal One, a penetrating conviction that the Gospel is the only cure for sin, the supreme solace for sorrow, and the exclusive ground of hope in the prospect of death. They seem to have been scarcely, if at all, troubled by such doubts and difficulties as beset us in these days of inquisitiveness and controversy. They lived "on the sides of eternity." Not in poetry, but in truth, heaven was to them a home; and to die was only to pass through a divinely opened door from one room to another.[1] And it should not be overlooked that in the sphere of labour which they selected they went far beyond what had ever before been attempted by English missions. The Society for the Propagation of the Gospel had confined itself to British dominions, and to countries which had recently been part of the empire, the Methodists were at work in the same field, the Baptists had chosen our Indian dependency as the sphere of their operations; but this new movement was planned in a spirit of the boldest religious adventure, in harmony with the original law of Christianity, "Go into all the world"; and the *Duff* and the *Nautilus* ploughed far-off seas to visit savage islands in the darkest depths of pagan ignorance and superstition.

---

[1] In words much the same as those I have here used these men were described to me by those who had known them well, or had lived much among their immediate descendants. Some allowance is to be made, of course, for the idealizing effect of distance and tradition, but no doubt the description is substantially correct.

The enterprise, however, did not at first win sympathy from all Evangelical Dissenters. Some felt doctrinal difficulties arising from perverted views of the subjects of election. Others thought miracles were needful to secure success in preaching the Gospel to the heathen; and some unfavourably regarded the comprehensiveness of the scheme.[1] The former objections could be easily disposed of, but no doubt difficulties might be discerned looming ahead, if Churchmen in any large numbers continued to co-operate when wide fields of labour were at command, and the directors had not only to provide for preaching the Gospel, but also for gathering converts into fellowship. The principle laid down in

---

[1] In illustration of this point I cannot do better than quote a passage from the Autobiography of my friend, the Rev. William Walford. Speaking of the Rev. Thomas Towle, pastor of an Independent Church in Aldermanbury Postern, he says (p. 108) :—" His religious opinions, which he held with the firmest tenacity, were highly orthodox, strictly Calvinistic and Athanasian ; so that he would admit none to his communion whom he judged to be defective in such points. He was a determined Nonconformist, and immovable in his regard to the strict discipline of regular Dissent, and in the highest degree averse to what he termed Methodistical irregularities. During the time of my intercourse with him, the London Missionary Society was formed, the constitution of which he in the highest degree disapproved, chiefly on the account of the union in it between Churchmen, Dissenters and Methodists, as he styled the followers of Lady Huntingdon and Mr. Whitefield. He held also an opinion that it would prove a failure for want of miraculous powers, which he conceived to be indispensable for the conversion of heathens."

the original plan, and still retained in the published constitution, was intended to give an unsectarian character to the Society. It runs as follows: "That it should be entirely left with those whom God might call into the fellowship of His Son among them, to assume for themselves such form of government, as to them shall appear most agreeable to the Word of God." But the practice would have been found less simple than the theory, had Episcopalians with other denominations continued to exercise a large amount of influence in the proceedings. Union in conducting a magazine, and union for other objects hereafter to be noticed, presented no formidable obstacles; but union in establishing churches would before long have proved a strain too hard to bear. The problem can scarcely be said to have been ever practically worked out; for the Church Missionary Society—to be noticed presently—attracted to itself such Churchmen as were not satisfied with the Propagation Society, and had felt inclined to join in the institution just described. No very large number of such persons ever belonged to it, and when, in no unfriendly spirit, some withdrew to support a society established within their own Church, the management of the earlier society, as a matter of course, fell almost entirely into the hands of Nonconformists; as Independents rallied round it by degrees in large numbers, and the relative proportion of Presbyterians diminished, the Congregational form of Church polity came to be practically followed in mission stations, although the comprehensive principle continued, in theory, to be professed.

Notwithstanding the circumstance that Scotland lies beyond the scope of this volume, it is pertinent here to add, that on the same principle as that of the London Missionary Society, another was founded in Edinburgh, in the year 1796. The Glasgow Missionary Society originated the same year and stood on the same basis. They agreed not to interfere with each other's operations, or to clash with the proceedings of their neighbours in the English metropolis. Indeed, though the effort proved unsuccessful, the Scotch attempted to co-operate with their English brethren in a mission to Sierra Leone. After this failure the North pursued its own course, but remained faithful to its original understanding with the South.

If I may be permitted for a moment to glance across the Atlantic, I would call attention to the important fact that from the stimulus afforded in London there arose missionary efforts in New England. A General Association was formed in Connecticut to "Christianize the heathen in North America, and to support and promote Christian knowledge in the new settlements of the United States." A minister, David Bacon, was forthwith despatched to the tribes on the shores of the broad Erie Lake, and a report of the progress made was sent to the

Evangelical clergyman at Hackney, John Eyre, informing him of the harmony and affection which reigned among the Trustees of the Society, and that they had "one heart to promote their benevolent design." "I believe," says the famous Dr. Hopkins of Newport, in a letter to Andrew Fuller, dated October, 1799, that "all the missionary societies lately formed in America owe their rise to those formed in England and their extraordinary exertions. There are five of these societies now in New York, Connecticut, and Massachusetts States."[1]

Rural preaching is another object which at the same period members of different churches united to promote. The Society they formed bore the name of the *Village Itinerancy.* A few wealthy persons undertook the direction of the work, and contributed towards it in a princely manner, one of them pledging himself to the amount of £500 a year. The plan included the employment of qualified men in supplying destitute neighbourhoods with religious instruction, and the education of young men in such elements of learning, including the Greek of the New Testament, as would fit them for preaching to rustic congregations. Hence an academy of this unpretending description was established at Hackney, to which Mr. Eyre gave his sanction and aid, having the

---

[1] Waddington's "Congregational History," 1700–1800, pp. 708–11.

satisfaction of uniting in the appointment of a suitable president.[1]

In those days many more villages were destitute of spiritual instruction and care than at the present period. The parochial system, of course, was in full existence, but in numerous cases the administration of it, from the inconsistencies of clerical life, a want of zeal, and an utter neglect of spiritual or benevolent oversight, failed to produce any large beneficial effects. Nor, except by the Wesleyan Methodists and by a few other Nonconformist ministers and laymen, was much accomplished outside the Establishment for the welfare of the rural population. Wales, in this respect, afforded a remarkable contrast; for, through the labours of Howel Harris of Trevecca, who preached in the open air, assisted by ten clergymen and fifty lay preachers, three hundred churches and religious societies were formed in the southern part of the principality. Charles of Bala also threw his energies into home missionary work, and carried the religious excitement which had been kindled from south to north, penetrating by its power not only the neighbourhood in which he lived, but other contiguous districts.[2] Such an agency as that of the Village Itinerancy for England, therefore appeared of

---

[1] The Rev. George Collison, an Independent minister.

[2] " Cyclopedia of Christian Missions," p. 194. See also Rees' " History of Nonconformity in Wales," chap. v.

great practical importance in the estimation of Evangelical Churchmen and orthodox Dissenters. The latter were roused to activity, much to the vexation of persons opposed to irregular proceedings, and who thought that the entire instruction of the people should be left in the hands of the parochial clergy. Bishop Horsley attacked all itinerant efforts, and was regarded as the instigator of legislative enactments for their repression; in consequence of which Mr. Eyre, in the *Evangelical Magazine*,[1] came forward as a defender of village preaching on the plan adopted by the Hackney Institute. The right reverend prelate had classed all unparochial agencies with Jacobin and infidel proceedings, in reply to which the Homerton incumbent affirmed that they were advancing State interests, " by turning the attention of the people from political debates, to subjects of higher importance and of everlasting interest." In all probability, Mr. Eyre and some of his co-operators were as disinclined to encourage political inquiry among the lower class as any bishops on the bench could be. Robert Hall, as a representative, not only of Baptists but of Nonconformists generally, took up his pen against the redoubtable assailant, and vindicated the liberty of prophesying, in his own eloquent style, tearing into shreds the webs of intolerance. In answer to the allegation that efforts of the kind

---

[1] For March and April, 1801.

condemned were inimical to the Establishment, he remarked, that the promotion of piety was its professed object, and to suppress the efforts of good men for the attainment of the same result was to counteract the very purpose for which the Establishment was avowedly framed. He regarded the Establishment as too powerful to be threatened by a few village itinerants, and pointed out the true peril—"secularity, and dissipation, which may first greatly impair its influence, and finally endanger its existence." Where religion declined, it was to be imputed to the neglect of the clergy.[1]

The Religious Tract Society is a further example of united action. The Society in connection with the Church of England for Promoting Christian Knowledge had for a century issued books and pamphlets upon the truths of Christianity, and in 1750 a society embracing different denominations had been instituted for promoting religious knowledge among the poor. Individual efforts in the same direction may be traced in the lives of several persons. Hannah More, for the space of three years, at the commencement of the French Revolution, published *Cheap Repository Tracts*, three a month, most of them written by herself, and committees were formed to secure their circulation.[2] John Wesley included within the

---

[1] Fragment on Village Preaching. Hall's Works, vol. iii. pp. 346–356.

[2] " Life of Mrs. More," vol. iii. p. 61.

plans which he vigorously carried out, the preparation and circulation of tracts. A lady at Clapham, named Wilkinson, about 1792, enlisted in the same kind of service, and employed the press of "The Philanthropic Society" to such an extent as to provide nearly half a million of small religious publications. Simeon of Cambridge, and an active Independent minister at Kingsland, John Campbell, made themselves useful in a similar way. George Burder of Coventry originated the New Society in 1799, after having printed and circulated tracts on his own account in several counties besides Lancashire and Warwickshire, in which he successively resided. On a visit to London, the year just mentioned, when attending the London Missionary Meeting in May, he secured the co-operation of Rowland Hill and other ministers in the formation of a permanent society for publishing religious books. On the very morning after his first proposal, he held a meeting in St. Paul's Coffee House, St. Paul's Churchyard,[1] where of old Protestant books and Scripture versions had been cast into the flames; and a committee was appointed to draw up rules for the projected undertaking. The Religious Tract Society sprung up in 1799, under the shadow of the London Missionary Society: and as the *Evangelical Magazine* had recommended the earlier, so also it

---

[1] "Jones' "Jubilee Memorial of the Tract Society," p. 14.

advocated the later institution.[1] In the first publication issued [2] the general character of its successors is foreshadowed, as not containing the shibboleth of a sect, nor as aiming to recommend one denomination more than another. When some objection was taken by Hannah More to a tract on the subject of Regeneration, Joseph Hughes wrote a letter, stating " that the sentiments of the committee were neither novel, nor confined to vulgar theologians, which might be evinced by an appeal, not only to a Watts and a Doddridge, but to a Beveridge, a Hopkins, an Ussher, and a Hall." [3] At the same time it could not be concealed, indeed the founders of the Society did not wish to conceal it, that their instructions and appeals proceeded not on the line of Anglo-Catholic, but on that of Evangelical Theology.

Crossing the threshold of a new century, we meet in 1802 with a movement which issued in the estab-

---

[1] An appeal on its behalf is found in the July number, 1799, p. 307.

[2] This tract was composed by Dr. Bogue, and has frequently been called the Society's "Act of Parliament." "Vivian's Dialogues" and Dr. Watts on the End of Time were printed " as commencing tracts." In the course of the first year thirty-four tracts were issued, in the second year twenty-seven, in the third only one. The twelve persons who formed the committee and officers at the Society's formation were all living in 1824 when the twenty-fifth anniversary was held (Jones' "Jubilee Memorial," pp. 18, 23–117). Legh Richmond was an early friend, and in 1813 became a secretary of the Society.

[3] Quoted in Jones' "Jubilee Memorial," p. 37.

lishment of the British and Foreign Bible Society. The circulation of the Scriptures had been promoted by the Christian Knowledge and Propagation Societies. In the seventeenth century Lord Wharton's Trust, and in the eighteenth century the Coward Trust, had given copies of the English Bible to poor people; and in 1779, there arose an effort which has not secured the notice it deserves. An unknown Quaker, named John Davis, wrote to another Quaker, George Cussons, proposing to distribute small pocket Bibles among the privates of the regular and militia troops. The well-known John Thornton encouraged the idea, and in the same year it took shape as a "Bible Society," since known as the " Naval and Military Bible Society." At the time of the Gordon Riots, in 1780, the soldiers encamped in Hyde Park were furnished with Bibles, and soon afterwards the Society was found steadily at work. John Newton, Rowland Hill, Bishop Horne, and William Wilberforce, promoted its objects, and, in later days, the Duke of Wellington appeared as president. This organization provided for a particular class; the world at large needed the same kind of effort on a corresponding scale. The story of Charles of Bala and the little Welsh girl, who "could not get to read the Bible"; and of his interview with Joseph Hughes, when he proposed a Bible Society for Wales, and was met with the suggestion: "Why not for the empire and the world?" is now a legend current throughout Christendom, and has given a key-note to countless speeches on Bible platforms. It was at a committee meeting of the Tract Society that the interview between Charles and Hughes occurred; and in its early minute book are recorded the steps which led to the inauguration of its noble associate in the enterprise of philanthropy. Several of the most prominent names noticed in the last few pages of this history appear in the preparatory proceedings, together with those of Wilberforce and Dr. Steinkopff —one of the first secretaries. Owen, an honoured Evangelical clergyman of that day, rejoiced to find himself "surrounded by a multitude of Christians, whose doctrinal and ritual differences had for ages kept them asunder, and who had been taught to regard each other with a sort of pious estrangement, or rather of consecrated hostility." And describing the early circumstances of the Society, he says: "The scene was new; nothing analogous to it had perhaps been exhibited before the public since Christians had begun to organize amongst each other the strife of separation, and to carry into their own camp that war which they ought to have waged in concert against the common enemy."[1]

---

[1] Owen's "History of the Bible Society," vol. i. p. 44.

The connection between the Tract Society and the Bible Society is often overlooked. It is interesting to read the following entries in the minute book of the former Society:—

"Tuesday, December 21, 1802.—The secretary read a paper

This narrative of the religious organizations which sprung up at the close of the last century or the beginning of the present would not be complete without some notice of the origin of the Church Missionary Society. The founders were all Evangelical clergyman, and amongst them Wilberforce took a prominent part. He was anxious to promote missionary operations, beyond the sphere occupied by the Propagation Society, and on different religious principles from those which it maintained. He

---

on the importance of forming a Society for the distribution of Bibles in various languages.

"Resolved—That a special meeting be holden next Tuesday, at 8 o'clock, as preparatory to a general meeting to promote that end."

The committee met, and this minute is recorded :—

"The object of the intended Society was maturely considered and determined unanimously to be : to promote the circulation of the Holy Scriptures in foreign countries, and in those parts of the British dominions for which adequate provision is not yet made : it being understood that no English translation of the Scriptures will be gratuitously circulated by the Society in Great Britain."

"January, 1804.—A special meeting was held for the purpose of promoting the Bible Society, when it was resolved that the title of the Society should be 'The British and Foreign Bible Society,' agreeably to the suggestion of the secretary, and that he be requested to prepare a circular letter on the subject."

It is afterwards stated that there was "reason to conclude that several respectable members of the Society called Quakers would attend the public meeting, and exert themselves on behalf of the excellent object."

These entries, with several others, are printed in Jones' "Jubilee Memorial," pp. 48-51.

deplored the neglect of the East India Company in reference to the natives under their control, and moved a resolution in the House of Commons, that it was a bounden duty, by all just and prudent means, to promote the religious improvement of the native Indians; but the Company, alarmed at his proposal, succeeded in striking this clause out of the India Bill of 1793.[1] This left no course open but to establish a voluntary society for spreading Christianity in the East, and such a society found an eloquent advocate in the illustrious philanthropist just named. Other circumstances at the time favoured the project. A sum of £4000 had been left by a gentleman of the name of Jane, to be expended "for the best advantage of the interests of religion." A few Evangelical clergyman in the country met and decided that the bequest could not be better applied than to the sending out of missionaries. The Eclectic Society of London, comprehending ministers of the Evangelical type with a sprinkling of Dissenters, discussed the question but with a different result. Only two or three agreed with Mr. Simeon in his view, which accorded with that of the country brethren. But a renewed discussion in 1799 led to a more favourable opinion, and by an interesting coincidence the Castle and Falcon in Aldersgate Street, which

---

[1] "Life of Wilberforce," by his Sons, vol. ii. p. 25 and Appendix.

had been the cradle of the London Missionary Society, witnessed the birth of its younger sister. Sixteen clergymen and nine laymen pledged themselves to support the new enterprise.[1] Without manifesting any antagonism to the Societies for Promoting Christian Knowledge and for the Propagation of the Gospel, it fixed itself upon a different foundation; and without recognising any control on the part of the Episcopal rulers of the Church, it simply made an annual contribution the ground of membership, and vested the power of administration in the hands of seven governors and a treasurer, chosen by the members, together with a committee of twenty-five elected in the same way. It was subject at first to no Episcopal authority. It was "rather a Society *within* the Church of England than a Society *of* the Church of England."[2] Its earliest agents were not espiscopally ordained, they were Lutherans or members of some other Reformed Church on the Continent. Its practice of late years has been quite different. Its missionaries are now all of the Episcopalian order. Designed originally for the East and for Africa, it has long since enlarged the field of its operations, carrying with it the sympathies and the support of a much larger number of Churchmen than at first espoused its interests. As intimated already,

---

[1] "Life of Simeon," by Carus, pp. 107, 167.
[2] Perry's "History of the Church of England," vol. iii. p. 489.

it affected the London Missionary Society to some extent, it drew off some of the original supporters of that institution, but at the commencement, as afterwards, it rallied round it Evangelical clergymen and laymen who never would have identified themselves with a thoroughly undenominational organization, or one largely conducted by Dissenting bodies.

Changes in methods of activity, described in the present chapter, were far more important and significant than is generally supposed. They took a large amount of religious work out of the hands of the Church, properly so called, whether in its established or its voluntary form, and entrusted that work to the care of societies each responsible *alone* to its own constituency. We see that not only did a number of Dissenters unite in some of these enterprises, but Churchmen did the same; and when they withdrew from early comprehensive institutes, to conduct others confined to their own particular views, they still proceeded upon the principle of independent action. They did not hold themselves responsible to the dignitaries of their own Church, except as those dignitaries became connected with them in associations voluntarily created and sustained. As corporate bodies they stood outside the Establishment, though as individuals the members remained within its enclosure. So likewise Nonconformists simply as Christians, not as Church members, constructed methods of missionary and benevolent procedure entirely free from any control exercised by the bodies to which they respectively belonged—so far at least as any real ecclesiastical authority could be concerned. Perhaps an exception occurs in the case of certain missionary proceedings amongst Wesleyan Methodists and Presbyterians; with regard to other sections of Nonconformity the remark is undoubtedly true. There has thus come into existence a new mode of spiritual influence unanticipated by the Church of former days, whether Mediæval or Reformed, whether Anglican or Puritan, whether Presbyterian or Independent. Born in the eighteenth, it has marvellously grown in the nineteenth century. It is displaying now a force which, immense as it is, promises to be still more immense, outstripping in activity anything purely ecclesiastical. In Protestant Christendom the power of religion is becoming greater and greater, the power of the Church is becoming less and less.

CHAPTER XXVIII.

1700–1800.

A GENERAL review of the state of religion at the end of the last century, compared with what it was at the beginning, may appropriately conclude the history in these volumes.

A decided change occurred before the end in many Established and Nonconformist pulpits : a wave broke on shores of silence ; a fountain opened amidst the hills, watering dry and thirsty fields. The old Hebrew cry rose from the lips of not a few, " Watchman, what of the night ? " The echo was caught up and repeated in churches, chapels, and barns ; it was a reaction against cold formality, indolence, and apathy; also against the neglect of doctrines dear to Reformers and Puritans. Sermons had been argumentative, and the logic wrought in them, if not quite frozen, was very dry. Scarcely any attention was paid to popular composition. Where style received much attention, it took a polished surface adapted to ears polite. A hard manner of treatment prevailed amongst even the thoughtful and earnest class of preachers. Bishop Horne amongst Churchmen, William Jay amongst Dissenters, wrought a decided and extensive change. Their sermons mark a transition period between the old and new in homiletic literature. We find in them less of argument and more of illustration; quiet sober fancy rather than great imaginative vigour takes the place of elaborate reasoning. Style became more didactic than logical, and piety insinuated itself through strains of affectionate statement and persuasive appeal. This method, whether from conscious imitation or from a spirit floating in the air, came to be widely adopted by preachers just before the commencement of the present century. Some, indeed, rose far above their brethren in eloquence and power. Horsley the Churchman, and Hall the Nonconformist, were men of erudition and eloquence, formed by nature to excel in any kind of oratory they might choose to adopt. Newton, Scott, Romaine, and others, made themselves felt more through the richness of their Scripture knowledge, the homely force of their instruction, the common sense of their appeals, and their large acquaintance with human nature, than by any speciality of style or superiority of rhetoric. On the whole, volumes of discourses published at the end of the century afford a striking contrast to those issued at the beginning.

Extra services, and particularly public meetings, mark a further change in the popular religion of the day. Before the rise of Methodism, the Common Prayer Book and the written sermon were the only forms of religious utterance within the pale of an English parish; and the meeting-house witnessed little or nothing beyond formal Sunday discourses, the singing of Watts' and Doddridge's hymns, and the offering of extempore prayer. But Methodism carried preaching out of consecrated buildings into private houses, public halls, city streets, and village greens. It gave a new impetus to prayer meetings on week-days; it led to gatherings for religious conversation. Classes and love feasts were not adopted by the old Dissent any more than by the orthodox Church; but a tendency to social spritual engagements, beyond those of the stereotyped order, was, doubtless, one of the effects produced by the Methodistic revival. Assemblies among religious people, such as we understand by the term public meetings, seem to have originated in the last decade of the century. Chairmen, secretaries, strings of resolutions, and a succession of speakers, come before us in connection with the birth of the London Missionary Society.

In September, 1795, Sir Egerton Leigh presided in the large room of the Castle and Falcon, when the ministers and laymen present received and considered a plan for the constitution of the new Institute; and the next day people crowded within the doors of Spa Fields Chapel in such numbers, that multitudes remained outside, unable to gain admission. Sobs and tears accompanied the singing: and the place of worship close to which the Countess of Huntingdon, its foundress, had died four years before—not dreaming of such a new outburst of religious energy—became a scene of unprecedented excitement. A sermon, however, had been deemed essential to the solemnity of the occasion, and it was not until that had been delivered, that a meeting was held, and the plan of the Society propounded to the congregation. For some time meetings were modest affairs, supplementary to accustomed forms of worship. Movers and seconders of resolutions slowly took their places. The chair was kept in awe by the reading desk, and timidly the platform crept out under the shadow of the pulpit. Meetings were counted an innovation, and some old worthies looked upon them askance. Speeches were held in small esteem, and were put far below the level of sermons. Some of the brotherhood, powerful in the pulpit, would never make their appearance on a platform; but by degrees the new instrumentality attained reputation and power. "The fathers and founders" did what Watts and Doddridge never dreamed of doing; and the former, in their turn, little thought of the Exeter Hall of the present century. The expenditure of an enormous amount of time and trouble upon committee business is of later origin.

Sunday Schools, founded by Raikes, took a new form before his death. Payments were at first made to persons employed in the instruction of the children. From 1786 to 1800, the Sunday School Society paid upwards of £4000 for that purpose, but unpaid labourers took a share in the good work before the death of their great leader and example in 1811; and the monitorial system had come into existence before 1794. In that year Raikes says to a friend:—

"In answer to your queries, I shall, as concisely as possible, state—that I endeavour to assemble the children as early as is consistent with their perfect cleanliness—an indispensable rule; the hour prescribed in our rules is eight o'clock, but it is usually half after eight before our flock is collected. Twenty is the number allotted to each teacher; the sexes kept separate. *The twenty are divided into four classes. The children who show any superiority in attainments are placed as leaders of the several classes, and are employed in teaching the others their letters*, or in hearing them read in a low whisper, which may be done without interrupting the master or mistress in their business, and will keep the attention of the children engaged, that they do not play or make a noise." He adds, "Their attending the service of the Church once a day has to me seemed sufficient; for their time may be spent more profitably, perhaps, in receiving instruction, than in being present at a long discourse, which their minds are not yet able to comprehend; but people may think differently on this point. Within this month the minister of my parish has, at last, condescended to give me assistance in this laborious work, which I have now carried on six years with little or no support. He chooses that the children should come to church both morning and afternoon; I brought them to the church only in the afternoon."[1]

---

[1] "Gloucestershire Tracts," Robert Raikes, p. 14.

These institutions, now so popular, had then in some cases to encounter much opposition; and when the Nonconformists at Lancaster, five or six years after Raikes began his labours, imitated his example, the walls of the town were placarded with bills bidding the inhabitants beware, "lest the cunning people at High Street should kidnap their children."[1] Sunday Schools, at first, sustained no close relationship to particular congregations. They were conducted in common by persons connected with different churches and chapels, on the new principle of extra parochial and extra ecclesiastical activity. The instruction given included the elements of reading, writing, and even arithmetic; Bible instruction for awhile was much neglected. Religious knowledge was chiefly conveyed through catechisms; little room was allowed for the exercise of free religious conversation with the pupils, and the warm play of spiritual affections. Distinct schoolrooms rarely existed at first, children were taught in the pews or in the aisles, and not until after several years of this century had elapsed did the system take an elaborately organized form. Sunday Schools, as they are met with in the north of England, are creations of a comparatively recent date. But the foundations were laid nearly a hundred years ago; and Raikes opened an era in the religious efforts of England

---

[1] "Memoirs of W. Alexander," by his Son, p. 3.

which has been followed on a still larger scale, and, it may be said, in a still more brilliant style, on the other side the Atlantic. His work marks a notable point of progress in the middle of the reign of George III.; and as early as 1784, we catch an echo of joyful achievement in the *Gentleman's Magazine*. "The schools lately established at Leeds in Yorkshire, for the instruction of the children of industrious parents who keep them employed all the week, have been found to answer all the good purposes intended by those who formed the plan. There are, it is said, nearly 1,800 already admitted, and when the plan is completed there will be more than 2,000." [1]

Theological literature gave signs of progress at the close of the period which we have passed in review. As already noticed, no such burning and shining lights appeared in the ecclesiastical heavens, at the close, as in the middle of the century; yet theology, as a science, made some advance. The controversial work of Bishop Tomline threw no new light upon old Calvinistic questions; but Scott, his antagonist, grappled with them in a way superior to many of his predecessors, and evinced a common-sense mastery of the difficult subject, in connection with a strong and masculine apprehension of Evangelical principles. Bishop Marsh, as a critic, opened up a new field of investigation, through his acquaintance with German

---

[1] *Gentleman's Magazine*, vol. iv. p. 377.

literature, and inquired into the origin and relation of the Four Gospels, also into the classification of Scripture MSS., after a manner somewhat new amongst English divines; and Dr. Hey at Cambridge, in his lectures on Systematic Divinity, on the whole surpassed his predecessors in acuteness, breadth, and impartiality. It is refreshing to turn from the dry and prolix dissertations of Ridgely, and even from the mathematical formularies of Christian knowledge in Doddridge, to the trenchant handling of dogmas, and the incisive style of expression adopted by the able Norrisean professor. In extensive reading, and in profound reflectiveness, he also went beyond Beveridge and Burnet, the two chief luminaries of the Church shining across the threshold of the last century. The Church Evangelicals, with the exception of Scott, were experimental and practical, rather than critical, systematic, or speculative. They simply sought to exhibit Divine truth so as to touch the consciences of their readers, and awaken within them religious affections; and they accomplished their object after a manner which bears favourable comparison with authors in a like department three generations before.

Robert Hall was an eloquent writer, and by the brilliant flow of his compositions made, as stated before, a deep impression upon the reading public of his day, including distinguished literary circles; but he can scarcely be said to have extended the boundaries of theological thought, or to have penetrated far into the depths of religious inquiry. Two of his Nonconformist contemporaries, as appears from what has been said already,[1] excelled him in this respect. Andrew Fuller and Edward Williams, whatever may be said of the conclusions at which they arrived, must be regarded, if judged fairly, as amongst the most original and vigorous theological thinkers of their day. Fuller, it will be remembered, had little learning, and perhaps the learning of Williams was not varied; they had neither of them the depth of Butler, or the boldness of Warburton, but they investigated the foundations of Evangelical doctrine, and exhibited some of its aspects in a way which had not been previously attempted. Of the two, I should regard Andrew Fuller as the more effective and valuable teacher. Well known to Nonconformist readers, his reputation, I suspect, has not far extended within Church circles; but I know that of late he has obtained attention in literary quarters, where his merits, before unknown, have received the admiration which they deserve.

It is worth while to notice the effect of American theology upon both these writers. Fuller, in a letter to Hopkins, a celebrated transatlantic divine, who has stamped his name upon a school of thinkers amongst his countrymen, remarks:

---

[1] See pages 244 and 296 of this volume.

"I have enjoyed great pleasure in reading many of your metaphysical pieces, and hope those who can throw light on Evangelical subjects in that way will continue to write. But I have observed, that whenever an extraordinary man has been raised up, like President Edwards, who has excelled in some particular doctrines or manner of reasoning, it is usual for his followers and admirers too much to confine their attention to his doctrines or manner of reasoning, as though all excellence was there concentrated. I allow that your present writers do not implicitly follow Edwards as to his sentiments, but that you preserve a spirit of free inquiry; yet, I must say, it appears to me that several of your younger men possess a rage of imitating his metaphysical manner, till some of them become *metaphysic mad*. I am not without some of Mr. Scott's apprehensions, lest by such a spirit the simplicity of the Gospel should be lost, and truth amongst you stand more in the wisdom of man than in the power of God." [1]

Fuller thought for himself, and had a keen eye for defects in the teaching of his day; and he will be regarded as having here hit the right nail on the head. Williams was more receptive, and more disposed to become the disciple of another, adding to *his* instructions comments, criticisms, and conclusions of his own. He could revere a Socrates, but it was after the fashion of a Plato. Williams adopted Edwards's theory of the will, with modifications and expansions quite original; and at the same time showed the

---

[1] Quoted in Waddington's "Congregational History," 1700–1800, p. 701. Where the letter is found does not appear.

influence of an American, and the independent speculativeness of an English divine. Dr. Watts would have found in him a congenial spirit, and would have been delighted to listen to what he would have called his "ingenious" thoughts.

There were other teachers abroad of a very different character from Jonathan Edwards. Kant and Lessing were beginning to be read in England at the latter part of the period under consideration. Lessing frankly acknowledged, "we have pulled down the old wall of separation, and under the pretence of making rational Christians have made most irrational philosophers." Again, speaking of the defenders and opponents of Christianity, he remarked : " It has often seemed to me as if these gentlemen, like death and love in the fable, had exchanged their weapons. The more closely one presses me with the proofs of Christianity, the more I am filled with doubts. The greater the insolent triumphs with which the other would trample it in the dust, the more disposed I feel to sustain it erect, at least in my heart." Yet, with these signs of better things, he could publish the celebrated Wolfenbüttel fragments, pronounced by no narrow minded judge "the boldest assault yet made on the received faith of the Christian world, and particularly on the credibility of the resurrection." [1]

German writers of this school have had an appre-

---

[1] Tayler's "Religious Life of England," p. 309.

ciable effect upon English theology during the present century, but the tide began to set in at an earlier period. The writer just quoted further observes:—

"While the theology and philosophy of England were yet obeying the impulse originally given to them by Locke, the speculative intellect concentrated in the universities of Germany was silently imbibing the spirit of the Jewish pantheist [Spinoza]. Herder, Lessing, Eichhorn, Paulus, Schleiermacher—all names which mark successive steps in the development of German theology, indicate in their writings and opinions the sway exercised over their thoughts by this subtle and meditative thinker. Perhaps to no circumstance can the different direction which theological inquiry has taken in England and in Germany be so immediately ascribed. In the two countries the mixture of a philosophical system with a yet unbroken rigidity of Scripturalism produced different but analogous results. In England the miracle was retained, to invest with a Divine authority the religious and ethical wisdom which the letter of the primitive record was made to yield. In Germany, where miracle was not reconcilable with the prevalent philosophy, while the letter of Scripture was still accepted with reverence, it was so interpreted as to bring miracle within the limits of natural law. In both there was a straining of Scripture language, in both an exegesis was tolerated that would have been considered admissible in no other book; but it was in a different way, and for a different purpose, in the two countries."

The bearing of these remarks upon England relates to the present more than the past century. Spinoza was read by our countrymen, probably a small number, for a hundred years, chiefly that he might be refuted; but few as his followers were for a long time, there could not be wanting even then some who sympathised in his spirit, and were influenced by his lucubrations. The Germans came within the acquaintance of English readers three-quarters of a century or so later, and early exerted a guiding power over inquisitive persons, such as William Taylor, the Norwich Unitarian, and his friends. For what are called rationalistic views of miracles, preparations had been made by Woolston and others; and though repeatedly met and forcibly exposed, they did not disappear, but were reinforced by foreign as well as home influences, to be carried forward to later times. What, however, may be emphatically denominated the infidelity of England, at the time now referred to, was of indigenous rather than exotic growth. Hume and Gibbon, far beyond any Dutch or German writers, promoted disbelief in this country; and among the vulgar Thomas Paine won a large following, the number of his disciples being vastly increased by the identification of his religious with his political opinions, and by the prejudice excited against Christianity, through despotic principles upheld by some of the rulers of the Church.

Between Church and Dissent relations were both friendly and unfriendly. Newton and Scott, we have seen, cultivated intimacy with Nonconformists; some Evangelical clergymen preached in Dissenting pulpits : in the London Missionary Society, the Religious Tract Society, and the British and Foreign Bible Society, they united with probably more warmth and depth of affection than has been seen at any period since. In other provinces of beneficent action a still more comprehensive combination could be found.

"In achievements of practical philanthropy inspired by deep religious enthusiasm," says an author just cited, "the power of the Evangelical body both in and out of the Establishment has been conspicuous. One pleasing feature distinguished the grand movement against the slave trade, as if the Spirit of Christ had converted for once the gall of theology into the milk of human kindness. Its leaders were of all religious persuasions, and yet acted together in perfect harmony and with mutual esteem. The Evangelical Churchman and the Unitarian fought side by side against oppression, on the floor of the House of Commons; and in the intervals of the strife Clarkson and Wilberforce, and Smith, Macaulay, Thornton, and Stephen took righteous counsel together in the communion of private friendship."[1]

At the same time mutual relations might be met with of a far different kind. A Yorkshire clergyman denounced Nonconformists in the bitterest terms, calling them wild beasts and savage brutes. They had been, he said, the greatest opposers of the most religious of the clergy, and to beguile the unwary introduced politics into their prayers, and employed their schism shops to stir up strife and sedition.

---

[1] Tayler's "Religious Life of England," p. 301.

They supported democratic candidates at elections, and circulated democratic publications in book clubs; begot by sedition they fostered an offspring of their own character, and with their superabundant piety were convicted of short weights and stinted measures. To finish the black list, they are called children of the devil.[1] Answers to such attacks were written with dignified forbearance, as well as with just indignation; but, no doubt, there were cases in which Dissenters failed to manifest the wisdom of meekness, and so provoked abusive retaliation.

Beyond ephemeral publications of local interest, very little issued from the press bearing on the main difference between Churchmen and Dissenters. Leading Evangelical Nonconformists were absorbed in the study of other questions. Robinson, of Cambridge, occasionally took up his pen to deal with ecclesiastical politics in his own trenchant style; but the book which to the end of the century took the lead in defending the principles of Nonconformity was "Towgood on Dissent." An able review of ecclesiastical establishments in Europe, by a Dissenting minister at Newcastle, named William Graham, and published in 1792, was, I believe, the first book to break ground in that department of the grand dispute which has

---

[1] These are words used in a tract entitled "A Candid Enquiry into the Democratic Schemes of the Dissenters." This inexcusable publication indicates the political activity of the party assailed.

attained such large dimensions in the present day; but twenty years elapsed before a second edition appeared.

As at the beginning, so at the end of the century, we can lay our hand upon the statistics of Dissent. Dissenters are stated by Dr. Edward Williams to be in comparison with Churchmen about one to eight, whereas a hundred years before they were about one to twenty-two.[1] The comparison, if accurate, shows a large increase. Some congregations are described as stationary, those among the less orthodox as on the decrease, whilst others were on the advance, both as to the size of the old and the creation of the new. Unitarian Dissenters are condemned for being political; the orthodox are spoken of with favour for confining "themselves more to religion." Arianism is declared to be almost extinct, having become merged in Socinianism. One out of eight among Dissenters are stated to belong to the unorthodox division, and the writer goes on to say that their struggles for greater enlargement of liberty made them obnoxious to government. "It is remarkable," he says, "that amongst all their complaints of hard treatment noticed in their sermons and publications (which by the way are fondly nursed by the reviews in general) we hear of no extra meetings for prayer among them, nor humiliation before God, seek-

---

[1] "Church of the Restoration," vol. ii. p. 207.

ing relief from Him,—no, not during or after those riots in which they were the principal sufferers."[1] Dr. Williams was pastor of an Independent Church at Birmingham, and by thus plainly referring to his neighbour, Dr. Priestly, he shows that he cherished no sympathy with him in his political sentiments. Evangelical Nonconformists generally were at that period by no means conspicuous in the assertion of national rights.

Nor did some orthodox Congregationalists look with favour upon their Wesleyan brethren. The latter were accused of being enemies. "They go to the greatest lengths," it is said, "in blaspheming our doctrine." The Independent preaching in a barn treated as a troubler one who said "horrid things of Calvinism."[2] The spirit thus manifested was as bad as that condemned.

It remains for me to adduce illustrations of diversities in spiritual life amongst Englishmen of different denominations.

One of the most beautiful instances, in addition to some already cited, occurs in the life of Henry Martyn. Just about the time that Carey commenced his career at Calcutta, Martyn—who had been educated in the grammar school of Truro, his

---

[1] Gilbert's "Memoirs of Williams."
[2] Waddington's "Congregational History." Continuation to 1850, p. 49.

native town, and had entered St. John's College, Cambridge—was known as "the man who had not lost an hour," so assiduous were his habits of industry, an industry which won the highest crown of academic honour. Religious impressions rested on his mind amidst his most eager studies. "A friend," he said, "attempted to persuade me that I ought to attend to reading, not for the praise of men but for the glory of God. This seemed to me strange but reasonable. I resolved therefore to maintain the opinion thenceforth, but never designed, that I remember, that it should affect my conduct." Yet still he read the Bible and "said a prayer or two rather through fear than from any other cause." But light gradually broke on his mind, and spiritual truth by degrees entered his heart. "Seekest thou great things for thyself? seek them not," were words which flashed across his memory as he entered the senate-house to compete for academic distinction. The emptiness of it he learned as soon as it was won. "I obtained my highest wishes, but was surprised to find I had grasped a shadow." Soon we find him asking, "Who that reflects upon the rock from which he was hewn, but must rejoice to give himself entirely and without reserve to God, to be sanctified by His Spirit? The soul that has truly experienced the love of God will not stay meanly inquiring how much he shall do, and thus limit his service, but will be earnestly seeking more and more to know the will of his heavenly

Father, that he may be enabled to do it." He did not lose his early predilections. " Since I have known God in a saving manner, painting, poetry, and music have had charms unknown to me before. I have received what I suppose is a taste for them, for religion has refined my mind, and made it susceptible of impressions from the sublime and beautiful." Country scenes awakened in him the purest joy; every breeze, he said, seemed to breathe love into his heart. He would sit at evening out of the reach of all sounds but the rippling of the water, and the whistling of the curlew. " Several of the poetic images in Virgil, especially those taken from nature, together with the sight of the moon rising over the venerable walls and sending its light through the painted glass, turned away his thoughts from present things, and raised them to God."[1] Charles Simeon remarked one day to the Senior Wrangler, that Carey, who had come to be much talked of, exemplified the good which might be done by a single missionary; and the effect produced by that observation was followed up by the perusal of David Brainerd's memoirs. Martyn determined to go to India, to spend his whole life there in missionary work. " He went forth," says his biographer, " to preach the Gospel to the heathen, and it was his fixed resolution to live and die amongst them. When he left England he left it wholly for

---

[1] Sargent's " Memoir " of Martyn, pp. 19, 24, 65, 80, 94.

Christ's sake, and he left it for ever."[1] As he thought of the voyage before him he could write in his journal: "Had I been going of necessity it would have almost broke my heart, but I go from choice."[2] A more sensitive nature there never was, for during his journey from London to Portsmouth he fainted, and fell into convulsions at the inn where he slept, as he thought of the friends whom he should leave behind, especially one whose life was bound up with his own. This shows the amount of self-sacrifice involved in the devotion of this extraordinary man, at a moment when zeal of this description was only beginning to revive in the English Church. His self-sacrifice has rarely been equalled. He was content to be nothing, to be unseen, to be forgotten. "If I never should see a native converted, God may design by my patience and continuance in the work, to encourage future missionaries." He was willing to lose his life, if only a breach could be made in the strongholds of Asiatic heathendom. He was willing to die on the walls, if he could only cheer on, in the track of victory, succeeding soldiers of the Cross.

I cannot resist the temptation to introduce here the following story. Some years since an English gentleman spent several weeks at Shiraz; while there, he met one day, at dinner with Mohammed Rahem, a Persian of middle age, with a thoughtful, gentle

---

[1] Sargent's "Memoir," p. 113.   [2] Ibid., p. 108.

countenance. The Englishman was full of levity. Mohammed silently reproved him with a look of surprise and sorrow. Our countryman was informed that the Persian was a learned priest, who had ceased to officiate, and who lived in retirement; and at a subsequent interview ascertained from him the particulars of his story. He said a beardless English youth, enfeebled by disease, had some time before come to that city, and dwelt there a year, teaching the religion of Christ. Mohammed treated with contempt the Christian teacher, but the latter persevered with so much love and gentleness as to convert Mohammed's contempt into esteem and affection. He gave him a tract, and entreated him to read it, and the result was the Persian felt the English youth was right. But fear and shame withheld the avowal of that conviction, and the Mohammedan shunned the society of the Christian. "But just before he quitted Shiraz," said the Persian, as he told this story, "I could not refrain from paying him a farewell visit. Our conversation sealed my conversion. He gave me a book: it has ever been my constant companion; the study of it has formed my most delightful occupation; its contents have often consoled me." Upon this, the narrator put into the Englishman's hands a copy of the New Testament in Persian; on one of the blank leaves was written, "'There is joy in heaven over one sinner that repenteth.' *Henry Martyn.*"

Martyn commenced his course at St. John's College

in October, 1797. That year another Cambridge man, Legh Richmond, who had entered Trinity in August, 1789, received deacon's orders in the Church of England. He was a type of the same Evangelical class as the Indian missionary whose early career has just been noticed, but he was designed by Providence for a longer life and a different kind of usefulness. The story of his conversion had best be told in his own words. It occurs in his memoir, in connection with a reference he makes to one of his beloved children,—

Speaking of his son Wilberforce, he remarks: "He was baptized by the name of Wilberforce in consequence of my personal friendship with that individual, whose name has long been, and ever will be, allied to all that is able, amiable, and truly Christian. That gentleman had already accepted the office of sponsor to one of my daughters; but the subsequent birth of this boy afforded me the additional satisfaction of more familiarly associating his name with that of my family. But it was not the tie of ordinary friendship, nor the veneration which in common with multitudes I felt for the name of Wilberforce, which induced me to give that name to my child: there had for many years past subsisted a tie between myself and that much-loved friend of a higher and more sacred character than any other which earth can afford. I feel it to be a debt of gratitude, which I owe to God and to man, to take this affecting opportunity of stating, that to the unsought and unexpected introduction of Mr. Wilberforce's book on 'Practical Christianity' I owe, through God's mercy, the first sacred impression which I ever received as to the spiritual nature of the Gospel system, the vital character of personal religion, the corruption of the human heart, and the way of salvation by Jesus Christ. As a young minister, recently ordained, and just entrusted with the charge of two parishes in the Isle of Wight, I had commenced my labours too much in the spirit of the world, and founded my public instructions on the erroneous notions that prevailed amongst my academical and literary associates. The scriptural principles stated in the 'Practical View' convinced me of my error; led me to the study of the Scriptures with an earnestness to which I had hitherto been a stranger; humbled my heart, and brought me to seek the love and blessing of that Saviour who alone can afford a peace which the world cannot give. Through the study of this book I was induced to examine the writings of the British and foreign reformers. I saw the coincidence of their doctrines with those of the Scriptures, and those which the word of God taught me to be essential to the welfare of myself and my flock. I know too well what has passed within my heart, for now a long period of time, not to feel and confess that to this incident I was indebted originally for those solid views of Christianity on which I rest my hope for time and eternity. May I not then call the honoured author of that book my spiritual father? and if my spiritual father, therefore my best earthly friend?"

Directing our thoughts to another communion we meet with an example of serene piety and unobtrusive usefulness in the life of Cornelius Winter, the disciple of George Whitefield and the tutor of William Jay. He has been already mentioned, in connection with the history of Congregationalism in Wiltshire. From the town of Marlborough, in that county, he removed to Painswick, in Gloucestershire, and by many in both neighbourhoods his name is still pronounced with reverence. Not educated amongst Dissenters, and quite disposed in early life to enter the Church of England but for difficulties thrown in his way,[1] he was led by the discipline of circumstances into the ecclesiastical position he occupied,—though what might be attributed first to accident became afterwards an object of preference. He comes before us amidst the quietude of country life, with no ambition secular or ecclesiastical, destitute of any craving for popularity, content with a modest salary of £50, eked out by his wife's small income, going week by week from the study to the pulpit, and day by day from his books and his students, to the homes of his people and the cottages of neighbouring peasants. Of a meek and gentle spirit, he generally disarmed opposition, though there were persons who, unpropitiated by candour and generosity, resented the good man's fidelity. It is as curious as it is pleasant to find one who entertained strong views of the depravity of human nature declaring, "I am never with this man without being reminded of paradisiacal innocence;" another, whose theology was of the same stamp used to say, "Mr. Winter would make the worst devil of any man in the world;"[2] and a friend, very

---

[1] See p. 269 of this volume.
[2] The two men were Matthew Wilks and Rowland Hill. "Memoirs of Winter," p. 327

remote from adulation and of very discriminating judgment, more than once said, after Winter had been the subject of conversation, " I have long thought he is more like Jesus Christ than any man on earth."[1] This can scarcely be considered too high praise, when the purity, patience, candour, and benevolence of the man are taken into account. Rising above the sectarianism of the age, he, though a Calvinist, cultivated acquaintance with Wesley, and often spent days together with Fletcher, to whom he wrote brotherly letters, afterwards published. The erection of a Methodist chapel in Painswick gave him no offence, but on the contrary elicited catholic sympathy, and in a letter to Lady Huntingdon he remarked :

"All distinctions that now divide the people of God will be lost in heaven. Though we are now distinguished by our peculiarities, we should not forget that we are but as so many tribes in the same Israel and as so many families in the same tribes." Again : "It is not always necessary to take sides, and yet it is almost impossible, often, to be indifferent. When brought into such a dilemma, a tender mind feels perhaps more than the contending parties." And yet again : " I have always considered the Church rather through the medium of Catholicism than as in party detachments ; and am persuaded that if that generosity and real candour which make no inconsiderable part of our religion were mutually cultivated, our joint object would be, more to spread the gospel than to divide its professors into parties."

" Memoirs," p. 327.

"Come and see me," he wrote to a young friend puzzled with the Canticles; "we will talk over the matter, and if we cannot unite in sentiment we will agree to differ; we will not quarrel about Solomon's Song, if you will agree to love a greater than Solomon."[1] "Recollect," he would say, "that it is possible to defend your own fort without storming another's battery. Maintain by scriptural argument your own principles and practices with modest confidence; but rail not, insinuate no reflection on your opponents; name them not, unless with respect." "A Dissenter from conviction, before he had established his seminary he sent one student to Oxford and another to Cambridge. He admired the liturgy, and was attached to instrumental music in the service of God."[2]

In the dockyard at Sheerness, hard by the fort rebuilt after being shattered in Charles the Second's reign by the daring assault of the Dutch in the Medway, there worked, about the middle of the last century, an industrious ship carpenter, bearing the inharmonious name of Shrubsole. Reading a book on "Looking to Jesus," by Ambrose the Puritan, he was led to adopt its evangelical sentiments, and to join himself to a little company of people who worshipped together on Sunday afternoons. Whitefield visited Sheerness, and gave fresh life to this community; and the ship carpenter, at their request, read sermons to them every week. Preachers from the Tabernacle in London sometimes went down to address them, but

---

[1] "Memoirs," p. 341.   [2] Ibid., p. 332.

the zealous artisan persevered in his services, officiating with timidity, and using parts of the Common Prayer-Book. He does not appear to have adopted Nonconformist principles, but only desired more evangelical instruction and more animated worship than he met with at church—a form of religious experience very common in those days. The upper storey of a large brick tenement, capable of accommodating three hundred people, and afterwards known as the Old Meeting House, became a place of worship, and the congregation invited Shrubsole to be their pastor. Embarrassed by his dockyard employment, he shrunk from this new office, lest he should forfeit promotion or fail in his religious duties. But encouraged on all hands, and forbidden by none, he went on in a double capacity, using his tools on week-days, and ascending the pulpit on a Sunday. "I am accounted a phenomenon," he would say, "there never having been, I believe, a preaching mastmaker before. However, I know there has been a preaching Carpenter of the most exalted rank, and this blessed Person I am determined, by the grace of God, to imitate while I live." Government, not offended by these unusual proceedings, appointed him master mastmaker in Woolwich Dockyard. But he soon returned to Sheerness, after which a chapel of considerable dimensions was erected for his use, and there he officiated gratuitously till the time of his death. His popularity attracted the notice of those who had no sympathy with Dissent: first a clergyman, and next a member of the government, urged him to conform, promising ordination and preferment, but he declined their flattering offers, and continued faithful to his humble charge until his death, in 1797. The artificers of the dockyard carried their master to the grave, and he left behind him a cherished memory illustrative of one peculiar phase in the religious life of that period.[1]

Before this good man had done all his work in his majesty's dockyards, there went to live at Lancaster a young Scotchman, who as a carpenter worked in the same shop as did the father of Dr. Whewell, Master of Trinity. He, like his contemporary just noticed, had at first no preference for Independency; and under the instruction of a clergyman—"Mr. Simeon's first convert, or eldest son," as he was called —came to adopt evangelical views. When that clergyman removed, William Alexander, for that was the carpenter's name, enrolled himself as a member of the Independent Church in the town, over which soon afterwards there presided a minister described as "a man of decidedly Calvinistic theology, of somewhat formal but gentlemanly manners, of ready wit and repartee, rich in anecdotes, faithful and affectionate in his friendships, an exemplary Christian, and a good minister of Jesus Christ." Alexander went

---

[1] Timpson's "Church History of Kent," pp. 482-6.

about holding religious conversations with his neighbours, and so acquired reputation as "a rare talker." He would also read and expound a chapter in the New Testament, which, of course, led to his being asked to preach, and he soon began that employment in one of the villages—for a time attending the parish church on Sunday morning, and then preaching in a house on Sunday afternoons. Later on, after toiling at the bench for six days, he would walk on the seventh thirty-two miles, "often in the midst of wind and rain, and in the course of which he preached at never less than three, and frequently at four different places." When attacked as a schismatic, he would defend himself by an appeal to the Thirty-nine Articles and parts of the Homilies, which he had learned by heart. He met with a good deal of persecution, but continuing steadfast, he at length, with the sanction of neighbouring ministers, accepted the call of an Independent Church to become its pastor, To give a glimpse of the religious habits of his class, as well as himself, it may be mentioned that he would on no account tolerate novels. "Even the 'Vicar of Wakefield,'" says his son, "was placed in the *index expurgatorius*, and I remember his scolding me severely for having it in my possession. But, as he himself delighted in history, especially in the history of Scotland, in the times of John Knox and the Covenanters, and of England from the Reformation downwards, especially the ecclesiastical parts, we had free access to such books."[1] He did not believe in spoiling the child by sparing the rod, and if a voluntary in ecclesiastical principle he appears a coercionist in religious education, for when the time came for repeating the famous Scotch formulary of religious knowledge, he would say, "Now go and fetch the Catechism—and the rod." His anxiety about the spiritual welfare of his children was very great, and though strict he was not severe. After all, the rod does not seem to have been much used.

One more illustration of the varieties of religious life at that period presents itself. At Stowmarket, in the county of Suffolk, a young man named William Walford was entering the Congregational ministry, as successor to William Godwin, who for a short time had been pastor there, with no prophecy of be-

---

[1] "Memoirs of the Rev. William Alexander," by his son, John Alexander, p. 76. John Alexander was an early friend of mine, and used to talk of William Whewell as one of his schoolfellows —rather daft, the boys thought; but his subsequent career, John Alexander would say, showed how daft they were to say so. His mother was a shrewd woman, and a good type of Calvinistic Dissent, arguing strenuously for her favourite dogmas. She was also something of a politician. William Pitt was then minister, and when he put an additional tax on salt, she was very indignant at such an interference with her domestic concerns. "That Billy," said she, "is going everywhere, and now he has got into the salt box." There was a large oak salt box hanging on the kitchen wall, and after this utterance of the good housewife, her children would slowly and timidly lift up the lid, to see what sort of a Liliputian Billy was.

coming a world-known philosopher, novelist, and historian. Indeed, Godwin could then preach after the fashion of his age, and moralize on the story of Hazael, taking for his text, "Is Thy servant a dog that he should do this great thing?" Failing to catch the exact meaning of that often misunderstood passage, he expatiated on the changes which occur in human character, little expecting that he should avow himself an atheist in the very town where this sermon was delivered. William Walford had some mental peculiarities resembling those of his predecessor, for he was independent in judgment, acute in reasoning, as perspicuous in style as he was perspicacious in thought, knowing exactly what he meant to say, and how to say it. But instead of wandering into metaphysical mazes without any Divine clue, he kept fast hold of the thread of revelation; and amidst all his inquisitiveness retained a faithful attachment to Gospel truth. He met, in the country town where he lived, with hearers in whose minds doubts as to Christianity were seething in perilous ways, and vainly strove to remove them; but he received testimonies of the growing acceptableness of his services, which inspired "a hope that they would be conducive to the religious and moral improvement of his flock." One effect which intercourse with people unsettled in faith had upon the young pastor's mind is worth noticing.

"It added very considerably to my information, and threw some of my opinions into a better mould; but what was chiefly valuable was the habit it formed of listening patiently to objections urged against my own notions, and of replying to them calmly and without irritability." [1]

One who could write in that way differed somewhat from many of his brethren. So he did also in another particular.

"The many branches of study which I thought it desirable to pay some attention to, had almost entirely abstracted me from attending to the art of preaching, and the composition of sermons, of which I had not more than half a dozen in my possession when I entered on the occupation which demanded two or three sermons every week." But he soon conquered this defect, and devoted himself to the preparation of discourses, which he delivered from analyses,—a habit agreeable to himself and engaging to his audience; "as the reading of a written sermon," he observes, "very often proves flat and uninteresting, an evil which is rather increased than diminished by committing it to memory, and reciting it without notes." He adds, "I universally found that a free prayer before preaching had the happiest effect on my feelings; and though I am of opinion that a beneficial alteration would be effected in our public services by the introduction of some short, simple, and pathetic forms into them, I should deprecate in the strongest terms, the relinquishment of free and extemporaneous prayer, as what cannot fail to be productive of extreme evils to both the minister and his hearers." [2]

William Walford, in point of intellect and education,

---

[1] "Autobiography of William Walford," p. 127.
[2] Ibid., pp. 118, 121, 122.

was very unlike the two men who in Kent and Lancashire combined artisanship with preaching; he differed, too, in many respects from the self-educated minister at Marlborough and Painswick; but he, as well as they, was deeply imbued with the spirit of evangelical religion, and in later life he rendered important services to the cause of English Nonconformity.[1]

It would be difficult to find at the end of the eighteenth century men of the same stamp as we find at the beginning; or at the beginning men of the same sort as we meet with at the end. No doubt there remained numerous drones in the hive, some worse than drones; but clerical character in the Establishment towards the latter half, though not painted by contemporaries in brilliant colours, yet loses some of the darkest shadows which cross it during the former;[2] and Nonconformist ministers, never charged with gross vices, or with much addictedness to the fashionable follies of the world, became much more earnest in their religious duties as time rolled on. A hundred years wrought a great change. Old-fashioned scholars, dryasdust antiquaries in parsonage and manse, cosy, respectable, ease-loving teachers of different denominations, were

---

[1] He became classical professor at Homerton College, and the author of useful commentaries on Scripture.

[2] See pp. 81 and 82 of this volume.

largely disappearing. A new race had risen up. Religious revivalists, if not ecclesiastical reformers, were on the increase and coming to the front. Methodism was infusing its spirit into the minds of men who dwelt outside its borders. The names of Wesley and Whitefield, in the second quarter of the century reviled as "the filth of the earth and the offscouring of all things," were in the fourth beginning to be pronounced with respect, and even with honour, by people altogether unsuspected of fanaticism. It is true persecution had not come to an end, but the assailants of Methodist preachers on village greens, during the last ten years, did not equal in numbers and fury those who attacked and burnt Dissenting meeting-houses during the first ten years of the period. Also there were popery riots, and political riots in 1780 and 1791; but in breadth of extent, and as to sympathy evinced by the upper classes, they did not attain the pitch of popular excitement reached in the days of Daniel Defoe and Dr. Sacheverell.

In history, as in commerce, the balance sheet is needed; losses and gains have to be reckoned up. Something was lost during a hundred years. The literary glories of the age of Anne passed away, through one of those inscrutable changes in history which perplex the philosophical student. There cannot be found in the reign of George III. the same amount of theological genius as in the reign of George II. Faith in Christianity, among the lower classes, received a ruder shock from Thomas Paine than it ever had from the critical attacks or sentimental speculations published by Collins and Shaftesbury. There was a wider separation, a more serious diminution of sympathy between class and class, especially in large English towns, after the outbreak of the French Revolution than before. Some of the measures of William Pitt, with a view to the suppression of seditious movements—especially the trials of the political martyrs of Scotland in 1793 and 1794, and the trials of Tooke and Thelwall about the same time, with the concurrent suspension of the Habeas Corpus Act —wrought untold mischief amongst the middle and lower classes; directly, by increasing disaffection to government, and indirectly, by strengthening a suspicion that religion is inimical to political freedom, because Church and State were arrayed against liberty of discussion. But very much more was gained than lost in the eighteenth century. The revival of evangelical religion, popular preaching, Sunday schools, and new religious societies, were immense gains. They not only produced immediate effects conspicuous on the surface, but they penetrated efficaciously into the depths of society, so as to render the continuance of certain existing evils almost impossible. People had believed that killing and burning a calf would bring good luck into a parish, and cure murrain among the cows. A boy in the weald of Kent had fancied an exciseman, with an inkbottle at his buttonhole, to be an officer of God Almighty, sent to take account of children's sins; and when Hannah More first went to Cheddar, she "saw but one Bible in all the parish, and that was used to prop a flower pot."[1] Such ignorance, superstition, and treatment of Scripture, could not but diminish, before the work carried on by village evangelists, by Sunday school teachers, by distributors of religious tracts, and by visitors connected with the Bible Society. And beyond all this, multitudes were converted to the faith and the practice of the Gospel, so as to live in virtue and benevolence, and die in the hope of eternal life.

The preceding pages are intended to assist in tracing various agencies, instruments, and influences which served to produce the beneficial results thus indicated. The immediate causes of moral and religious progress may, after diligent search, be pretty accurately ascertained, but there lies something beyond and above them all. More or less of mystery is connected with all grand effects produced in the Church and in the world. No great man appears in history, with regard to whom common enquiry is not found at fault in reference to the causes of his high position, and mighty power. The same may be said with regard to momentous revolutions and improvements in society. In addition to the action of human influence there re-

---

[1] See Lord Mahon's "History of England," vol. vii. p. 332.

mains much which is incapable of explanation upon any theory commonly called philosophical. Step by step we go on in our researches, pointing out one link after another in the chain of causation, till we are constrained to acknowledge some invisible and mysterious staple ring, lying outside social sequences, to which they are all attached, on which they all depend. When foiled in attempts to account fully for the formation of some of the characters, and for the origin of some of the events, we have attempted to review, we are thrown back on the conviction that there were Divine as well as human elements at work— the former shaping, controlling and giving life to the latter. The inexplicable residuum left in the crucible when the analysis of intellectual and social causes has been exhausted, is fully and purely *Divine*. The Presence, the Providence, and the Spirit of God are traceable, as in all the ages of Christendom, and all the ages of the world, so likewise, and that conspicuously, under particular aspects, in the history now submitted to the judgment of intelligent readers.

INDEX.

Abbadie, i., 365.
Abney, Lady, i., 203, 217-219, 348.
Abney, Sir Thos., i., 218.
Academies, ii., 214-217, 233-239, 262, 279, 334.
Acts, Toleration, i., 15, 241; ii., 24; Test, i., 19, 227, 234; for naturalizing foreign Protestants, 66; Test and Corporation, 108, 109, 242; ii., 39-41, 46; exempting Quakers and Moravians from taking oaths, i., 361.
Adair, Sergeant, ii., 52.
Adams, Thos., i., 282.
Addington, Dr., ii., 237.
Addison, Joseph, i., 94, 140, 159-164.
Aiken, Dr., ii., 211, 216.
Alderson, Robert, ii., 228.
Aldrich, Dr., i., 26.
Alexander, William, ii., 389-391.
Allix, Peter, i., 365.
America, i., 310, *et seq.*; war for independence, ii., 65; episcopacy in, 65-74; methodism in, 181; missionary societies in, 348.

Amory, Dr., ii., 214.
Anglesey, Earl of, i., 21.
Anne, i., 25, 31, accession of, 3; marriage of, 4; intimacy with Duchess of Marlborough, 4, 5; her speeches, 5, 6, 12, 50; her coronation, 7-9; at Oxford, 9; at St. Paul's, 10; opens Parliament, 17; her bounty, 48, 207; her letters to the Archbishop, 53, 54; death of her husband, 63; at Sacheverell's trial, 70; her death, 80, 84, 91; her attendance at church, 154-156.
Antinomianism, ii., 169, 285.
Arianism, i., 113, 115, 196; ii., 234, 377.
Arminianism, i., 214, 215, 224; 227, 395; ii. 160.
Arminius, James, ii., 298.
Armistead, Dr., i., 21.
Asbury, Francis, ii., 181-184.
Ashurst, Sir William, i., 313.
Ashworth, Dr., ii., 234.
Athanasian Creed, i., 81, 112.
Atterbury, Bishop of Rochester and Dean of Westminster, i., 33, 54,

70, 92, 161, 170; his vindication of his party, 36; his controversy with Wake, 37, 38; advocate of Schism Bill, 77; chosen prolocutor, 80; his "Representation," 81-83; suggests that James Stuart be proclaimed, 89; at coronation of George II., 93; his arrest, 119; his trial and condemnation, 120; his devotion to the Pretender's cause, 122; his banishment, 123; his sermons, 129.
Ayscough, Dr., i. 346.

Bacon, ii., 106.
Badock, Samuel, ii., 119.
Bagot, Bishop of Norwich, ii., 118.
Bala, Charles of, ii., 355.
Balguy, John, i., 134.
Balmerino, i., 254.
Bampton, John, ii., 119.
Bangorian Controversy, i., 110-112, 115, 301.
Baptists, i., 6, 115, 196, 199, 204, 211; associations, 212; divisions among, 214-216; numbers, 221; General, ii., 273; New Connexion, 276; articles of faith, 277; Particular, 278; churches, 284; ministers, 286, 294-302; missionaries, 289; societies, 292.
Barbadoes, i., 314.
Barbauld, Mrs., ii., 227.
Barber, i., 191.
Barclay, Robert, ii., 320.
Barker, John, i., 337.
Bath, ii., 151.
Bathurst, Lord, i., 120, 320; ii., 33.
Baxter, Margaret, ii., 230.

Baxter, Richard, i., 349, 350, 351; ii., 218-220, 230, 298.
Beauchamp, Lord, ii., 39.
Beaufoy, ii., 39.
Beauvoir, i., 100, 101.
Beddome, Benjamin, ii., 286.
Bedford, Row Chapel, ii., 104.
Bedford, Hilkiah, i., 170.
Belsham, Thos., ii., 215, 235.
Bendish, Bridget, i., 203.
Benion, Dr., i., 209.
Benson, Joseph, ii., 159, 160.
Bentley, Richard, i., 130, 139, 151.
Berkeley, George, Bishop of Cloyne, i., 318-324.
Bermudas, i., 320-322.
Berridge, John, ii., 154, 157, 158.
Beveridge, Bishop of St. Asaph, i., 308.
Bicknell, ii., 35.
Bill, Conformity, i., 19-25, 29-31, 41, 108, 109; Land tax, 42; Regency, 50; Schism, 77-80, 93, 108, 109, 210; for taxing Roman Catholics and Nonjurors, 123.
Binks, Dr., i. 42, 54.
Birch, Dr., i., 144.
Birmingham riots, ii., 49-51.
Bishops, i., 31; appointments of, 125-127, 246-249, 260-268; American, ii., 69-75; charged with nepotism, 79, 80.
Bisse, Philip, Bishop of Hereford, i., 125.
Blackbourn, Launcelot, Archbishop of York, i., 127.
Blackbourne, John, i., 176.
Blackburne, or Blackburn, Francis, Archdeacon of Cleveland, i., 264; ii., 17-19.

INDEX.

Blackhall, Bishop of Exeter, i., 127. 129.
Blackwell, Anthony, i., 139.
Blaize, Bishop, ii., 78.
Blayney, ii., 88.
Blenheim, battle of, i., 11.
Bogue, Dr. David, ii., 333-336.
Bohemia, i., 354.
Böhler, Peter, i., 376.
Bois, Abbé du, i., 102.
Bold, John, i., 128.
Bolingbroke, Lord, i., 21, 24, 25, 89; advocate of Schism Bill, 77, 78.
Boothroyd, Dr., ii., 243, 244.
Bossuet, Bishop, i., 105.
Boswell, ii., 121, 122.
Bourdillon, Jacob, i., 366.
Bowyer, i., 301.
Boyle, Hon. Robert, ii., 118.
Bradbury, David, ii., 267.
Bradbury, Thomas, i., 89-91, 93, 113-116, 195, 328.
Bradford, ii., 78.
Bray, i., 308, 317.
Brett, Thomas, i., 140.
Brighton, ii., 151.
Bromley, William, i., 21, 24, 41.
Broughton, Thomas, i., 298.
Browne, Simon, i., 192.
Brydges, Dr. Henry, i., 131.
Buddeus, Dr., i., 355.
Bull, William, ii., 99, 238.
Burder, George, ii., 266, 271, 353.
Burgess, Daniel, i., 179-181.
Burke, Edmund, ii., 20, 25, 44-48, 51.
Burnet, Gilbert, Bishop of Salisbury, i., 3, 6, 28, 57; ii., 18; references to his "Own Time,"
i., 22, 23, 48, 64; sends message of Anne's death to Bradbury, 91; his death, 97; his preaching, 129.
Bute, Lord, ii., 12.
Butler, Alban, ii., 35.
Butler, Joseph, Bishop of Durham, i., 208, 260, 276, 288; his Durham charge, 264; a favourite of Queen Caroline's, 248, 249, 264, 277; his "Analogy," 277-279.

Cadogan, Hon. ii., 333.
Calamy, Dr. Edmund, i., 16, 64, 113; visits Scotland, 60-62, 65, 107; Salters' Hall Sermons, 116; presents copies to George I., 117; his pastoral work, 185, 186; his church, 226.
Calcutta, Bishopric of, ii., 73.
Calvin, John, ii., 298.
Calvinists, i., 214, 227; ii., 160, 235, 284, 297.
Cambridge University, i., 151, 294; ii., 115.
Campbell, John, ii., 353.
Canada, ii., 74.
Cappoch, James, i., 251.
Carey, William, ii., 290-293, 378, 380.
Carolina, South, i., 312; North, 315.
Caroline, queen of George II., i., 323; her character, 232; her interview with Hoadley, 236; her death, 245; bishops made during her life, 246-249; anecdote of Zachary Pearce and, 266.
Carstairs, William, i., 62.
Carte, i., 300.
Cathedral services, ii., 77-80.

Cecil, Richard, ii., 104-106, 333.
Chandler, Edward, Bishop of Durham, i., 99, 125, 134, 246.
Chandler, Dr. Samuel, i., 193, 254-258, 330-333.
Charden, Sir John, i., 308.
Charlett, Dr., i., 151.
Charlotte, queen of George III., ii., 5, 6.
Cheshunt, ii., 162.
Church, deficiencies of the established, i., 289-292; Methodism in relation to the, ii., 205; compared with Presbyterianism, 208.
Churches, i., 144-147, 285; behaviour in, 154-159, 163; worship in, ii., 80.
Church-in-danger cry, i., 40, 49, 69, 95, 155; ii., 48.
Clark, Matthew, i., 64.
Clarke, Adam, ii., 177-179.
Clarke, Dr. Samuel, i., 84, 112, 134-136.
Clarkson, Thomas, ii., 133, 339.
Clayton, John (Churchman), i., 281.
Clayton, John (Noncon.), ii., 249.
Clergy, i., 127-132; writers, 132-140, 269-280; preachers, 280-284; character of the, 140, 286; ii., 80, *et seq.*, 394; theologians, 91; evangelicals, 93, *et seq.*
Cobden, Archdeacon, i., 155.
Codrington, General, i., 314.
Coke, Thos., ii., 176-178, 182-184.
Cole, William, i., 269.
Collet, Samuel, ii., 275.
Collier, Jeremiah, i., 171-175.
Collins, Anthony, i., 133, 134.
Comenius, i., 353.

Commons, House of, i., 19, 22-25, 44; Occasional Conformity Bill, 41; impeach Sacheverell, 68; Schism Bill, 77-80; debate on repeal of Schism Act, 110; bill against Atterbury, 120.
Comprehension, i., 255-258.
Compton, Bishop of London, i., 50, 51, 75.
Conder, Dr., ii., 237.
Connecticut, Bishopric of, ii., 74; missionary society in, 349.
Controversies, Bangorian, i., 110-112, 301; Salters' Hall, 112-116; deistical, 132-135; doctrinal, 135.
Convocation, House of, i., 13, 14, 234; right of prorogation, 26; contention between upper and lower houses, 26-29, 42; meetings of, 26, 32, 80; renewed disputes, 52-58; Atterbury's "Representation," 81-83; new differences, 83; Bangorian controversy, 110.
Conybeare, Bishop of Bristol, i., 134, 135.
Cornbury, Lord, i., 307.
Cornwallis, Archbishop of Canterbury, ii., 14, 22, 56.
Courayer, Dr., i., 102.
Coward, William, his trust, i., 341, 394; ii., 236, 355.
Cowper, Lord, i., 120, 123.
Cowper, William, ii., 124 129, 238.
Cox, Archdeacon, ii., 85.
Crabbe, George, ii., 85, 86.
Crisp, Dr., ii., 172.
Cumberland, Richard, Bishop of Peterborough, i., 126.
Cussons, George, ii., 355.

INDEX. 403

Cutts, Lady, funeral sermon for, i., 129.

Darracott, Risdon, i., 348–350.
David, Christian, i., 354.
Davis, John, ii., 355.
Dawes, Sir William, Archbishop of York, i., 108, 124.
Dawson, Jemmy, i., 252.
Deacon, Dr., i., 252–254.
Deistical controversy, i., 132–135.
Delany, Mrs., i., 369.
Derham, William, i., 139.
Devonshire, Duke of, i., 23.
Dibdin, Dr., ii., 98.
Doddridge, Dr. Philip, i., 222, 264, 338, 357, 394; his sermons, 342; his hymns, 343, 409; his academy, 344; also ii., 218, 234, 256; his opinions, i., 345; his works, 346; friendship for Warburton, 347; his correspondence, 347.
Dodwell, Henry, i., 166–168.
Douglas, Dr., Bishop of Carlisle, i., 273.
Drake, Dr., i., 43, 51.
Drummond, Dr., Archbishop of York, ii., 11.
Dryden, ii., 100.
Duff, the ship, ii., 340–342.
Duncan, Lord, ii., 334.
Duncombe, John, ii., 93.
Dunning, ii., 30.
Dunton, John, i., 334.
Dupin, of Sorbonne, i., 100–105.
Dury, John, i., 105.

Edmundson, William, ii., 314.
Edwards, Jonathan, ii., 221, 222, 224, 372.

Elections, i., 49, 50.
Eliot, i., 314.
England, Union with Scotland, i., 58.
England, George, i., 272.
Episcopalians, i., 12–15, 20, 50, 51, 94, 104; bitter feeling against Dissenters, 40–47; English and Scotch, 61; societies, 303, *et seq.*; simoniacal practices, ii., 53; separation between Church in England and in America, 67; unite with Dissenters in instituting Missionary Society, 335; preachers, 362; theological literature, 368; their relation to Dissent, 374; illustrations of spiritual life, 378.
Epworth, i., 381, 382.
Erastians, i., 12, 14.
Erskine, Lady, ii., 162.
Evans, Dr. Caleb, ii., 280.
Evans, Hugh, ii., 280.
Evans, Dr. John, i., 184.
Evans, John, Bishop of Bangor, i., 98.
Evelyn, i., 308.
Exeter, i., 112–115.
Eyre, John, ii., 332–334, 336, 349, 351.

Fabiens, Daniel, i., 199.
Fawcett, Benjamin, i., 350.
Fenelon, i., 104.
Finch, i., 24.
Findlater, Earl of, i., 62.
Fleetwood, William, i., 125, 126.
Fletcher, John W., Vicar of Madeley, ii., 156–159, 171–176.
Foe, Daniel de, i., 20, 59; his

satires, 44-47, 49, 142; his trial and punishment, 47; his novels, 164.
Foskett, ii., 280.
Foster, Dr. James, i., 333, 334.
Fothergill, Marmaduke, i., 176.
Fowler, Edward, Bishop of Gloucester, i., 126.
Fox, Charles James, ii., 39, 40, 51.
Fox, George, ii., 320.
Frampton, Bishop of Gloucester, i., 168.
France, revolution in, ii., 41-47, 60.
Francke, i., 305.
Franklin, Dr., ii., 43.
French Protestants, i., 363-367.
Fuller, Andrew, ii., 292, 293, 294-299, 349; his theological writings, 370, 371.
Fulneck, i., 360.
Furneaux, Dr., ii., 211, 213.

Gale, Dr. John, i., 182, 183.
Gallican Churches, i., 100-104.
Gambold, John, i., 298, 359, 360.
Gardiner, Colonel, i., 251.
Gardner, Dr., i., 308.
Garrick, ii., 153.
Gastrell, Francis, Bishop of Chester, i., 126.
Gaudy, Henry, i., 299.
Gentleman, Robert, ii., 217.
George I. proclaimed king, i., 91; coronation of, 93; Dissenters present addresses to, 106-108; Calamy presents sermons to, 117; Royal bounty for Dissenters, 118; death of, 231.
George II., his accession, i., 231-233; queen's influence over him, 232, 246; his death, ii., 3.

George III., i., 346; ii. 12, 27; his accession, 4; his character, 7; his letter to Archbishop of Canterbury, 16.
George IV., ii., 137.
George, Prince of Denmark, i., 4, 25, 31; his death, 63.
Georgia, i., 317, 371-373.
Gerardin, Piers de, i., 101.
Gibbon, i., 301; ii., 113, 374.
Gibbons, Dr., ii., 237.
Gibson, Edmund, Bishop of London, i., 127, 134, 268.
Gifford, Dr., ii., 279.
Gilbert, Archbishop of York, ii., 11.
Gill, Dr., i., 338.
Godolphin, Lord, i., 25, 31, 42, 68, 70.
Godwin, William, ii., 391.
Gooch, Dr., Bishop of Norwich, i., 254-256.
Goodman, Dean, i., 260.
Gordon, Lord George, ii., 31-34, 145.
Gouge, i., 225.
Graham, William, ii., 376.
Green, Bishop of Lincoln, ii., 11.
Grenville, ii., 12, 13.
Grey, Zachary, i., 270.
Griffin, John, ii., 340.
Grimshaw, William, ii., 169.
Grosvenor, Dr., i., 115.
Grove, Henry, i., 209.
Grove, Thomas, ii., 261.
Grundler, John Ernest, i., 304.
Guyse, Dr., i., 338, 342.
Gyles, Dr., i., 209.

Hackney, Academy, ii., 214, 351.

Haime, John, ii., 188.
Haldane, Robert, ii. 334.
Halifax, Bishop of Gloucester, ii., 118.
Halifax, Lord, i., 24, 50, 79.
Hall, Clement, i. 315, 316.
Hall, Robert, ii., 47, 56, 234, 294; his preaching, 299–301; his writings, 351, 369.
Hampden, i., 78.
Handel, Festival, ii., 76.
Harbin, Dr. George, i., 170.
Harcourt, Sir Simon, i., 69.
Hardcastle, Joseph, ii., 339.
Hardwicke, Earl of, i., 244.
Hardy, ii., 47.
Hare, Bishop, i., 249.
Harle, Dr., ii., 231.
Harmer, Thomas, ii., 240–243.
Harrington, Lord, i., 239.
Harris, Howel, ii., 350.
Hartopp, Sir John, i., 203.
Hastings, Lady Betty, i., 321.
Haweis, Dr., ii., 155, 161, 162, 336, 341.
Hearne, John, i., 150.
Henley, Orator, i., 142, 143.
Henry, Matthew, i., 181.
Herbert, Lord, i., 133.
Hernhut, i., 354, 355.
Herring, Archbishop of Canterbury, i., 251, 256, 260, 336.
Hervey, Lord, i., 238, 244.
Hervey, James, i., 281, 298.
Hesketh, Lady, ii., 128.
Hey, Dr. John, ii., 90, 369.
Hickes, George, Bishop, i., 168–171, 173.
Highbury, College, ii., 236, note.
Hildesly, i., 282.

Hill, Richard, ii., 172.
Hill, Rowland, ii., 143–146, 160.
Hinchcliffe, Bishop of Peterborough, ii., 30.
Hindmarsh, Robert, ii., 324.
Hoadley, or Hoadly, Benjamin, i., 51, 68, 135, 263; raised to Bishopric of Bangor, 98; advocates repeal of Schism Act, 109; his sermon which produced Bangorian controversy, 110–112; raised to Hereford, thence to Salisbury, 127; interviews with Queen Caroline and Walpole, 236–238; promoted to Bishopric of Winchester, 246; his death, ii., 11.
Hobart, Bishop, i., 313.
Hogarth, William, i., 270.
Hoghton, Sir Henry, ii., 24, 25, 39.
Holt, John, ii., 215.
Homerton Academy, ii., 236, note.
Hooper, Bishop of Bath and Wells, i., 33, 51, 59.
Hopkey, Miss, i., 372.
Hopkins, Dr., ii., 349.
Horne, George, Bishop of Norwich, ii., 61–64, 114, 362.
Horneck, Dr., i., 297.
Horsey, John, ii., 235.
Horsley, Samuel, Bishop of St. Asaph, ii., 58–61, 63, 91.
Hough, Bishop of Worcester, i., 51, 99, 125.
Houghton, Pendlebury, ii., 228.
Howard, John, ii., 252–254.
Howe, John, i., 20.
Howell, i., 173.
Hoxton Academy, ii., 236–238.
Hubbard, Thos., i., 340.
Hughes, Joseph, ii., 280, 354, 355.

Huguenots in London, i., 364-367.
Hume, David, i., 273, 274; ii., 374.
Hunter, Dr., ii., 230, 336.
Huntingdon, Selina, Countess of, ii., 15, 95, 268, 315; patroness of the Methodist movement, 146; co-operates with Whitefield, 146; her Connexion, 150, *et seq.*; her death, 162.
Hurd, Richard, Bishop of Worcester, ii., 27, 28, 57, 83, 118.
Huss, John, i., 352.
Hutchinson, John, ii., 62.
Hutton, Dr., Archbishop of Canterbury, i., 261.
Hutton, James, i., 359.

Independents, i., 6, 115, 196, 310, 326; numbers, 221; ministers in London, 223; compared with Presbyterians, ii., 207, 232; academies, 233-239; literary ministers, 239-246; distinction between old Independency and new Congregationalism, 246; pastors, 248; *et seq.*
India Bill, ii., 358.
Ingham, Benjamin, i., 298, 359, 360.
Inglis, Dr., ii., 70, 71.
Iroquois, i., 307.

Jablonsky, Daniel, i., 354.
Jablonsky, Figulus, i., 354.
Jacobites, i., 95-97, 110, 149, 153, 171, 233-240, 251.
Jamaica, Bishopric of, ii., 73.
James, John, i., 208.
James, Stephen, i., 209.
Jane, ii., 358.

Jansenists, i., 100.
Jay, William, ii., 269, 362.
Jebb, ii., 113.
Jefferson, ii., 66, 67.
Jekyll, Sir Joseph, i., 78.
Jenkin, Dr., i., 299.
Jenkins, Dr. Jenkyn, ii., 217.
Jennings, Dr. David, ii., 214.
Jerome of Prague, i., 352.
Jesuits, i., 100, 102, 399.
Johns, Captain Pierce, i., 216.
Johnson, Dr. Samuel, i., 7, 71, 186, 301; ii., 34, 100, 121-124, 153.
Jollie, Timothy, i., 209.
Jones, Jeremiah, i., 193.
Jones, Samuel, i., 193, 208.
Jortin, i., 276.

Kant, ii., 372.
Keith, George, i., 310.
Ken, Bishop of Bath and Wells, i., 8, 168, 169.
Kennet, White, Bishop of Peterborough, i., 80, 91, 109, 126, 145, 308.
Kennicott, Dr., i., 385; ii., 61, 87.
Kidder, Bishop of Bath and Wells, i., 8, 39.
Kilham, Alexander, ii., 202, 203.
Killingham, i., 224.
Kilmarnock, Lord, i., 255.
Kimberley, Dr., i., 21.
Kinchen, Charles, i., 298.
King, Archbishop of Dublin, i., 155.
King, Sir Peter, i., 78.
Kinghorn, Joseph, ii., 302.
Kingswood colliers, i., 389.
Kippis, Dr., ii., 210-214, 219, 224.

INDEX.   407

Lambert, George, ii., 337.
Lancashire, Nonconformity in, ii., 262.
Langford, Dr., ii., 217.
Lansdown, Lord, i., 109.
Lardner, Dr., i., 113, 330-333.
Lavington, George, Bishop of Exeter, i., 265, 393; ii., 252.
Lavington, Samuel, ii., 251.
Law, William, i., 300, 301, 375.
Leibnitz, i., 105, 232.
Leigh, Sir Egerton, ii., 271, 338, 364.
Leslie, i., 15.
Lessing, ii., 372, 373.
Lindsay, i., 300, 301.
Lindsey, Theophilus, ii., 111-113.
Lippe, Countess, i., 355.
Lloyd, Dr., Bishop of Worcester, i., 18, 19, 35, 98, 168.
Locke, i., 294.
Loggerheads, the, i., 223.
London, neighbourhood of, ii., 136-138.
Lords, House of, i., 19, 22, 23-25, 108, 109.
Loughborough, Lord, ii., 54.
Louis XIV., i., 366.
Lovat, Lord, i , 254.
Love, Dr., ii., 335.
Lowth, Dr., Bishop of London, i., 276; ii., 57, 333.
Loyola, Ignatius, i., 399.
Lusatia, i., 354.
Luther, i., 374.
Lyttleton, Lord, ii., 101.

Macaulay, Thomas Babington, i., 121.
Macaulay, Zachary, ii., 133.

McQuhae, James, ii., 265.
Madan, Martin, ii., 154.
Maddox, Bishop of Worcester, i., 246, 362.
Madeley, ii., 156-159, 175.
Magazines, ii., 331-335, 351, 353, 368.
Man, Isle of, i., 316, 317.
Manningham, Dr., i., 156.
Mansfield, Lord, ii., 23, 32, 34, 213.
Marlborough, John Churchhill, Duke of, i., 10, 25, 31, 42, 70, 119; ii., 57.
Marlborough, Sarah, Duchess of, i., 4, 5, 25, 31, 63; ii., 57, 146.
Marriott, Dr., i., 223.
Marryat, Dr., i., 340.
Marsh, Bishop, ii., 368.
Martin, Joshua, ii., 318.
Martineau, ii., 212, 229.
Martyn, Henry, ii., 189, 378-382.
Massachusetts, ii., 349.
Mather, Alexander, ii., 185.
Mather, Cotton, i., 313.
Mather, Increase, i., 313.
Matthews, i., 172.
Maxfield, Thos., i., 402, 404.
Mead, Matthew, i., 224.
Meredith, Sir William, ii., 19.
Methodism, ii., 260, 263, 326-328, 363; Wesley, founder of, i., 367, *et seq.*; organization of, 399; first chapel, 401; conferences, 404; ii., 199, 202, 208; the circuit, i., 405; local preachers, 405; hymnology, 408; progress of, ii., 163-193; preachers, 193-195; ordination and administration of sacraments, 200; the new connections, 203; spiritual work, 204; rela-

tion to the Established Church, 205.
Methodists, i., 266, 393; ii., 7, 11, 157, 257.
Middleton, Conyers, i., 272.
Milner, Dean of Carlisle, ii., 144.
Milner, Joseph, ii., 106, 107.
Mitchell, John, i., 406.
Mitford, ii., 37.
Missionary Society, institution of, ii., 335, 364; first expeditions, 340-345; constitution of the, 347.
Moody, James, ii., 271.
Moore, Dr., Archbishop of Canterbury, ii., 57.
Moore, Henry, ii., 185.
Moravia, i., 353, 354.
Moravianism, i., 352-363, 373; band meetings, 403.
More, Hannah, ii., 352, 354, 397.
Morell, Thos., i., 270.
Morgan, George, ii., 228.
Mortmain, Statute of, i., 48.
Morton, John, i., 139.
Musgrave, Sir Christopher, i., 35.

Neal, Daniel, i., 114, 337, 342.
Nelson, Robert, i., 168, 176.
New Brunswick, ii., 74.
Newdigate, Sir Roger, ii., 21.
New England, i., 310; ii., 348.
Newfoundland, i., 314; ii., 74.
Newton, Dr., Bishop of Bristol, ii., 11, 12, 14.
Newton, James, ii., 280.
Newton, John, ii., 96-101, 109, 124, 127, 129.
Newton, Sir Isaac, i., 161, 208.
New York, Missionary Society in, ii., 349.

Nicholson, Bishop of Carlisle, i. 106.
Nitschman, David, i., 354, 355.
Nonconformists, i., 13, 15, 20, 22, 23, 112, 234-239, 310, 394; bitter feeling towards the Church, 41-47, 49; address to the queen 58, 59; addresses to George I., 105-108; their schools, 154; preachers, 179-194; ii., 362; preaching, i., 194-196; places of worship, 196-203; congregations, 203, 221-226; services, 204; choice of ministers, 206; incomes, 206; academies, 207-210; social life, 216; census, 220; state of Dissent, 227-230; Deputies, 239-243; ii., 39; active supporters of the Government, i., 252; deficiencies of, 292; lecturers, 328; education of students. 339; address to George III., ii., 8; deputies active in obtaining religious liberty, 22-25; concession to, 25; attempt to obtain repeal of Test and Corporation Acts, 39-41; persecution of, 257; spread of, 258-272; views of Christian union, 327; periodicals, 331; institute Missionary Society, 335; public meetings, 363; Sunday schools, 365; theological literature, 368; relations with the Church, 374; statistics, 377; illustrations of spiritual life, 378, *et seq.*; character of ministers, 394.
Nonjurors, i., 13, 15, 92, 110, 123, 166-178, 360; sympathize in rebellion, 251; support Prince Charles, 252; decline of, 298-302; Moravian, 361.

Norris, i., 139.
North, Brownlow, Bishop of Winchester, ii., 26, 28.
North, Lord, ii., 26.
Norwich, Mediæval Pageantry in, ii., 77.
Nottingham, Lord, i., 73.
Nova Scotia, Bishopric of, ii., 70-74.
Nowell, Dr. ii., 21.
Nye, Stephen, i., 134.

Oglethorpe, General, i., 317, 356, 361.
Oldfield, Dr. Joshua, i., 114, 208.
Olivers, Thomas, ii., 187-189.
Olney, ii., 97-99, 127.
Onslow, i., 123.
Opie, Mrs., ii., 229.
Ormond, Duke of, i., 94.
Orton, Job, ii., 218-220.
Osbaldeston, ii., 11.
Owen, James, i., 209.
Owen, John, i., 200.
Oxford, Lord, i., 94.
Oxford University, i., 9, 10, 148-151; ii., 114, 115; revival at, i., 294-297.

Paine, Thomas, ii., 51, 374, 396.
Pakington, or Packington, Sir John, i., 18, 30, 59.
Paley, Archdeacon, ii., 88-90.
Palmer, Samuel, ii., 248.
Parker, Samuel, i., 299.
Parkins, Samuel, i., 340.
Parliament, i., 17, 50; Occasional Conformity Bill, 19-25; repeal Schism Act, 108; bill for taxing Roman Catholics and Nonjurors, 123; attempt to repeal Test and Corporation Acts, 241; ii., 39; Quakers petition for relief from tythe laws, i., 243; act for exempting Quakers and Moravians from taking oaths, 361; subscription to Thirty-nine Articles, ii, 19-21; concession to Dissenters, 25.
Parr, Dr., ii., 83, 119.
Parsons, Edward, ii., 337.
Patrick, Bishop of Ely, i., 49, 51.
Pearce, or Pierce, Samuel, ii., 287, 292.
Pearce, Zachary, Bishop of Rochester, i., 134, 266.
Peck, Francis, i., 269.
Pegge, Dr. Samuel, i., 270.
Penn, William, ii., 320.
Pennsylvania, i., 310; Bishopric of, ii., 74.
Percy, Dr., ii., 22.
Pinners' Hall, i., 224, 333.
Pitt, Earl of Chatham, i., 362; ii., 9, 25.
Plasterers' Hall, i., 340
Plumer, i., 242.
Plutscho, i., 304.
Poley, i., 43.
Pomfret, Samuel, i., 183.
Porteus, Beilby, Bishop of Chester, ii., 22, 28.
Potter, John, Bishop of Oxford, i., 126; afterwards Archbishop of Canterbury, 246-248, 356; his death, 260.
Powis, Sir Thomas, ii., 24.
Prayer Book, revision of, ii., 21.
Presbyterians, i., 6, 196, 204, 206, 211, 235; English and Scotch, 59-61, 96; numbers, 221; ministers, in London, 223; accused of being

leaders of Rebellion, 254; lecturers, 330, *et seq.*; compared with Independents, ii., 207, 233; compared with Episcopalians, 208; learned men, 210-214; academies, 214-217; ministers, 217; decline of, 229; Scotch, 230-232.
Pretender, the, *see* Stuart.
Prettyman, *see* Tomline.
Price, Dr. Richard, i., 226; ii., 47, 210, 211; his political discourses, 41-45; his theology, 222-224, 226, 227.
Prideaux, Dean, i., 308.
Priestley, or Priestly, Dr. Joseph, ii., 41, 58, 284; his literary labours, ii., 210-212; his theology, 224-227.
Priestley, Timothy, ii., 266.
Primatt, Dr., ii, 113.
Prior, i., 321.

Quakers, i., 212, 310, 322, 361; petition Parliament, 243-245; ii., 52; their convictions, 303; testimonies, 305; legislation, 309; religious life, 316; in Norwich, 321; yearly meetings, 323.
Quebec, Bishopric of, ii., 73.

Rahem, Mohammed, ii., 381.
Raikes, Robert, ii., 130, 131, 365-368.
Ramilies, battle of, i., 11.
Rankin, Thomas, ii., 185.
Ray, John, ii., 337.
Read, i., 224.
Rees, Dr., ii. 214.
Regium Donum, i., 118.
Reynolds, John, i., 209.

Reynolds, Sir Joshua, ii., 77.
Rhode Island, i., 322, 323.
Richmond, Legh, ii., 383.
Ridgley, Dr. Thomas, i., 208, 339.
Robins, Thomas, ii., 234.
Robinson, Benjamin, i., 185.
Robinson, John, i., 76, 124.
Robinson, Robert, ii., 281-284.
Roby, William, ii., 267, 337.
Roche, de la, ii., 70
Romaine, William, ii., 94-96, 154.
Roman Catholics, i., 123; ii., 29-31, 33, 35-38.
Rosewell, Samuel, i., 183, 184.
Routh, Dr., ii., 114.
Rundle, Dr., i., 267.
Rutland, Duke of, ii., 55,
Ryland, Dr. John, ii., 280, 288, 289.
Ryland, John Collet, ii., 288.

Sacheverell, Dr. Henry, i., 16, 67-72, 89.
Sackville, Sir George, ii., 20.
Saffery, ii., 293.
St. John, *see* Bolingbroke.
St. Paul's, i., 144, 156, 376; ii., 77.
Salters' Hall, i., 113-116, 336, 337.
Sandemanism, ii., 297.
Saurin, James, i., 364, 366.
Savage, Dr., ii., 214, 236.
Saville, Sir George, ii., 20, 24, 30.
Schimmelpenninck, Mrs., ii., 315.
Schism Bill, i., 77-80, 93; repealed, 108, 109, 210.
Schomberg, Marshal, i., 365.
Schools, charity, i., 152-154; Sunday, ii., 365-368.
Schulze, i., 305.
Schwartz, Frederic, i., 305.

INDEX. 411

Scotland, union with England, i., 58; consecration of American bishops in, ii., 68, 69; Missionary Society founded in, 348.
Scott, James, ii., 239, 259.
Scott, Sir William, ii., 52.
Scott, Thomas, ii., 99-103, 109.
Seabury, Dr., ii. 68, 69.
Secker, Archbishop of Canterbury, i., 208, 271, 288, 326; ii., 73; his character, i., 261-263; his account of funeral of George II. and accession of George III., ii., 3-7; his death, 13.
Seed, Jeremiah, i., 284.
Sellon, William, ii., 155.
Shaftesbury, Lord, i., 133, 134.
Sharp, Granville, ii., 339.
Sharpe, or Sharp, Archbishop of York, ii., 8, 50, 77, 124.
Shelburne, Lord, ii., 55.
Shephard, James, i., 173.
Sheridan, ii., 144.
Sherlock, Bishop of Salisbury, i., 248, 255, 260, 362; afterwards Bishop of London, 263, 325; his death, ii., 11.
Shirley, ii., 171.
Shirley, Lady Fanny, ii., 148.
"*Shortest* Way with the Dissenters," i., 44.
Shrubsole, William, ii., 338, 387-389.
Sierra Leone, ii., 75, 348.
Simeon, Charles, ii., 117, 116, 353, 380.
Simpson, Dr. Robert, ii., 237, 265, 266, 337.
Smallbrook, Bishop of Lichfield and Coventry, i., 134, 246.

Smalridge, George, Bishop of Bristol, i., 126.
Smith, William, i., 140.
Societies: Christian Knowledge, i., 303; S.P.G., 305, *et seq.*, 355, 371; ii., 345; King's Head, i., 339-341; ii., 236, 237; for Furtherance of Gospel, i., 358; London Missionary, ii., 335-348, 364; Religious Tract, 339, 352, 353; Hibernian and British and Foreign Bible, 339, 355; Village Itinerancy, 349; Naval and Military, 355; Church Missionary, 357; Eclectic, 358.
Socinianism, ii., 284, 296, 377.
Somerset, Lord, i., 24.
Sophia, Princess, i., 74.
South, Dr., ii., 51.
Southey, Robert, i., 199, 280; ii., 212.
Southgate, Richard, ii., 92.
Spa Fields Chapel, ii., 153-155, 161.
Spectator, the, i., 140, 157-161, 163, 164.
Spilsbury, John, i., 350.
Spinkes, i., 171, 175.
Spinola, i., 105.
Spinoza, i., 133; ii., 373.
Spitalfields, i., 364-366.
Sprat, Thomas, Bishop of Rochester, i., 130.
Stanhope, Dr., i., 84.
Stanhope, Earl, i., 108, 121-123.
Stark, ii., 229.
Steadman, ii., 293.
Steele, i., 158, 159.
Steinkopff, Dr., ii., 356.
Stennet, Dr. Samuel, ii., 286.

Stennett, Joseph, i., 180.
Stephens, James, ii., 133.
Sterne, Lawrence, i., 371.
Storey, George, ii., 188.
Strange, Thomas, ii., 256.
Strype, i., 139.
Stuart, Charles Edward, i., 250–253.
Stuart, James Edward, i., 89, 95, 122, 250.
Sutcliff, John, ii., 287, 289, 292.
Swedenborg, Emanuel, ii., 324–326.
Swift, Dr., Dean of St. Patrick's, i., 5, 159, 235, 236.
Sykes, Arthur, i., 272.

Tahiti, ii., 341–343.
Talbot, John, i., 310.
Talbot, William, Bishop of Durham, i., 127.
Tanner, Thomas, Bishop of St. Asaph, i., 246.
Tatler, the, i., 160.
Taylor, Daniel, ii., 275, 278.
Taylor, Dr. John, i., 340; ii., 211, 215, 216, 220–222, 228.
Taylor, Edward, ii., 229.
Taylor, Thomas, ii., 191–193.
Taylor, William, ii., 212.
Tenison, Archbishop of Canterbury, i., 3, 8, 28, 306; at Convocation, 53–55; crowns George, I., 93; his death, 99.
Terrick, Dr., Bishop of London, ii., 12, 14.
Thelwall, ii., 47, 396.
Thomas, Dr., Bishop of Salisbury, ii., 11, 60.
Thornton, Henry, ii., 133.
Thornton, John, ii., 129, 238, 355.

Thorpe, John, ii., 261.
Thurlow, Lord Chancellor, ii., 59.
Tindal, Dr., i., 133, 134, 192.
Toland, John, i., 133, 134.
Toller, Thomas, ii., 255.
Tomkins, Martin, i., 191.
Tomline, Bishop of Lincoln, ii., 57. 368.
Tonbridge Wells, ii., 152.
Tong, William, i., 184.
Tooke, ii., 47, 396.
Tookie, Dr., i., 146.
Toplady, ii., 173-175, 225.
Tories, i., 12, 50, 59, 73, 93–96.
Torrey, Josiah, i., 313.
Towgood, ii., 376.
Townsend, George, ii., 337.
Townsend, John, ii., 337.
Townsend, Lord, i., 79.
Trelawny, Bishop of Exeter, i., 11, 34.
Trevecca College, ii., 156–160, 333.
Trinitarians, i., 113–117; ii., 234.
Tucker, Josiah, Dean of Gloucester, ii., 213.

Union, i., 100–105; views of Christian, ii., 327, *et seq.*
Unitarians, i., 196; ii., 51, 374, 375, 377.
Universities, i., 148–152, 294–298.
Unwin, Mrs., ii., 125.
Utrecht, Peace of, i., 11.
Uvedale, i., 139.

Vanderkemp, Dr., ii., 343.
Venn, Henry, ii., 94, 95, 154, 260, 261.
Village itinerancy, ii., 349.

Virginia, church of, ii., 66-68.

Wake, Dr., i., 246, 355; his controversy with Atterbury, 37, 38; made Archbishop of Canterbury, 99; his correspondence with Beauvoir, 100-105.
Wakefield, Gilbert, i., 262; ii., 211, 215.
Walford, William, ii., 346 note, 391-394.
Walker, George, ii., 210.
Walker, Samuel, i., 282.
Walpole, Horace, i., 144, 262, 362; ii., 3, 152.
Walpole, Sir Robert, i., 78, 123, 234-238, 241, 321.
Walter, Nehemiah, i., 313.
Warburton, William, Bishop of Gloucester, i., 249, 274-276; ii., 9-11, 28, 118.
Warren, Samuel, i., 209.
Warton, Joseph, ii., 83, 84.
Warton, Thomas, ii., 83, 84.
Warwickshire, religious revival in, ii., 271.
Washington, George, ii., 66.
Waterland, i., 136, 276.
Watson, Robert, Bishop of Llandaff, ii., 55, 56.
Watts, Dr. Isaac, i. 114, 160, 348, 395; ii., 372; account of him, i., 186-191; his meeting house, 197, 226; his income, 207; at Lady Abney's, 218; a Coward trustee, 342; his hymns, 343, 409.
Waugh, Dr., ii., 230.
Weigh House, ii., 249, 250.
Wellington, Duke of, ii., 355.

Wesley, Charles, i., 392, 396, 399; his hymns, 408-412.
Wesley, John, i., 301, 386, 388; ii., 132, 154, 314; at Oxford, i., 295-298, 369; early life, 368; his ordination, 370; a missionary at Georgia, 371; his connection with Moravians, 373; a high Churchman, 374; his mysticism, 375; his conversion, 375-377; his theology, 377-381; his preaching, 382-386, 395, 396, ii., 152; his interview with the Bishop of London, i., 392; his visits to Cornwall, 394; his controversies with Whitefield, 397; founder of Methodism, 399; his egotism, ii., 160; progress of his work, 163, *et seq.*; his old age, 195; his death, 197; his funeral, 198; character of his preaching, 199.
Wesley, Samuel, i., 49, 85, 137, 381.
Wesley, Susanna, i., 49.
Westminster Abbey, i., 143, 161, 259; ii., 60, 61, 76.
Weston, Stephen, Bishop of Exeter, i., 127.
Wharton, Lord, i., 79, 93.
Wharton, Lord, ii., 355.
Wheatley, James, ii., 164, 165.
Whewell, Dr., ii., 389.
Whigs, i., 12, 15, 47, 49, 72-75, 96, 234.
Whiston, William, i., 112, 131; his doctrinal views, 81, 82, 135, 136, 151; extracts from his memoirs, 191, 248; ii., 274.
White, Gilbert, ii., 86.
Whitefield, George, i., 296, 394,

ii., 14, 143; his preaching, i., 146-157, 314, 386, 389-391, 396; his conversion, 387; his character, 388; controversies with Wesley, 397; his labours, ii., 139; his death, 141; places where he preached, 142; Lady Huntingdon's co-operation with, 146-154; effects of his preaching, 267-269; relics of, 268.

Wilberforce, William, ii., 105, 115, 131-136, 356, 357.

Wilks, Matthew, ii., 142, 337, 338.

William III., i., 3, 5, 7, 13, 154, 305, 365.

Williams, Dr., i., 93, 181.

Williams, Dr. Edward, ii., 239, 244-246, 370-372, 377.

Williams, Joseph, i., 350.

Williams, Roger, i., 322.

Willis, Bishop of Gloucester, i., 109, 126.

Wilson, Captain James, ii., 340.

Wilson, John, ii., 338.

Wilson, Thomas, Bishop of Sodor and Man, i., 280-282, 316, 317, 359.

Wilson, Thomas, ii., 238.

Wilton, Dr. Samuel, ii., 248, 249.

Wiltshire, Nonconformity in, ii., 269.

Winter, Cornelius, ii., 269, 384-387.

Wits, i., 159.

Woolston, i., 133, 134, 192, 264, 273.

Wotton, Dr., i., 134.

Wren, Sir Christopher, i., 144, 147, 149; ii., 77.

Wright, Dr., i., 336.

Wyndham, Sir William, i., 78.

Yale College, i., 323.

Yonge, Bishop of Norwich, ii., 11.

Yorkshire, Nonconformity in, ii., 259.

Young, Dr., ii., 123.

Ziegenbalg, i., 304.

Ziegenhagen, i., 355.

Zinzendorf, Count, i., 354-362, 374; ii., 180.

ERRATA.

Vol. I. page 175, line 26, *for* "Hickes" *read* "Spinkes."
,, ,, 317, running title, *for* "Nelson" *read* "Wilson."
,, ,, 359, line 8, *for* "James" *read* "Benjamin Ingham."
Vol. II. ,, 229, running title, *for* "Octogan" *read* "Octagon."

Butler & Tanner, The Selwood Printing Works, Frome, and London.

BY THE SAME AUTHOR.

THE ECCLESIASTICAL HISTORY OF ENGLAND.
IN 2 VOLS., DEMY 8VO, PRICE 25s.
THE CHURCH OF THE RESTORATION.
IN 1 VOL., DEMY 8VO, PRICE 12s.
THE CHURCH OF THE REVOLUTION.

"Even for the Court of Charles II., we appeal from Lord Macaulay to the most recent and able historian of Nonconformity, Dr. Stoughton. From his pages we may perceive that even within that precinct were to be found lives and practices of sanctity, no less remarkable than the pollutions with which they were girt about."—The Right Hon. W. E. GLADSTONE, in "THE QUARTERLY REVIEW."

From DEAN STANLEY'S *Speech at Kensington Chapel, April* 1875:—

"He was there also to express the obligations of dear old friends of 200 years ago—Chillingworth, Jeremy Taylor, Sir Matthew Hale, Cudworth, and others. All these were now near friends, who but for Dr. Stoughton would never have been known to them. He had also to express his obligations to Dr. Stoughton for making him acquainted here with men whom he should know so well above—he meant Howe, Owen, and others. They had, before Dr. Stoughton's time, histories of the Puritans, in which they read of nothing but Puritanism; histories of the Church of England, in which was nothing but the glories of the Church of England. The work of Dr. Stoughton's was the first work which had brought together men famous in their different classes, within the four corners of the same book. He only trusted that, when the twenty-first century should come, future historians of the reign of Queen Victoria would treat of men of our time with the same candour and fairness.

"His wise reserve in passing judgment, his earnest desire to deal fairly with every subject that passes under his view, are qualities by no means so common as they ought to be; and since Dissenters are sure to study this part of our Church history, we are quite content that they should do so under the guidance of one so intelligent, so calm, so unfeignedly truthloving as our author."—SATURDAY REVIEW.

"A markedly fair, charitable, and large-minded history. . . . A careful search into original and contemporary documents and authorities—a habit of placing the actual men of the time before us, as far as may be, in their own words, and avoidance of the rounded and general descriptions, written for literary effect, under which the school of Hume disguised and concealed the truth, and the substitution for them of life-like pictures of individual men, fairly chosen and from all sides; and, above all, the most thoroughly Christian and honest watchfulness to narrate without partiality or prejudice—such are the characteristics of Dr. Stoughton's work."—GUARDIAN.

HODDER AND STOUGHTON, 27, PATERNOSTER ROW, LONDON.

BY E. DE PRESSENSÉ, D.D.

I.
JESUS CHRIST:
HIS TIMES, LIFE, AND WORK.
SIXTH EDITION, CROWN 8VO, CLOTH, 9s.

"*One of the most valuable additions to Christian literature which the present generation has seen.*"—CONTEMPORARY REVIEW.

"*On the whole, a most noble contribution to the cause of truth, for which the deep gratitude of all sincere Christians cannot but be due to its accomplished author.*"—CANON LIDDON'S BAMPTON LECTURE.

II.
THE MARTYRS AND APOLOGISTS.
8VO, CLOTH, 14s.

"*A most valuable and important addition to our Church histories.*"—SUNDAY MAGAZINE.

"*A most fascinating and trustworthy history of the struggles of the early Church, narrated in a style of lofty and impassioned eloquence.*"—CHURCHMAN.

III.
HERESY AND CHRISTIAN DOCTRINE.
8VO, CLOTH, 12s.

"*This is the third volume of a series in which Dr. Pressensé has undertaken to describe the history of the Church during the first three centuries of the Christian era. His style is good, often eloquent, always perspicuous. It brings out the varying phases of belief which prevailed in the earliest centuries without indulging in harsh condemnation. The translation is good and reads well.*"—ATHENÆUM.

IV.
CHRISTIAN LIFE AND PRACTICE IN THE EARLY CHURCH.
8VO, CLOTH, 12s.

"*His style as a writer is admirably clear, correct, and compact, and persuasive by the force of its sincerity. His principal contribution to ecclesiastical literature has been his exhaustive 'History of the First Three Centuries of the Christian Church.' The present is the closing volume of the series, and by no means the least interesting. It well deserves the honours of the Index at the Vatican.*"—DAILY NEWS.

HODDER AND STOUGHTON, 27, PATERNOSTER ROW, LONDON.

www.ingramcontent.com/pod-product-compliance
Lightning Source LLC
Chambersburg PA
CBHW022108290426
44112CB00008B/588